Bondarch

War and F

Bondarchuk's
War and Peace

Literary Classic to Soviet Cinematic Epic

DENISE J. YOUNGBLOOD

UNIVERSITY PRESS OF KANSAS

Published by the University Press of Kansas (Lawrence, Kansas 66045), which was organized by the Kansas Board of Regents and is operated and funded by Emporia State University, Fort Hays State University, Kansas State University, Pittsburg State University, the University of Kansas, and Wichita State University

Library of Congress Cataloging-in-Publication Data

Youngblood, Denise J. (Denise Jeanne), 1952–
Bondarchuk's War and peace : literary classic to Soviet cinematic epic / Denise J. Youngblood.
pages cm
Includes bibliographical references and index.
ISBN 978-0-7006-2005-0 (cloth)
1. Voina i mir (Motion picture) 2. Bondarchuk, Sergei, 1920–1994—Criticism and interpretation. 3. Tolstoy, Leo, graf, 1828–1910—Film adaptations. I. Title.
PN1997.V577Y88 2014
791.43'72—dc23
2014020684

British Library Cataloguing-in-Publication Data is available.

Printed in the United States of America
10 9 8 7 6 5 4 3 2 1

The paper used in this publication is recycled and contains 30 percent postconsumer waste. It is acid free and meets the minimum requirements of the American National Standard for Permanence of Paper for Printed Library Materials z39.48–1992.

To Kevork Spartalian, who shares my love
of the movies and much more

CONTENTS

ACKNOWLEDGMENTS

As always, I am pleased to acknowledge the people and institutions that helped me complete this project. Michael Briggs planted the idea for a book about Bondarchuk's *War and Peace*. Frank Manchel encouraged me to persevere, patiently reading the manuscript in its earliest stages, providing invaluable insights, and sharing his inestimable knowledge of cinema art. Later on, the manuscript benefited enormously from careful readings by Peter Kenez, Anna Lawton, and Stephen M. Norris. My husband, Kevork Spartalian, was a most exacting copy editor and participated in endless dinner-table discussions about *War and Peace* that sharpened my thinking. I also benefited from the work of my capable research assistants: Nadezda Berkovich, Oleg Ershov, Jessica Fuller, and Forrest Parsons. Jess Fuller was particularly essential to the project.

My home institution, the University of Vermont, was very supportive of this work. The College of Arts and Sciences provided a sabbatical leave in fall 2013 that enabled me to finish writing, as well as a Lattie F. Coor research assistantship. The UVM Department of History, a most collegial working environment, gave me a grant to cover the cost of the still photographs.

Libraries and archives were also central to the project. I thank the Bailey-Howe Library at UVM for its great interlibrary loan services; the Russian, East European, and Eurasian Center at the University of Illinois–Urbana-Champaign for continuing to offer its summer research laboratory, despite funding cuts; and the Russian State Archive of Literature and Art for its cooperation.

NOTE ON TRANSLITERATION AND TRANSLATION

The transliteration in the notes and bibliography is according to the Library of Congress system, for the benefit of specialists. Transliteration in the text has been modified to facilitate pronunciation for non-Russian speakers: *y* instead of final *ii*, *ye* instead of initial *e*, *yu* instead of initial *iu*, and so on. The soft and hard signs, ' and ", have been omitted altogether. Well-known Russian names are rendered in the standard English spelling, for example, *Leo Tolstoy* rather than *Lev Tolstoi*. Translations from the Russian are mine unless otherwise indicated.

Bondarchuk's
War and Peace

INTRODUCTION

Sergei Bondarchuk's *War and Peace* (*Voina i mir*, 1965–1967) is perhaps the most grandiose film ever made, as well as the most expensive, costing an estimated $700 million in today's dollars. But it is more than a blockbuster: of the many adaptations of Leo Tolstoy's classic novel, it is clearly the best. It was also the first Soviet picture to win an Oscar for Best Foreign Language Film. Although it has certainly earned its place in the history of world cinema, it is important for another reason. Conceived as an "answer" to King Vidor's *War and Peace* (1956), Bondarchuk's film is arguably the major artifact of the cultural Cold War waged by the USSR against the United States.

War and Peace was in production from 1961 to 1967, a signal period in Soviet history, and its historical context is quite important. These were transitional years for the USSR in general and for Soviet cinema in particular, spanning both the Khrushchev and Brezhnev eras. Nikita Khrushchev's tenure as first secretary of the Communist Party of the Soviet Union (1953–1964) was marked by a series of largely unsuccessful reforms, particularly in agriculture, but also in the party structure and government operation. The era is most remembered, however, for three reasons. First, the Secret Speech of 1956 and subsequent de-Stalinization were unquestionably significant. However, for purposes of evaluating *War and Peace*, the other two reasons are probably more important, as chapter 1 explains. Second, there was the continuation of the Cold War and, indeed, a heightening of Cold War tensions. Third, there was the Cold War's polar opposite, the relaxation of cultural restrictions known as the Thaw (*ottepel*). In contrast, Khrushchev's successor, Leonid Brezhnev (1964–1982), represented "stagnation" (*zastoi*), a refreezing of Soviet culture as well as a paradoxical attitude toward the Cold War. Brezhnev was, after all, an architect of détente but also of the "second Cold War" in the early 1980s.

Before embarking on our examination of *War and* Peace, a brief overview of the historical context is in order to understand the backdrop against which *War and Peace* came into being. It emerged not out of a vacuum but rather from the vagaries of post-Stalin cultural politics. After all, its director, born in 1920, was a product of the Stalin era and was certainly affected by the contorted course of de-Stalinization under Khrushchev and the attempt to re-Stalinize certain aspects of Soviet life under Brezhnev.

From Khrushchev to Brezhnev

When Stalin died on 5 March 1953, he left the nation rudderless. The first order of business was to find a successor, and Nikita Khrushchev, Lavrenty Beria, and Georgy Malenkov struggled for sole power.[1] The cultural Thaw, which is inextricably linked to Khrushchev, did not begin with the death of Stalin, nor did it end with Khrushchev's ouster by Brezhnev in 1964. The Thaw was a relatively quiet cultural revolution, but its impact on Soviet society was at least as important as that of the earlier cultural revolution of 1928–1932. On the one hand, according to historian Miriam Dobson, the Thaw was "forward-looking, ambitious, and full of hope"; on the other hand, it was "disorienting and potentially unsettling."[2]

A few months after Stalin's death, changes were noticeable in the press as party leaders began the "overt encouragement of stylistic reform."[3] Stalin's name began to disappear, and the strident rhetoric of late Stalinism was toned down. Censorship was relaxed, and journalists began to criticize social and economic problems such as shoddy goods, crime, alcoholism, and hooliganism. In 1954, following Ilya Ehrenburg's novel *The Thaw* (*Ottepel*), several other novels appeared that offered mild critiques of the Soviet culture of bureaucracy and corruption.[4] At the same time, there were also signs of a thaw in foreign relations with Yugoslavia and China. Khrushchev and US president Dwight Eisenhower met for the first time at the Geneva summit in July 1955 to discuss arms control and European security issues.

Then came the Twentieth Party Congress of February 1956 and Khrushchev's Secret Speech, "On the Cult of Personality and Its Consequences." This four-hour speech detailed the illegal arrest, torture, and imprisonment of Communist Party members, criticized Stalin for the Red Army's defeats in the summer of 1941, denounced the deportation of national minorities that had occurred during and after the war, and blamed Stalin's egotism for the break with Yugoslavia. The speech was published the next day in Italian newspapers and quickly circulated in samizdat format in the USSR. In the summer of 1956 there was a mass amnesty of political prisoners, with 7 million to 8 million released by the end of 1957. Prominent members of the KGB were forced into retirement.

According to Polly Jones, a specialist on Soviet culture, de-Stalinization meant that "the very ideas of stability, control, and authority were thrown into question."[5] The rewriting of history books began. Some city names that had been sovietized were renamed to sound more Russian; Stalingrad became Volgograd. The Stalin Prize became the Lenin Prize. Some Bolshevik victims of the Great Terror of the 1930s were exonerated. The political fallout was immediate. The party faithful were demoralized if they were innocent, terrified if they were not. In 1956 Hungary rebelled against Soviet power, an uprising the USSR crushed by force.

Not surprisingly, cinema was greatly affected by this upheaval. The cinema of the Thaw marked the first time since the 1920s (Soviet cinema's golden age) that cineastes outside the USSR took serious notice of Soviet movies and their makers.[6] The cinematic Thaw was part of the European transformation in film art known as Neorealism in Italy and the New Wave in France. However, because of Soviet cinema's centrality to the state's political project, one might argue that this cultural transformation had even greater societal impact in the USSR than it did elsewhere. The Thaw's effect on cinema was marked first and foremost by humanism (with the individual, not the group, placed front and center) and second by a reflective questioning of the Socialist Realist aesthetic and its canon. As film scholar Alexander Prokhorov writes: "During the Thaw, film privileged visual expression over narrative and sound."[7]

At the time of Stalin's death, Soviet film production was so low as to be almost nonexistent. Of the dozen or so studios, only Mosfilm, Lenfilm, and Soiuzdetfilm/Gorky Studio were producing movies with any regularity. The number of movie theaters was on the rise, but nearly a decade after the end of World War II, there were few new Soviet films to be seen. Ten days after Stalin's death, the government abolished the Ministry of Cinematography and replaced it with the Main Administration on Cinema Affairs, located within the Ministry of Culture.[8] This was a welcome move as far as the cinema community was concerned. Because it took cinema out of the direct line of fire by the party and the government, filmmakers might be less fearful of possible repercussions and more encouraged about new productions. Although the literary debate about Socialist Realism's efficacy as the state's aesthetic doctrine had begun very cautiously by late 1953, the new thinking did not trickle down to the studios until the end of 1954.

In 1954 Ivan Pyrev, who had been director of the Mosfilm studio during the war, regained that position. Unpredictable and autocratic but a good judge of authentic talent, Pyrev brought new energy and initiative to the filmmaking enterprise. Under Pyrev, an influential director in his own right, Mosfilm was rebuilt and expanded and became the home of many bright young talents, including Bondarchuk. Pyrev was also adept at bending the numerous rules that still existed in the Main Administration on Cinema Affairs, if doing so would benefit his filmmakers.

When the new Five-Year Plan was unveiled in 1955, it called for substantial investment in all aspects of cinema, with a target of 75 new titles to be produced in 1956.[9] By the late 1950s, Soviet studios were turning out more than 100 films annually. In 1959 the number was 137, up from 9 in 1951.[10] For the first time in more than twenty years, people who loved movies had real choices, and cinema surged in popularity. Studios began to organize film festivals that encouraged genuine public discussion of the pictures screened. *Cinema Art* (*Iskusstvo kino*), which had been transformed in the late 1940s as an agent of the "cult of personality" surrounding Stalin, once again published film criticism of genuine merit. The long-defunct fan magazine *Soviet Screen* (*Sovetskii ekran*) was brought back to life in 1957; although the reborn publication was mainly a pictorial devoted to developing a star culture, it also translated some of the critical debates for its readership, the nonprofessional moviegoing public. In terms of censorship, studios were given more authority to govern themselves, rather than being subjected to central oversight.[11]

Artistically revolutionary pictures appeared during this era, such as Mikhail Kalatozov's *The Cranes Are Flying* (*Letiat zhuravli*, 1957), Sergei Bondarchuk's *The Fate of a Man* (*Sudba cheloveka*, 1959), Grigory Chukhrai's *The Ballad of a Soldier* (*Ballada o soldate*, 1959), and Andrei Tarkovsky's *Ivan's Childhood* (*Ivanovo detstvo*, 1962). Not only did these pictures make history in the USSR; they also made waves in the West for their artistic achievements. The fact that they were hailed abroad and won prizes at international film festivals was a point of special pride for filmmakers and the Soviet public alike. The majority of the artistically renowned films of the late 1950s and early 1960s "revisioned" World War II, moving away from generals, maps, and complaints about the Allies and toward the human cost of the conflict. Individualism was the hallmark of the Thaw in film, and directors cautiously put their individual stamps on these films without breaking wholly from the conventions of Socialist Realism.

Alongside this exciting cultural ferment, however, the Cold War heated up as the USSR began to flex its muscles. In 1957 the Soviets launched their first intercontinental ballistic missile and the satellite *Sputnik*; that year they also detonated a hydrogen fusion bomb, causing shock and consternation in the United States. Nevertheless, in June 1957 the Party Presidium voted Khrushchev out of office while he was vacationing in Finland. With the help of the KGB and the army, he managed to quash this attempted coup, but the Central Committee exacted a price: limits on the extent of de-Stalinization. A putative Khrushchev supporter, Leonid Brezhnev, saw his star begin to rise at this time.

Khrushchev continued to face opposition within the party, even among his supporters. This opposition was intensified by worries over international crises and domestic failures. Khrushchev flailed about in an inconsistent manner, and this did not inspire confidence among the party leadership or the rank and file. Indeed, as Jones notes, there was "no consistent commitment to liberalization on the part of the authorities, not even *within* the various cultural communities."[12] In 1958, for example, despite the cultural relaxation of the Thaw, Boris Pasternak's novel *Dr. Zhivago* was savagely attacked in the press after its publication in the West, and Pasternak was forced to decline the Nobel Prize in literature. Yet in 1962, Khrushchev personally authorized the publication of an equally incendiary novel, Alexander Solzhenitsyn's *One Day in the Life of Ivan Denisovich*. Khrushchev praised Stalin as a theoretician in 1959, but in 1961 he hinted that Stalin was responsible for the 1934 assassination of Sergei Kirov and ordered Stalin's body removed from Lenin's mausoleum in Moscow's Red Square.

By the end of 1962, the "fragility" of the Thaw and its "potential for reversal" were sadly obvious.[13] Censorship had once again become more stringent, and the press began to attack Solzhenitsyn. Dmitry Shostakovich's Thirteenth Symphony *Babi Yar*, based on Yevgeny Yevtushenko's poem about the World War II massacre of Jews in Kiev, was savaged in the press. The symphony could no longer be played, although Shostakovich was still allowed to perform some of his previously banned works.

After the fright caused by the Hungarian revolt in 1956, Khrushchev's foreign policy became increasingly erratic, alternating between diplomacy and belligerence. Given the Cold War face-off, relations with the United States were most important. Here too, we see Khrushchev's ambivalent policies and behavior. He first visited the United States in the fall of 1959, a friendly visit to set up cultural, educational, scientific, and sports exchanges. But the mood quickly soured due to events in 1960 and 1961. In May 1960, shortly before a scheduled summit in Paris, an American U-2 spy plane crashed on Soviet soil. In September 1960 Khrushchev famously banged his shoe on the table at a United Nations meeting in New York. In April 1961 the Berlin Wall crisis and the abortive Bay of Pigs invasion of Cuba both occurred.

The fiasco at the Bay of Pigs, and Khrushchev's low opinion of John F.

Kennedy, emboldened the Soviet premier to begin constructing missile silos in Cuba in the late summer of 1962. On 22 October Kennedy ordered a blockade of Cuba and placed US forces on high alert. After nearly a week of diplomatic gamesmanship, the silos came down on 28 October. As far as Soviet citizens were concerned, this was a clear victory for the United States. (*War and Peace* had begun filming in September 1962, just before the Cuban Missile Crisis began. Not surprisingly, the news greatly unnerved the cast and crew.) The Cuban Missile Crisis marked the beginning of the end of the Khrushchev era. Just before the second anniversary of the crisis, on 14 October 1964, the Central Committee met while Khrushchev was on vacation in the Black Sea and unanimously voted him out. Leonid Brezhnev became the party secretary.

Brezhnev was the anti-Khrushchev, a skilled politician with many friends in the party. He instituted a number of reactionary measures: he restored the party privileges that Khrushchev had worked hard to limit, cracked down on the arts, and restored Stalin's good name, especially as a wartime leader. But at the same time, he ended the influence of bogus scientific theories that had crippled Soviet science, such as Lysenkoism, and he stopped the bullying of the Russian Orthodox Church that had been prominent under Khrushchev.

By the time Khrushchev was ousted, the cultural climate was cooling down. Although Brezhnev was an unknown quantity to most filmmakers, politically astute directors understood that a return to greater cultural control was probably imminent. Brezhnev admired Stalin in many ways, and like him, Brezhnev preferred straightforward, representational art. He sought to harness the arts in pursuit of the state's goals and had little tolerance for artistic experimentation.

Nevertheless, the Thaw in cinema did not truly end until 1968 (the year of the invasion of Czechoslovakia), after *War and Peace* was finished. Indeed, the Thaw and Brezhnev's policy of détente effectively inhibited neo-Stalinist efforts to turn the cultural clock all the way back to Stalinism. However, an important step in the hardening of the cinematic line occurred in 1963, when the Main Administration on Cinema Affairs was abolished in the Ministry of Culture and ministerial status was restored to cinematography by the reestablishment of Goskino, headed by Aleksei Romanov. Goskino was answerable to the State Council of Ministers on economic matters and to the Communist Party's Central Committee on ideological matters. In mid-1965 Goskino turned down a number of scripts intended to critically explore the late Stalin era.[14] By the late 1960s, a number of films, particularly several about the Russian Civil War, had been banned outright.

Important to the success of Bondarchuk's film was Brezhnev's desire to promote patriotic culture in the USSR and raise the military's profile. His central focus was to expand the nascent cult of World War II into a massive state enterprise, with Victory Day as a major national holiday.[15] Although films about World War II were privileged, films with other military-patriotic themes were also welcome, especially one about Napoleon's 1812 invasion.

In the Brezhnev era, filmmakers also faced increasing pressure to make movies with mass appeal. By this time, a large number of Soviet citizens owned televisions, and television began to compete seriously with the movies. As the cinema box office began its downward spiral in the mid-1960s, Goskino began to pay attention to audience preferences.[16] As a result, it vigorously promoted the work of directors who catered to the public's taste for lighter genres such as comedies, science fiction, detective films, and melodramas.[17] This atmosphere helps explain the mixed reception of *War and Peace*, a decidedly artistic film.

Why *War and Peace*?

Why write a book about Bondarchuk's *War and Peace*? A masterpiece of epic filmmaking, it is certainly Bondarchuk's most ambitious picture in his storied forty-year career in the movies. More important is the complexity of the film, which operates on a number of different levels: as the biggest epic in an era of film epics, as an admirable attempt to adapt Tolstoy's sprawling novel for the screen, and as a historical film of grand proportions. Bondarchuk took literature and history seriously, striving to make a historically authentic film that was also true to the spirit of Tolstoy's novel. Furthermore, Bondarchuk's *War and Peace* exemplifies the transition from the intimacy of Thaw-era cinema to the monumentalism of many of the films of the Brezhnev era. This means that an analysis of Bondarchuk's *War and Peace* has the potential to illuminate an important but less studied aspect of Soviet cultural politics.

This film is also a significant artifact of the cultural Cold War between the United States and the USSR. From its genesis as a response to American director King Vidor's *War and Peace* (1956) to its afterlife as a film much admired in the West (more so than at home), Bondarchuk's film offers a concrete look at how Soviet patriotism was constructed during the Cold War.

Moreover, the film is emblematic of growing Russian nationalism, intended to unify the country under the umbrella of an all-wise Mother Russia. But instead, it exacerbated the state's already troubled relations with its many ethnic minorities, contributing to its demise in 1991.

This book is organized thematically. Chapter 1 covers the making of *War and Peace*, a story that is almost as interesting as the film itself. It examines the fraught history of the film's production. Bondarchuk was a complicated man who liked to think of himself as a demanding but reasonable "actor's director." However, many of his cast and crew felt that he was in fact a tyrant, which led to exceptional volatility during a production process that seemed to drag on forever. This chapter also demonstrates the Soviet state's involvement in film production, particularly how Minister of Culture Yekaterina Furtseva interceded in the filmmaking at key junctures. Finally, this chapter explicates the ambivalent reactions to the film, which greatly disheartened the cast and crew, who were very proud of their work, especially Bondarchuk. Although we cannot know what Soviet audiences thought, we do know that they decided not to see parts three and four, despite the large turnout for parts one and two.

Chapter 2 analyzes the film as an epic, particularly as a Soviet epic. It would be a serious mistake to characterize Bondarchuk's picture as a crassly politicized version of Tolstoy's novel. Bondarchuk had too much respect for Tolstoy. However, it is also true that Bondarchuk chose to focus on aspects of Tolstoy's philosophy in *War and Peace* that were congenial with Soviet ideology. Therefore, the film definitely emphasizes Russia as the motherland and Russian patriotic culture. Although these characteristics were present in the script from the beginning (it was finished in early 1962, before Khrushchev's ouster), they became a hallmark of the finished film in terms of both style and content. Therefore, Bondarchuk's film became a bulwark of Brezhnev's political culture, which privileged the military and sought to inculcate Soviet citizens with patriotism.

Chapter 3 studies the film as a literary adaptation, to examine how Bondarchuk's *War and Peace* fits into adaptation theory and to assess its fidelity to Tolstoy. Everyone—cast, crew, and critics—acknowledged that Bondarchuk and cowriter Vladimir Solovev made every effort to be faithful to the novel. Indeed, the first title on the screen—"Leo Tolstoy, *War and Peace*"—pays homage to the author. Only after this does Bondarchuk get credit as the director. The question is, how could any film, even one with a 250-page script and that ran for seven hours, be faithful to a 1,200-page book that is literature and philosophy in almost equal measure?[18] Obviously, Bondarchuk and

Solovev had to engage in extensive cutting, and what they omitted from the film is as revealing as what they included.

Chapter 4 examines the film as an independent historical work. Bondarchuk immersed himself in historical as well as literary sources. The point of this chapter is twofold: to evaluate how well the film operates as a "big picture" history of 1812 and its epoch, and to examine how well the film conveys Tolstoy's idiosyncratic philosophy of history, which downgrades human volition and autonomy in favor of large impersonal forces that supposedly determine the course of history. Filming the "history" was arguably the trickiest aspect of Bondarchuk's *War and Peace*, given that the official Soviet politicization of history was grounded in Marxism.

Chapter 5 compares Bondarchuk's film with its nemesis, King Vidor's 1956 version of *War and Peace*, an Italian-American coproduction. Although Vidor was constrained by the Western model of filmmaking, which emphasized commercial returns and audience appeal, his film is a solid effort that found an audience in the USSR. There is no question that Bondarchuk's picture is more "Russian"—how could it be otherwise?—but is it better aesthetically or truer to Tolstoy? In other words, did Bondarchuk's *War and Peace* succeed in its goal of surpassing Vidor's effort?

Chapter 6 takes a look at Bondarchuk's next film after *War and Peace*, *Waterloo* (1970), which he considered an epilogue to the earlier picture. This film, an Italian-Soviet coproduction, was produced by Dino De Laurentiis (who also produced Vidor's *War and Peace*) and Mosfilm, the USSR's leading studio; it was distributed in the United States by Columbia Pictures. The film, which reportedly cost $38.9 million, was, like Bondarchuk's *War and Peace*, one of the most expensive films of its time. Despite its stellar cast—Rod Steiger as Napoleon, Christopher Plummer as Wellington, and Orson Welles as Louis XVIII—the picture was not as well received in the West as *War and Peace*. Bondarchuk's vaunted ability to work with actors was not in evidence in his only English-language effort. However, the battle scenes, Bondarchuk's forte, are magnificent. Nevertheless, this film can be considered Bondarchuk's "Waterloo," as it stymied his quest to become a major European director.

The conclusion ties up Bondarchuk's career after *War and Peace* and *Waterloo* and examines the recent history of the former. It also sums up the reasons why *War and Peace* belongs in the pantheon of great epic films.

CHAPTER ONE

FROM INCEPTION TO SCREEN

In 1959 American director King Vidor's 1956 adaptation of *War and Peace*, starring Henry Fonda, Audrey Hepburn (a favorite with Soviet audiences), and Mel Ferrer, was released in the USSR. It was one of a wave of American films imported following a US-Soviet cultural exchange agreement in 1958. Although some Soviet critics have claimed that the film was not well received by Soviet audiences, 31.4 million spectators bought tickets, putting it in second place for foreign films and tenth place overall, belying those claims.[1] Surprisingly, it was the only adaptation of Tolstoy's masterwork in the past forty-one years.

The first screen adaptation, a Pathé Frères/Khanzhonkov coproduction, appeared in 1912, two years after Tolstoy's death. It was directed by Pyotr Chardynin and featured the fabled star of the imperial Russian screen, Ivan Mozzhukhin, as Prince Andrei Bolkonsky and ballerina Vera Karalli as Countess Natasha Rostova.[2] It had 1,000 extras.[3] World War I led to renewed interest in Tolstoy's novel, and three versions were made in 1915, although only two were released. The first, titled *War and Peace* (*Voina i mir*) was produced by Thieman & Reinhardt's leading directors, Vladimir Gardin and Yakov Protazanov, with Olga Preobrazhenskaya (later a Soviet director) as Natasha. The Khanzhonkov studio and Chardynin took another stab at the novel in *Natasha Rostova*, with Karalli again playing Natasha but Vitold Polonsky playing Andrei this time; Mozzhukhin was cast as the cad Anatole Kuragin, who seduces Natasha. Apparently the market was sated, because Drankov & Taldykin's production, directed by Anatoly Kamensky and first mentioned in the press 1914, was never released.[4] Then came Vidor's Italian-American production after a four-decade hiatus.

Genesis

After the release of Vidor's film in the Soviet Union, sentiments began to grow that it needed to be "answered" with a bigger and better epic.[5] In the opinion of Russian film scholar Fyodor Razzakov, Vidor's *War and Peace* was a weapon in the Cold War, intended to show that the United States was richer than the USSR.[6] These rumblings increased in 1961 as the 150th anniversary of Napoleon's invasion approached and plans were made to open the Museum-Panorama "Battle of Borodino" on Kutuzov Avenue in Moscow.[7] There can be little doubt, however, that the primary impetus for a Soviet *War and Peace* was the cultural Cold War.[8] Some Soviet citizens were outraged that "their" masterpiece had been appropriated by the Americans, who presented merely a facsimile of Russian culture. In February 1961 the Central Committee of the Communist Party received a letter from scientists, cultural figures, and military officers complaining that an "American" *War and Peace* had appeared on Russian screens.[9] Shortly thereafter a group of leading cinematographers also wrote a letter demanding a Soviet *War and Peace*, stating: "As is well known, the American film, based on this novel, communicated neither the artistic nor the national aspects of Tolstoy's epic, nor the great, liberating spirit of the Russian people."[10] Bondarchuk himself wrote letters to friends and colleagues: "Why is it that this novel, the pride of Russian national character, was adapted in America and released in their cinema halls? And we ourselves are not able to adapt it? It's a disgrace to the entire world!"[11] The Central Committee took these complaints seriously and turned the project over to the minister of culture, Yekaterina Furtseva. The film was going to be a *goszakaz*, a state-ordered picture that guaranteed good distribution and lots of prestige.[12]

Many directors vied for this important assignment, chief among them Ivan Pyrev, formerly the head of Mosfilm. As Kristin Roth-Ey notes: "Bringing a movie to the screen in the USSR always entailed an intricate choreography of institutional relationships," and Pyrev had enemies among the Khrushchev-era reformers in the Kremlin.[13] Furtseva was loath to appoint him as sole director.[14] In their letter, the cinematographers had suggested Bondarchuk as director: "We must attract the best dramaturges and masters of cinema to work on it. The production of the film should be led by one of our best film directors. The most worthy candidate for us seems to be the laureate of the Lenin Prize, People's Artist of the USSR, S. F. Bondarchuk."[15] Bondarchuk reluctantly accepted Furtseva's offer.[16] Initially, Bondarchuk and Pyrev were supposed to codirect, but Pyrev abruptly left the project after a failed love affair with Liudmila Maichenko, an actress being considered for the part of Natasha.[17] That left Bondarchuk—unlike Pyrev, a non-Communist—to direct the film.[18]

Sergei Bondarchuk

Despite the opinion of the Soviet cinematographers, Sergei Bondarchuk was not an obvious choice to direct such a politically important film. Indeed, he recalled that his first response was fear; he consulted with writer Mikhail Sholokhov, the world-famous author of *Quiet Flows the Don* (*Tikhii Don*), as to whether he should take on the task.[19] After all, he had directed just one prior film, the touching psychological drama *The Fate of a Man* (*Sudba cheloveka*, 1959), based on a Sholokhov story about the travails of a Soviet prisoner of war in World War II. Granted, *The Fate of a Man* had been a major hit, but it was an intimate picture, about as far from an epic as any film could be. Yet Bondarchuk later reminisced, "If there hadn't been *Fate*, I don't think I would have dared film *War and Peace*.[20]

Born on 25 September 1920 in the small southern Ukrainian village of Belozerka, in Kherson oblast, Bondarchuk was a child of the revolution. He was the son of a worker from the southern Russian city of Taganrog, famous as Chekhov's hometown.[21] He came from a mixed ethnic background. In addition to having Ukrainian blood, one of his grandfathers was Bulgarian, and a grandmother was a Serb.[22] After spending his first seven years in the Odessa region, Bondarchuk and his family moved to the Taganrog area, where his father eventually became the chairman of a large collective farm.[23] The young Bondarchuk was therefore a country boy and remained one at heart.[24]

Bondarchuk wanted to be an actor from an early age and made his acting debut at age nine.[25] He also experimented with homemade "cinema": hand-drawn frames spooled between two bobbins.[26] Strongly influenced by one of his uncles, an amateur comic actor, Bondarchuk performed semiprofessionally with the Working Youth Theater and then with the Robinson Crusoe Theater.[27] He briefly left school to join a professional theater troupe in Yeisk, on the Sea of Azov, but eventually returned to Taganrog to finish his education.[28] Bondarchuk hoped to join the Okhlopkov Theater in Moscow, but in 1937 he entered the Rostov Theatrical College instead. There he performed in the Dvatsky Theater, which subscribed to the Stanislavsky acting method, a tradition he valued.[29]

When the German army invaded the Soviet Union in June 1941, Bondarchuk enlisted in Groznyi and was part of the defense force in the Caucasus. He entertained the troops by declaiming Russian and Soviet literary classics.[30] After his demobilization from the army he traveled, still in his soldier's uniform, to Moscow to attend VGIK, the All-Union State Institute of Cinematography.[31] The year was 1946. Bondarchuk was initially unsure about pursuing a career in cinema because of his love for the theater—VGIK had attempted to recruit him earlier when he was at the theatrical school in Rostov. But when he sat in on a class taught by leading director Sergei Gerasimov, he was sold on the idea of becoming a film actor. He passed twelve exams in one week and was accepted as a scholarship student in Gerasimov's third-year acting class.[32] Although he also attended lectures by Sergei Eisenstein and rehearsals with Vsevolod Pudovkin, Bondarchuk was profoundly influenced by Gerasimov's theory of acting: "Each actor should become the director of his role."[33] Bondarchuk graduated from VGIK with perfect grades; to earn his diploma, he appeared in Gerasimov's World War II film *The Young Guard* (*Molodaia gvardiia*, 1948), where he played the role of an elder, the "old Party underground worker" Valko.[34]

Bondarchuk entered Soviet cinema at its nadir, in terms of both quantity and quality.[35] (Cinema had been severely blighted during Stalin's final years, for economic and political reasons.) Now officially a professional film actor, Bondarchuk appeared in a number of films from 1948 to 1951, including *The Story of a Real Man* (*Povest nastoiashchego cheloveka*, Aleksander Stolper, 1948), *Michurin* (Aleksandr Dovzhenko, 1948), and *The Cavalier of the Golden Star* (*Kavaler Zolotoi Zvezdy*, Yuly Raizman, 1951), before being cast in the role that would make him a star, the eponymous hero in Igor Savchenko's *Taras Shevchenko* (1951).[36] It was Bondarchuk's mentor Gerasimov who recommended him for the role. Bondarchuk was deeply impressed by Savchenko, and he recalled: "For me [Savchenko] was an Academy. From him I learnt everything . . . everything . . . I did everything with him. So I can call myself his disciple."[37] Not surprisingly, the character Taras Shevchenko, which Soviet critics Galina Dolmatovskaya and Irina Shilova proclaimed "one of the best biographical roles in the history of Soviet cinema to the present day," was the first role Bondarchuk was really proud of.[38] In 1952, at the astonishingly young age of thirty-two and with only a few films to his name, Bondarchuk became a People's Artist of the USSR, the highest honor for an artist.[39] He also received Stalin's direct praise for his part in *Taras Shevchenko* and came to international attention when he won a prize at the Karlovy Vary film festival in Czechoslovakia.[40]

Following *Taras Shevchenko*, Bondarchuk took many roles in mediocre movies.[41] Then, in 1955, he played the part of the sensitive Dr. Dymov in Samson Samsonov's adaptation of Chekhov's *The Grasshopper* (*Poprygunia*), which was a great success. Next to Taras Shevchenko, this was Bondarchuk's second favorite role from his early career because of its psychological complexity. *The Grasshopper* was followed by the lead role in Sergei Yutkevich's *Othello* (*Otello*, 1955).[42] Then came Bondarchuk's directorial debut in *The Fate of a Man*, which won him many accolades, the grand prize at the Moscow International Film Festival, and international renown.[43]

Two years later, he found himself at the helm of what would become the most expensive film made to date and perhaps the most expensive film of all time. Estimates of *War and Peace*'s costs range from a low of $29 million to a high of $100 million, the equivalent of about $700 million today.[44] The true costs of the film will never be known because of the unprecedented level of "free" state support it received. For example, many Russian commentators have cited the *Guinness Book of Records*' claim that there were 120,000 extras in the film who were provided "practically free" by Mosfilm.[45] Moreover, it was "one of only a few Soviet films shot in 70mm format."[46] When the first of its four parts, "Andrei Bolkonsky," was released, 2,805 copies were made (a record for Soviet cinema) for an audience of 58.3 million.[47] The film was eventually shown in at least eighty countries and was seen by 250 million viewers worldwide.[48] Even Tolstoy's daughter Alexandra liked it.[49] As film scholar Elena Prokhorova writes: "In short, *War and Peace* was designed as a Soviet prestige object, demonstrating the superiority of Soviet cinema."[50] "We had to compete with America," recalled the film's composer, Viacheslav Ovchinnikov.[51]

Production

It is fitting that this epic film, intended to smite American dominance in cinema, had an epic production that went on for more than six years. Bondarchuk's *War and Peace* got the green light on 5 May 1961, when Minister of Culture Yekaterina Furtseva gave Bondarchuk 30,000 rubles—one-fifth of what he had asked for—in seed money.[52] Work on the script began immediately, with Bondarchuk and writer Vasily Solovev serving as coscenarists. Initially the film was approved for three parts; the writers received 4,000 rubles for the first part and 30 percent less for each succeeding part.[53] Some filmmakers advised Bondarchuk to go back to the historical sources for 1812 and write a "fresh" screenplay, but he was deeply committed to Tolstoy's text, as the finished film shows.[54] Nevertheless, Bondarchuk "scrupulously" researched his subject.[55] The two scenarists, who worked together harmoniously, wrote what was essentially a shooting script (Solovev recalls that the film could have been edited from it). It read, however, like a novel, at least in the opinion of literary scholar Evelina Zaidenshnur, who evaluated the script for the Ministry of Culture.[56] Historians and Tolstoy specialists gave it good reviews as well.[57] The film had expanded to four parts by the time Mosfilm approved the thoroughly reworked script on 27 February 1962; a little less than a month later, on 20 March 1962, the Ministry of Culture endorsed the making of the film as presented.[58]

There had been much debate. Should the film be shot in color? Should French be spoken in the film (as it was in the novel)? Should the skirmish at Schöngraben prior to the Battle of Austerlitz be excised?[59] Furtseva remained personally involved in the first two years of the production, which was generally a positive thing. On 26 March 1962, for example, she sent a letter to the assistant minister of agriculture requisitioning 900 horses for the production, and on 30 March she allocated nearly 1.4 million rubles to *War and Peace*—795,000 to cover the audition phase, and 600,000 for miscellaneous expenses.[60]

The auditions for the 300 speaking parts were arduous; thousands of actors read for Bondarchuk.[61] Even when he made a casting decision, there was trouble. His first choice for Prince Andrei, Oleg Strizhanov, backed out to accept a part at the Moscow Art Theater.[62] A furious Bondarchuk pleaded with Goskino, the state film administration, to force Strizhanov to return. He then turned to Furtseva, who called Strizhanov at home and even met with him personally, to no avail.[63] In the face of this defeat, Bondarchuk cast the extremely popular and gifted Innokenty Smokhtunovsky as Andrei, even though the actor wanted to play Pierre Bezukhov (a role Bondarchuk had taken for himself, to Smokhtunovsky's disgust).[64] However, director Grigory Kozintsev interfered and persuaded Smokhtunovsky to play the coveted title role in his own current film, *Hamlet*. After much wrangling with Kozintsev, Bondarchuk gave in, supposedly out of respect for the older generation, at least according to Solovev.[65] More realistically, it was probably because Kozintsev had highly placed friends on the Cinema Committee.[66] Bondarchuk then told Vasily Lanovoi that if he tried out for the part of Anatole Kuragin (even though Vadim Medvedev had already been cast), he could also try out for Andrei—a role Lanovoi was anxious to play.[67] But later, Bondarchuk crassly broke his word, telling Lanovoi in a telephone call that he could be Anatole or nothing.[68] The actor took the part.

With great reluctance, and at the insistence of Furtseva, Bondarchuk eventually cast his fellow student at VGIK, Viacheslav Tikhonov, as Andrei.[69] In addition to being in the same class at VGIK, Bondarchuk and Tikhonov had acted together in two films: Sergei Gerasimov's *The Young Guard* and Leonid Lukov's *It's Impossible to Forget This* (*Ob etom zabyvat nelzia,*

Bondarchuk cast himself as Pierre. (Courtesy Photofest)

1953).[70] Tikhonov had dreamed of playing Andrei, but he had given up hope when Bondarchuk failed to call him for a tryout.[71] For his eventual audition, Tikhonov (as Andrei) played opposite Bondarchuk (as Pierre Bezukhov, an act of self-casting that aroused some mockery) in a scene central to Andrei's internal evolution: the discussion of Good and Evil.[72] Although Bondarchuk accepted Tikhonov for this key role, he truly believed that a man "with worker's hands" who had once worked as a mechanic could not play the role of a prince.[73] Tikhonov joined the cast on 14 December 1962, three months after shooting started, when his commitment to *Optimistic Tragedy* ended.[74] Bondarchuk's hostility to and bullying of Tikhonov almost led to disaster, as Tikhonov was driven into a deep depression and frequently threatened to quit the film.

Despite the difficulties of finding an actor to play Andrei, the hardest part to cast was undoubtedly Natasha. Bondarchuk initially considered dozens of established professional actresses, the top contenders being Anastasiya Vertinskaya, Natalya Kustinskaya, and Natalya Fateeva.[75] When he decided to seek a fresh face, he called on the public to help him find his Natasha and received thousands of photographs of young women.[76] Finally, he settled on Liudmila Saveleva, an unknown, nineteen-year-old ballerina who had just graduated from the Leningrad Choreography School. Saveleva had been accepted by the Kirov Ballet as a soloist when Bondarchuk's associate, Tatiana Likhacheva, discovered her.[77]

Likhacheva had a hard time selling Saveleva to Bondarchuk, who had little respect for the acting abilities of ballerinas. But when Likhacheva showed him Saveleva's screen test for another movie, Bondarchuk reluctantly agreed to invite her for a tryout. Saveleva herself was uncertain whether she wanted the role, which she felt Audrey Hepburn "owned."[78] Bondarchuk was not impressed with Saveleva at first glance and thought she did not resemble Natasha at all, but when she played the marriage proposal scene with Smokhtunovsky as Andrei, Bondarchuk and the crew proclaimed with one voice, "There she is!"[79] She was a young woman the audience would "know and love . . . as Natasha."[80] Bondarchuk chose her because "she was like a clean white sheet of paper."[81]

Bondarchuk even had trouble casting the secondary actors. For example, the actress he wanted for the part of Prince Andrei's sister Marya, Antonina Shuranova, initially refused the role. In her last year at the Leningrad Institute of Theater, Music, and Cinematography, Shuranova intended to pursue a career in the theater and believed she was not particularly photogenic. There were other reasons for her refusal as well. She had not met Bondarchuk during the auditions and learned she had won the role only by reading it in a newspaper.[82] Another factor was the low pay, only twelve rubles a day, which was "not a big sum" even in those days, and she was financially strapped.[83] Shuranova eventually accepted because she wanted to work with the legendary actor Anatoly Ktorov, who had been cast as Prince Nikolai Bolkonsky, Andrei and Marya's father. Ktorov was her mother's favorite actor, and he beguiled Shuranova by calling her "Lady Tonya" at the tryouts. Likewise, Anastasiya Vertinskaya, who played Andrei's unhappy wife, Lise, also turned down the role at first.[84]

Difficulties with actors were only one part of the production story. Bondarchuk also had a serious problem holding on to his cinematographers. Vladimir Monakhov, the first director of photography, abruptly left *War and Peace* to work on Samsonov's *Optimistic Tragedy*. After this defection, Bondarchuk persuaded the husband-and-wife team of Aleksander Shelenkov and Iolanda Chen (Chen YuLan), famous for filming *Zoya* (*Zoia*, Leo Arnshtam, 1944), *Admiral Ushakov* (Vsevolod Pudovkin, 1953), and *The Communist* (*Kommunist*, Yuly Raizman, 1958), to be his cinematographers.[85] Trouble began almost immediately: Shelenkov and Chen were shooting thirty to forty takes of each scene, an inordinate number.[86] The couple exited the film on 20 May 1963 in the midst of a mini-scandal. They wrote a letter to the general director of Mosfilm, Vladimir Surin, stating that their initial joy while working on *War and Peace* had quickly vanished. They accused Bondarchuk of running the production like a dictator; he failed to form a creative collective, refused to work collaboratively, and reshot material without their permission. In sum, they claimed it was impossible to work with him. Surin tried, unsuccessfully, to resolve the problem and ended up accepting their resignations. Shelenkov and Chen were replaced by thirty-one-year-old Anatoly Petritsky, the second cameraman, who had shot only one film independently, *My Younger Brother* (*Moi mladshii brat*, Aleksandr Zarkhi, 1962).[87]

Petritsky's promotion was a stroke of much-needed good luck for *War and Peace*, as he proved to be not only extremely talented but also innovative. Petritsky had served for five years as an assistant cameraman and was eager to work on his own, so he had been reluctant to take another job as second camera, but Surin himself had offered him the job—an unusual step. Petritsky was well aware of the turmoil on the set. In addition to the first cinematographer, Monakhov, set designer Yevgeny Kumanov had resigned as well. By 1963, Petritsky had also left the picture, returning to Moscow to work with Ivan Pyrev on a movie project. Pyrev, who was probably jealous of Bondarchuk, urged Petritsky not to return to *War and Peace*. In March 1963, however, Surin urgently called him back, saying that Shelenkov was "ill" (an apparently frequent occurrence). Petritsky thought the difficulties between Shelenkov and Bondarchuk were a matter of generational conflict and that Shelenkov's "illnesses" were symptomatic of the larger problem. Even so, Bondarchuk was reluctant to accept Petritsky as director of cinematography after Shelenkov and Chen departed and insisted that he share the duties with another cinematographer such as Gherman Lavrov or Vadim Yusov. Petritsky steadfastly refused, and pressure from Surin convinced Bondarchuk to give in and allow Petritsky to be the sole director of cinematography.[88] However, relations between the two continued to be uneasy. After the tour de force scene of Natasha's ball, Petritsky tried to quit, thinking that Bondarchuk wanted him out. But Surin told Petritsky that if he insisted on quitting, he would never work again.[89] Bondarchuk recalled that Petritsky was inordinately sensitive, probably because he was not a war veteran.[90] Many years later, Petritsky admitted that he had perhaps been too egotistical as a young man.[91]

Finally, there were problems with Bondarchuk's choice for the film's composer, twenty-five-year-old Viacheslav Ovchinnikov.[92] Mosfilm's Artistic Council, the studio's censorship body, expressed grave doubts about his youth. Some Ministry of Culture bureaucrats did not want him because he was still a student, but Furtseva was in his corner.[93] Ovchinnikov immodestly argued that the Russian writer Mikhail Lermontov and Wolfgang Amadeus Mozart had accomplished great things at a young age.[94] Eventually, of course, Furtseva and Bondarchuk prevailed.[95]

Then there was the matter of the military history consultants to contend with. Minister of Defense Rodion Malinovsky ordered the General Staff to open its archives to the production, and he appointed as chief historical consultants General of the Army V. V. Kurasov and Major General P. A. Zhilin. Kurasov, director of the War Academy of the General Staff and a Hero of the Soviet Union, was in charge. As a sign of the Ministry of Defense's wholehearted support of the project, other high-ranking generals were also appointed as consultants. General of the Army Markian Markovich, twice a Hero of the Soviet Union and known as a lover of Russian literature, became the consultant on general military affairs. Lieutenant General and Hero of the Soviet Union Nikolai Oslikovsky, an economist by training and a former film producer, became the consultant on cavalry operations.[96] Marshal Vasily Chuikov, famous for the defense of Stalingrad, attempted to intervene in the production and objected to the formation of cavalry units for the film; Furtseva had to smooth things over.[97] And when the editing of the battle scenes was finished in December 1963, they were shown to the highest-ranking officers in the military for approval, including seventeen marshals, with colonel general the lowest rank in the entourage.[98]

As if having to please the generals were not enough, the film also had to pass muster with the political watchdogs at Mosfilm. These critics found the script's depiction of Pierre and his wife Hélène to be "somewhat banal history" compared with the battle scenes, and they called for better development of Natasha's brother, Nikolai Rostov, and the relationship between Prince Andrei and Captain Tushin.[99] There was also wrangling over how many parts the film would be divided into; Bondarchuk and Furtseva wanted two long parts, but others argued that three or four would be better for distribution.[100]

Then there was the task of gathering objects for the film. Bondarchuk was absolutely committed to historical verisimilitude, and he even called in a hairdresser from Paris to coif the cast for Natasha's ball.[101] Furtseva ordered the cooperation of all the historical museums and archives in the Soviet Union; all told, fifty-eight museums, ranging from the Armory of the Kremlin Museum and the Military-Historical Museum to the Tretiakov Gallery and the Tolstoy Museum, provided furniture, paintings, dishware and cutlery, decorative objects, sabers, rifles, and so on.[102] Production manager Nikolai Ivanov recalled that the film could not have succeeded without the help of the directors and staffs of the museums.[103] In addition, thousands of ordinary citizens sent personal period items for use in the film.[104] Irina Skobtseva, who played Pierre's wife Hélène and was Bondarchuk's real-life wife, remembered that all the jewelry in the film had been donated.

What could not be found had to be constructed. The crew built 272 sets and fabricated "100 historically accurate artillery pieces" and 60 wooden cannons that looked like the real thing.[105] Sabers were made from "undisclosed lightweight material to avoid injury" in the hand-to-hand combat scenes.[106] Costumes were copied from period textiles and included 9,000 soldiers' uniforms and 3,000 civilian costumes.[107]

Finding animals for the film was an even more difficult problem. As noted earlier, Furtseva had already requisitioned 900 horses from the Ministry of Agriculture, but at least 600 more would be needed to accommodate the 1,500 soldiers acting as cavalry in the Battle of Borodino. Bondarchuk asked private owners for help, as well as circuses and slaughterhouses.[108] They also needed dogs: sixty beagles and thirty borzois for the hunt scene.[109] The borzois—a quintessential Russian breed that had once been a symbol of the aristocracy—were all donated to the production after a public appeal.[110]

Meanwhile, a small creative group traveled to Transcarpathia in western Ukraine in April 1962 to prepare for shooting, which began symbolically on 7 September 1962, the 150th anniversary of the Battle of Borodino.[111] The first scene shot was the French soldiers executing the Muscovites outside the walls of the Novodevichi monastery.[112] After spending a month on this one scene, only 316 meters of film were usable, at a cost of 121,600 rubles.[113] In addition to the number of takes demanded by Shelenkov and Chen, even after extensive rehearsals, the poor quality of the Soviet-made 70mm film necessitated extra takes due to breakage.[114] Bondarchuk had wanted to use Eastman-Color, but for reasons of cost (and national pride), DS-5 and LN-5 film from the Shostinsky factory was employed.[115] Cinematographer Petritsky recalled that there were mosquitoes in the emulsion, and often the film perforations did not match up.[116] There were also difficulties with the Soviet-made 70mm cameras, especially with the fade and superimposition. Petritsky mused many years later: "The Americans could do it. Why couldn't we?"[117] The quality of the film stock, however, was the "scourge" of the production.[118]

The next scene to be shot was the hunt scene. The borzois were not trained to hunt and did not want to run, but the crew managed to excite them by using a pack of beagles.[119] Then came the battle scenes. Schöngraben and Austerlitz were both shot near the village of Mukachevo in Transcarpathia.[120] The first issue the filmmakers had to deal with was how to keep the inevitable signs of modernity, such as television antennae, out of the film.[121] Then there were delays because Prince Andrei had not been cast; as noted earlier, Tikhonov did not join the production until the end of 1962.

Next, winter intervened. On 26 February 1963 shooting stopped; it was so cold that the production's physicians barred the soldier-extras from working. In March Bondarchuk was called to Moscow for a meeting of government leaders, writers, and artists, and the pace of shooting slowed dramatically. From 15 March through 3 April, there were only six days of work; during this time, the average amount of usable film shot per day was 5.6 meters, at a cost of 120,000 rubles. Finally, on 17 May 1963, the shooting for these scenes ended; three days later, Shelenkov and Chen exited.[122]

The next scene shot was the Battle of Borodino, a technically difficult episode that cinematographer Petritsky was justifiably proud of. The actual battlefield had been turned into a national park, with many monuments, so the location filming could not be done there.[123] Instead, the battle was filmed near the village of Dorogobuzh in Smolensk province, in the Dnepr valley, a good stand-in for the real Borodino.[124] Preparation for the shoot began on 1 August 1963, and the main part of the filming took place over six weeks in September and October.[125] Hundreds of meters of rail had to be laid for the dollies used by the remote-control cameras.[126] A fifteen-meter-high tower was built on a rolling platform with cables for the camera, along with a "suspension road" for aerial shots.[127] The extras consisted of 13,500 infantrymen and 1,500 cavalrymen, all drawn from the Soviet army. The special effects were spectacular: 23 tons of explosives, 40,000 liters of kerosene, 12,000 aerial explosives, 10,000 smoke grenades. But the production did not rely entirely on modern effects; 1,500 antique weapons from Soviet museums were employed in the scene.[128] Amazingly, there were no injuries to the cast or crew, but some horses were hurt during the re-creation of the battle.[129]

After location shooting wrapped in October, the cast and crew returned to Moscow to shoot the interior scenes during December 1963 and January 1964. Here, Bondarchuk and Tikhonov famously tangled while shooting the scene that takes place in the corridor of Kutuzov's headquarters. After twenty takes, Tikhonov shouted, "No, Sergei, I'm leaving. I can't work with you. I don't have the strength for this role. No! No!" After another twelve takes, they had only thirty meters of usable film.[130]

Production continued mainly at the Mosfilm studio through 1964.[131]

Filming of the next important scene, Natasha's ball, began on 28 March 1964. Bondarchuk had originally hoped to use the large foyer of the Tauride Palace in Leningrad, but the electricity there was too unreliable for filming.[132] They had to settle for a set built on Mosfilm's stage 1—the largest pavilion, at 1,400 square meters. Gennady Miasnikov, one of the art directors, recalled that this set was a special challenge.[133] A large space was needed to accommodate the more than 500 dancers that appear in the scene.[134] According to Petritsky, the scene was filmed by four cameramen on roller skates using handheld cameras, but it was plagued by the exceptionally hot lighting system in the pavilion (the high temperatures melted the actors' makeup) and the low quality of the film stock.[135] Nevertheless, the scene is outstanding for its cinematography (a suspension rod was used for the overhead shots) and its choreography (Vladimir Burmeister, "very famous in ballet circles," was the dance master), even though Tikhonov was concerned about his dancing ability.[136]

In mid-June 1964 Bondarchuk traveled to Tolstoy's ancestral home, Yasnaya Polyana, to restore his flagging energies. He returned to Moscow in early July, and on 23 July the production was struck with a terrible blow. While watching a screening of Mikhail Kalatozov's new film *I Am Cuba* (*Ia Cuba*), Bondarchuk suffered a major heart attack. He was clinically dead for a few minutes, and doctors worked for more than two hours to stabilize him. Once he regained consciousness, his first words were that he wanted Sergei Gerasimov, his old mentor, to finish the picture. He was out of commission until 27 September.[137]

By 1965, the Ministry of Culture was getting anxious about the slow pace of production. The film had cost 8,165,200 rubles to date, not counting all the "free" support offered by various agencies of the government. The decision was made on 26 May 1965, against Bondarchuk's wishes, to send the first two parts to the IV Moscow International Film Festival, even though the film was unfinished. This decision forced the rapid editing of parts one ("Andrei Bolkonsky") and two ("Natasha Rostova").[138] The hard and hurried work paid off, because *War and Peace* shared the grand prize with a Hungarian film, Zóltan Fábri's *Twenty Hours* (*Húsz óra*, 1965).[139]

The first half of *War and Peace* was released to the general public in 1966, as shooting continued. The line at the Rossiya Theater, Moscow's largest, was a kilometer long.[140] The head of Goskino, Aleksei Romanov, recalled that "the first part was seen by 49 million people in only five months, although . . . our film *War and Peace* did not have a single advertisement."[141] This is true, but it did have a significant amount of preproduction and production publicity in the fan magazine *Soviet Screen* and even in the serious film journal *Cinema Art*.[142]

Shooting of the final scenes, including the magnificent Moscow fire episode, took place in the vicinity of the Iosifo-Volokolamsky monastery near the village of Teryaevo in Volokolamsk oblast.[143] An extraordinary stand-in for old Moscow was constructed. The set crew had begun planning in late December 1965, but the building did not commence until 25 July 1966.[144] The crew also built tracks for the camera dollies.[145] Perhaps mindful of the difficulties of being director and lead actor simultaneously, Bondarchuk used a double, Yury Devochkin, in some scenes.[146] At 2:30 p.m. on 6 October 1966, the burning of Moscow was filmed with six cameras (the cameramen wore flame-retardant clothing) and five fire engines, under the supervision of the production's pyrotechnics specialist V. A. Likhachev.[147] Petritsky feared that his cameras and film stock might melt, but fortunately, the scene proceeded smoothly, using SU and MIG-9 planes and helicopters for the aerial scenes.[148] There could be no second takes. On 25 October filming was complete, four long years after it had begun. All that remained to be done was sound, music, and editing, as well as the six-month-long process of organizing the return of all the objects loaned by the various museums.[149]

On 28 December 1966 Mosfilm approved the finished part three ("1812"), as work on part four ("Pierre Bezukhov") continued. Four months later, on 26 April 1967, part three was screened at the Cannes Film Festival, outside the competition. This showing—standing room only—was a "fantastic success."[150] The film was distributed to France, Japan, England, and Belgium before it was shown to the Soviet public.[151] When part three premiered at the Rossiya Theater on 21 July, the audience, perhaps tired of all the hype since its win at the Moscow International Film Festival, or perhaps disenchanted with its serious subject, stayed away. Only 21 million people saw part three, a decline of 37 million. This was a real shame, since the Battle of Borodino is one of the best battle scenes ever filmed. Part four premiered on 4 November 1967 to even fewer spectators—only 19.8 million. Perhaps Bondarchuk and Furtseva had been right: the film should have been shown in two parts.[152] Nevertheless, *War and Peace* was among the Soviet blockbusters of the 1960s and recouped its billed, as opposed to actual, costs.[153] Parts one and two ranked twenty-sixth and twenty-seventh as all-time Soviet box-office hits.[154] As the current head of Mosfilm, director Karen Shakhnazarov, observes: "Everybody wanted to see it," even though the response was mixed.[155]

Because the film was conceived as a weapon in the Cold War, and because

Soviets tended to compare their culture to the Americans', of special pride to the cast and crew was the Academy Award for Best Foreign Language Picture of 1968, presented in April 1969.[156] Only Saveleva attended the ceremony, ironically sitting next to King Vidor, who was gracious and praised the film lavishly.[157] It also won prizes at the Venice International Film Festival and from the New York Association of Film Critics.[158] As a whole, the cast was very proud of the film, and Saveleva hyperbolically called it a "gift to the Motherland like Tretiakov's gift of the gallery."[159]

Virtually everyone involved in *War and Peace* regarded their participation as an endurance test.[160] The chief reason was Sergei Bondarchuk, a workaholic who "lived in the studio."[161] Some of them were awestruck, considering him to be an "actor's director."[162] Bondarchuk thought of himself this way: he believed that, from an actor's perspective, the best director is one "who knows, understands, feels . . . the actor's creativity."[163] Kira Golovko, who played Countess Rostova, recalled: "In my point of view, no one worked with actors as he did. I understood right away: a Big Actor is rehearsing and shooting the film."[164] Nikolai Trofimov, who played Captain Tushin, liked the way Bondarchuk interacted with him and believed the director had "full faith in his artists." Trofimov called Bondarchuk his teacher, even though he was already an experienced actor.[165] Even Saveleva, who was intimidated by Bondarchuk and called him an "absolute commander," admired his efforts, like "the last of the Mohicans," to preserve Russian culture.[166]

These positive recollections are contradicted, however, by the memories of others who describe a very different Bondarchuk, an overweening authoritarian. The difficulty he had keeping cinematographers is a case in point; even his ultimate choice, Petritsky, had an on-again, off-again relationship with him. Shuranova described him as a "dictator" who made his actors, including her, very nervous on the set; she even lost her voice during the first take of her first scene, when Andrei is going off to war.[167] Bondarchuk himself wrote: "The director has studied all the material for the film; he alone knows everything. He is tsar and god."[168]

Definitely worst was Bondarchuk's treatment of Tikhonov. Trofimov reported that Tikhonov was forced to perform take after take. The scene where Prince Andrei defends Captain Tushin before General Bagration was reshot twenty-nine times.[169] Shuranova recalled that Tikhonov was even more nervous than she was.[170] Tikhonov believed that Bondarchuk's animus was caused by his belief that an actor from a working-class family could not play a prince. Tikhonov began to doubt himself, and after Bondarchuk repeatedly complained about the actor's large hands, he wore white gloves in an

The unhappy Viacheslav Tikhonov as Prince Andrei. (Courtesy Photofest)

effort to conceal them.[171] Bondarchuk's words—"Bolkonsky is completely different"—kept ringing in his ears, and he asked to be released from the film more than once.[172]

After the screening of the first two parts of *War and Peace* for the cast and crew at the Udarnik Theater, Bondarchuk praised everyone, especially Saveleva. To Tikhonov, he simply said, "You won the marathon."[173] In the end, Tikhonov faced a severe emotional crisis: "I didn't believe in myself."[174] He felt that his "individuality had been squashed out of him" and thought he should quit acting.[175] Nevertheless, the role was a real career booster for Tikhonov. Despite the critical ambivalence about Tikhonov's Andrei, *Soviet Screen's* 1966 readers' poll chose Tikhonov and Saveleva as best actors for their performances in part one.[176]

Reception

In a 1967 postmortem, part of the discussion centered on the paucity of reviews of the film; there were allegedly only four reviews about part one (there were actually a few more, depending on what one counts as a review). Goskino head Aleksei Romanov complained: "This isn't a lot, especially since there were nearly 7,000 articles published abroad about it."[177] As Russian film scholar Natalia Tendora put it: "Only in Russia was the success of the picture, as always, silenced."[178] According to Tendora, Bondarchuk's unpopularity with film critics and other filmmakers was one reason for this relative silence.[179]

The film's reception in the USSR was definitely mixed; given the status of Tolstoy's novel and the film's monumental sweep, it could hardly be otherwise.[180] Most critics found both good and bad in the film. As historian Stephen Norris notes: "Early reviews believed that Bondarchuk had for the most part captured the spirit of the times. They divided over whether or not he had captured Tolstoy's spirit."[181] The journal *Soviet Culture* (*Sovetskaia kultura*) was perhaps the most enthusiastic, calling the film a "big, exciting work . . . a national work, lofty . . . mighty, deep, Russian."[182] K. Zamoshkin also saw the film as very Russian and very patriotic; it was "big, serious, deep, innovative."[183] Although critic A. Sofronov, writing in *The Light* (*Ogonek*), called the film a "talented reproduction" rather than a true screen adaptation, he still praised it as an "achievement," especially the cinematography, the performances of actors Liudmila Saveleva and Anatoly Ktorov, and the film's "patriotism and authenticity."[184] Director Khamil Yarmatov was especially sympathetic, noting the amount of work that had gone into the production. He cited Bondarchuk's success in creating an "indelible spectacle" and wrote: "Without a doubt, the picture *War and Peace* is not only a great event in our cinematography but one of the most successful adaptations of a Russian classic."[185]

It seemed that everyone could agree on a few points. First, the battle scenes were magnificent.[186] Second, two of the cast members were outstanding: Anatoly Ktorov and Liudmila Saveleva. The casting of Ktorov as Prince Nikolai Bolkonsky was indeed a masterstroke. Ktorov, a major film star in the 1920s, had not acted in film in thirty years and had been working exclusively at the fabled Moscow Art Theater. He managed to achieve a purely Tolstoyan image of the old prince, who found happiness in endless activity.[187] There was also general agreement that Saveleva was the perfect Natasha. No one, however, could outdo Bondarchuk in his praise. The "very Russian, very national" Saveleva, he declared, did not act; she "lived" the film.[188] Scriptwriter Sergei Ermolinsky, who found the beginning of the film pretentious, saw Natasha as a "fresh breeze."[189]

Despite this praise, others considered the film a failure. One prominent critic was Lev Anninsky, who thought Bondarchuk's obsession with historical accuracy sapped the life from the film.[190] Even more strongly, dissident director Sergei Paradzhanov argued that *War and Peace* represented everything that was wrong with Soviet cinema; he saw it as indicative of an "amazing crisis" in the film industry.[191] The highbrow journal *Cinema Art* (*Iskusstvo kino*) was less direct in its attack. According to well-known director Georgy Daneliya, Bondarchuk and Solovev "chose the hardest but truest road. They *tried* to bring Tolstoy's thoughts to the screen. . . . Directors don't like to bring ideas to the screen for fear of boring the viewer . . . Bondarchuk wasn't afraid of *boring the viewer* [emphasis added]."[192]

The most scathing review came from Igor Zolotussky in the prominent literary journal *New World* (*Novyi mir*). Zolotussky argued that the film superficially reflected Tolstoy's novel because only the book's events (rather than the ideas) interested Bondarchuk. Zolotussky claimed that Bondarchuk's *War and Peace* was a "great spectacle," but for Tolstoy, "war was not an epic." For Bondarchuk, Zolotussky argued, "war is an epic without tragedy."[193] According to this critic, Bondarchuk had not captured the soul of the novel.[194]

European reviews, in contrast, tended to be positive. A French review, for example, praised the film as "deeply individual, rich, and poetic"; French director Claude Autant-Lara admired Bondarchuk's mastery of detail and thought the film transported the spectator into a richly nuanced world.[195] One of Tolstoy's grandchildren declared that it would have been "impossible to make it better."[196] British critic James Oldridge thought the picture captured the Russian soul (although he also thought the film could have been more dynamic to better suit contemporary tastes).[197]

Because Bondarchuk's *War and Peace* was directed in part toward the American audience as an answer to Vidor's film, the American response is particularly interesting. Soviet films had done poorly at the US box office in the late 1950s and early 1960s, and Hollywood distributors left the US-Soviet film exchange in 1963; art film distributors contracted directly with Soveksportfilm.[198] However, Bondarchuk's film was dealt with differently. As film scholar Tino Balio writes: "The biggest deal was Walter Reade's acquisition of Sergei Bondarchuk's epic *War and Peace*, the most expensive film ever made up to that time. In 1968, Reade released a slightly cut and dubbed version of the film specifically to bypass the art house circuit."[199] Reade's Continental Distributing paid $1.5 million for the rights and "spent the cost of a major film" on the dubbing and duplication of prints.[200] The six-hour film opened on 28 April 1968 at the DeMille Theater in New York;

it was shown in two parts, with a two and a half–hour intermission. The cost of a ticket for the benefit premiere was a colossal $125; ticket prices for the public ranged from $5.50 to $7.50, the highest ever for a film screened in the United States (the previous record was held by *Funny Girl*, at $6).[201]

As in the USSR, the reaction to the film was mixed. Critics were united in lambasting the dubbing.[202] Renata Adler of the *New York Times* wrote that the dubbing of such a long film may have been a feat, but it was also a terrible mistake: "It is that this particular movie, so quintessentially Russian, gains nothing by dubbing. It loses romance and authenticity."[203] *Variety's* "Beau" felt that the dubbing detracted from the emotional scenes in the film.[204] Stanley Kauffman, writing in the *New Republic*, noted that the dubbing had a "dead, studio quality."[205] Penelope Gilliatt in the *New Yorker* extensively bemoaned the decision to dub: "Dubbing a serious foreign picture is sometimes called 'making it commercially viable.' In the case of *War and Peace*, as usual, this turns out to be the gobbledygook phrase for letting sales chaps put a boot through it."[206] As far as the film itself was concerned, most American critics found it too long, especially the battle scenes. In the words of *Newsweek* critic Joseph Morgenstern, interest in the battle began "to pall after the 40,000th casualty."[207]

Although American reviewers had reservations about *War and Peace*, most of them thought the acting very good, especially Liudmila Saveleva as Natasha.[208] *Time* admired the painterly grandeur of the film.[209] "Mosk" in *Variety* wrote that "the costuming, sheer manpower, and the rattling din of violence overpower most critical reservations on this immense film."[210] Stanley Kauffman acknowledged that Bondarchuk "tried throughout to make a *film* of *War and Peace*, not merely a chronicle of the novel on film."[211] Although the reviews could have been better, there is no question that *War and Peace* had an impact both at home and abroad, demonstrating the might of Soviet cinema.

Most critics, both Soviet and American, called Bondarchuk's film an epic. As Soviet critic Elena Bauman wrote: Bondarchuk's "films resemble grandiose frescoes with many figures. They contain numerous human tragedies and battle scenes. A sense of the eternity and harmony of nature, they are permeated with subtle lyrical feelings and deep philosophical thoughts, . . . an acute sense of the concerns, emotions, and moods of his contemporaries, the call of the epoch."[212] An analysis of *War and Peace* as an epic that reflects the "call of the epoch" follows.

CHAPTER TWO

WAR AND PEACE AS A FILM EPIC

Bondarchuk's *War and Peace* fulfilled the Soviet state's desire for an international hit that would top Vidor's *War and Peace*. The large domestic audience for the first two parts of the Soviet film definitely qualifies it as a *blockbuster*, at least in the original meaning of the word: "something, such as a film or book, that sustains widespread popularity and achieves enormous sales."[1] Film scholar Raphaëlle Moine defines cinematic blockbusters differently, as "historical films set in ancient (and non-ancient) times that elevate spectacle"; *War and Peace* is a blockbuster in this sense as well.[2] Indeed, another film genre specialist, Barry Langford, calls *War and Peace* a blockbuster "on the postwar Hollywood model" or, more specifically, an "action blockbuster."[3] Like Moine, Langford conflates *blockbuster* with the usual definition of an *epic* film.

So what is a film epic? According to cinema scholar Constantine Santas, epics are "fictional tales that offer size, length, spectacle, and above all, unusual human feats—possibly of heroic proportions."[4] For Santas, the main characteristics of a historical film epic are as follows: (1) it is based on a historical era or episode, (2) it seeks to represent that period accurately, and (3) it is based on historical materials and its "scenes are more often than not filmed on the locations where events actually took place."[5] Moreover, according to Langford, in the epic films of the 1950s and 1960s, spectacle was the "stylistic dominant."[6] Finally, Robert Burgoyne observes that the "epic spectacle has often been seen as promoting the cause of nationalism."[7] As we shall see, Bondarchuk's *War and Peace* fulfills all these requirements.

Narrative

The first issue to consider is whether the narrative has epic scope. Clearly, Tolstoy's novel did, but Bondarchuk's *War and Peace* is a severely shortened version of the story. The film reduces the novel to four intersecting narrative arcs. It combines the stories of three aristocrats—Prince Andrei Bolkonsky, Countess Natasha Rostova, and Count Pierre Bezukhov—with the story of the Napoleonic Wars, especially the invasion of Russia in 1812. As discussed in the next chapter, Bondarchuk cut many narrative lines and characters from Tolstoy's novel in order to fit the material into the four films that constitute *War and Peace*, but the novel's epic narrative sweep has not been sacrificed.

Part one, "Andrei Bolkonsky," opens with panoramic shots of the Russian landscape before the credits roll, setting the stage for its antiwar and national themes. Thunder transitions to the sounds of bombs going off, horses neighing, men screaming. The story begins in 1805 in St. Petersburg, and the development of the three main characters takes place against the backdrop of the impending war to defend Russia against Napoleon. The purpose of part one is to establish foundations, not only for the characters but also for Tolstoy's favorite ideas about war and history. It opens in Anna Scherer's sparkling salon, with naïve Pierre Bezukhov arguing with other guests about Napoleon's greatness, while Andrei Bolkonsky's unhappy wife, Lise, wonders about the reasons for this "wretched [coming] war."

Later, when Pierre and Andrei continue their conversation at the Bolkonskys' home, the rift between Andrei and Lise becomes apparent; he treats her curtly, pretending she needs to rest because of her pregnancy while, in reality, he is just tired of her. Pierre and Andrei disagree about the war. Andrei says he "must go" to war, but not for any patriotic reasons. He is simply bored with his life in the heavily Westernized capital. Later, they walk along the banks of the Neva River talking about the meaning of life and whether each is fulfilling his potential. At the end of this conversation, Andrei advises Pierre, who has a reputation as a carouser, not to associate with the wastrel Anatole Kuragin, foreshadowing the role Anatole will play in Andrei's life.

Despite this warning, Pierre goes straight from the Bolkonskys' to Kuragin's drinking party, where he quickly becomes very drunk. (The camera sways, mimicking inebriation.) A soused Dolokhov (another foreshadowing, this time for Pierre) takes a bet that he can drink an entire bottle of rum in one gulp while standing on the sill of a broken window. Pierre, who is completely out of control, is about to attempt the same feat when Kuragin decides to move the uproarious party, which includes a captive bear, elsewhere.

There is an abrupt transition to Pierre's father, Count Bezukhov, who is dying. The next scenes are cut back and forth between old Bezukhov's deathbed, where sycophants and priests hover around him, and thirteen-year-old Natasha Rostova's name-day celebration, which includes a dinner

Liudmila Saveleva as thirteen-year-old Natasha. (Courtesy Photofest)

party and a dance. This parallel construction offers a nice contrast between life (the exuberant Natasha) and death (Bezukhov père); this contrast is a recurrent theme for both Tolstoy and Bondarchuk. Prince Vasily Kuragin, Anatole's father, is at the Bezukhov house, scheming to control the dying man's will. Finally, Pierre's cousin Catiche announces the old man's death. Pierre, who is an illegitimate son, inherits the count's title and great wealth because of his father's last-minute intervention with the emperor, Alexander I, to legitimize him and thereby approve the inheritance.

The stage setting continues. Cut to the Bolkonsky estate at Bald Hills. Here, we are introduced to Andreï's eccentric father, Prince Nikolai, who, as the narrator informs us, has been exiled by Emperor Paul (Alexander I's father) to his estate. We also meet Andrei's devout and obedient sister, Princess Marya. Relations between the old prince and his offspring are strained due to Nikolai's idiosyncratic, autocratic, even cruel behavior. About to leave for war, Andrei asks his father to send for a physician when his wife goes into labor. Nikolai responds angrily about the worthlessness of women but promises to do so nonetheless. The two men tentatively embrace in a subtly wrenching scene.

Then the film turns to the Battle of Schöngraben, in which Andrei will participate. Panoramic shots are overlaid by the sounds of many men, and the narrator provides an explanation: "Fifty thousand Russians marched into Austria to join General Mack." Bondarchuk spends a great deal of screen time on the army rank and file, to emphasize the collective nature of the Russian army. In this episode, he intercuts scenes of Andrei at General Mikhail Kutuzov's headquarters and Pierre at Scherer's salon in St. Petersburg with slow tracking shots of masses of soldiers marching, digging fortifications, and tramping through the mud. In the meantime, Pierre is introduced to his future wife, the empty-headed but voluptuous Hélène Kuragina, Anatole's sister.

The Battle of Schöngraben (1805) is well-crafted and exciting and is filmed on an epic scale. This is Bondarchuk's first chance to display his skill with the mass scenes that are so important to the Soviet film canon. First we see thousands of French soldiers entering the screen, followed by the Russians, before the two armies meet. Bondarchuk has expertly choreographed the episode to show the chaos and carnage of war: bodies everywhere, soldiers running, a cavalry charge, the air so thick with smoke that one can hardly see the action. General Pyotr Bagration, a historical figure, orders his men to fall back, but one officer, Captain Tushin (fictional), ignores this order and continues to fight; the sky is dark with smoke from the fires. Later, when night has fallen, Tushin is upbraided by Bagration for not obeying orders. Andrei, a staff officer, defends the lowly captain's courage. Tushin thanks Andrei for his intervention but receives no acknowledgment from the aloof, stone-faced prince.

Back home in Russia, life is gay. Pierre is at the Kuragins for Hélène's name-day party. (Her father has been contriving reasons to force them together, hoping to arrange an advantageous marriage for his daughter.) Pierre sits awkwardly with Hélène on a settee; a split screen shows her eavesdropping parents anxiously awaiting a proposal in an adjacent room. The impatient Kuragin senior, who cannot wait forever, enters and excitedly

Prince Andrei carries the regimental banner. (Courtesy Photofest)

proclaims his happiness about their impending marriage as he kisses them. Pierre, nonplussed, realizes he has been trapped into marrying the vacuous Hélène. He tries to convince himself that he is really in love with her.

Back to war. The next episode is the Battle of Austerlitz (also 1805). General Kutuzov is shown sleeping through briefings, which was not unusual for the real Kutuzov. He does not want to engage in battle; this is the emperor's obsession. In true epic fashion, we see masses of Russian soldiers marching through the fog before the emperor arrives and orders Kutuzov to give the command to start, even though some of the battalions are not yet in place. ("We're not at parade," Alexander says with a smug smile. Kutuzov tartly retorts, "That's precisely why we wait.") Again, as in Schöngraben, Bondarchuk emphasizes the chaos and tragedy of war, as well as Alexander I's major blunder in getting involved in the fight in the first place. Bondarchuk shows hand-to-hand combat by swordsmen, and there are many shots of their fallen horses. A particularly poignant symbol of the disaster is a herd of riderless horses crashing through the battlefield. When the defeated Russian soldiers attempt to flee the onslaught in panic, Andrei picks up the regiment's banner to rally them and rushes forward. He almost immediately takes a hit, which is followed by a black screen, then a close-up of a hand taking the religious medallion his sister Marya had given him. We see Napoleon on horseback in a long shot perusing Andrei's prone body and admiring his bravery ("That's a beautiful death"), followed by aerial shots of the battlefield to emphasize the carnage. It is not clear at this point whether Andrei is dead or alive.

Afterward, two survivors of the battle, Natasha's brother Nikolai Rostov and his friend Denisov, arrive at the Rostovs to general rejoicing. The scene is different at the Bolkonskys'. Nikolai Bolkonsky, at his lathe, informs his daughter Marya that, according to Kutuzov, Andrei is dead, even though his body has not been found. Marya tries to tell the very pregnant Lise this tragic news but cannot bring herself to do it.

Back at the Rostovs', life goes on as usual. Rumors about an affair between Pierre's wife and the cad Dolokhov are circulating, and Pierre has received an anonymous note. At a lavish, male-only dinner party to honor General Bagration, a waiter lays a sheet of paper before Pierre. Then Dolokhov, who is seated opposite Pierre, makes a sneering, suggestive remark about the husbands of pretty women and grabs the paper. Pierre snatches it from Dolokhov's hand and challenges him to a duel. In a remarkable scene, which makes good use of extreme close-ups and crane shots, a confused and scared Pierre surprisingly manages to shoot Dolokhov (not a mortal wound) while avoiding the downed man's return gunshot. This is followed by a ferocious argument over the duel between Pierre and Hélène, who denies having anything other than an innocent flirtation with Dolokhov. Enraged, Pierre takes a marble tabletop and brandishes it at her, threatening to kill her.

At this point, the film starts to resemble a soap opera. At the Bolkonskys', Lise is in labor, and it is going badly. To Marya's shock and happiness, Andrei suddenly arrives; he is too late to save his wife, but the baby boy lives. Prince Nikolai drops his iron mask and weeps with joy at his son's return, a remarkable display of genuine emotion for the flinty old man.

Bondarchuk next tries to bring in some of Tolstoy's philosophical ideas. Pierre and Andrei are seen walking through a grove of trees (shot at Tolstoy's estate, Yasnaya Polyana) discussing weighty matters of right and wrong, happiness and evil. Cut to the spring. Andrei is out in a carriage, headed for the Rostovs' country estate. (Natasha's father is Marshal of the Nobility in the area, and Andrei has some estate business to discuss with him.) As he rides along, Andrei contemplates an old oak tree that shows no signs of life and muses that he is like the oak. At the Rostovs', Andrei catches a glimpse of Natasha and later overhears Natasha and her cousin Sonya chattering, as young girls do. ("There's never been such a beautiful night," exclaims

Andrei and Pierre discuss the meaning of life. (Courtesy Photofest)

Natasha.) Andrei is entranced, and when he leaves the Rostovs', the old oak tree is now (amazingly) in full bloom, a portent that "life is not over at thirty-one." (Nature is a recurring motif for Bondarchuk, as it was for Tolstoy, symbolizing life and the motherland.)[8] Triumphant music swells.

Part one not only lays the groundwork for the narrative; it also offers epic spectacle through the two battles. It allows Bondarchuk to disseminate some of Tolstoy's philosophy of right and wrong and his attitude toward war. Part two, "Natasha Rostova," centers on the story of the star-crossed lovers Natasha and Andrei. This time, the credits unfold against a mysteriously black screen, with birds loudly chirping.

"Natasha Rostova" opens with the Treaty of Tilsit (1807), which seems to be mentioned only to date the action; its historical import is unclear in the film. Natasha cuddles up in bed with her mother, talking about her infatuation with Boris Drubetskoy (an insignificant character in the film). During the conversation, Natasha mentions that Pierre is a Freemason—the only such reference in the entire film, although this is a major plot point for Tolstoy.

The film jumps ahead several years; the next episode is dated New Year's

Natasha and Prince Andrei at the ball. (Courtesy Photofest)

Eve, 1810. Natasha is coming out at her first ball, and Bondarchuk shows the excited preparations as Natasha dresses, flitting back and forth. The ball is a big event, and Natasha is very nervous. When the emperor arrives, the other guests crowd around him. As Natasha watches the dancers in awe, a tremulous look comes over her. Will no one ask her to dance? The screen blurs as Natasha watches the festive scene through unshed tears. Pierre, lost in thought, suddenly notices Natasha's discomfiture and asks Andrei to dance with her. In what is arguably the film's single most famous scene, Andrei sweeps Natasha off her feet. Cinematographer Petritsky chose to film them in close-up, with the other dancers slightly out of focus; it is intensely romantic and very beautiful. The camera is constantly moving, thanks to those cameramen on roller skates. Then the dance floor fills, and there is a traveling overhead shot of the entire scene. Cut to Pierre, who is watching the pair sadly, thinking of his own loveless marriage and envying his friends' evident happiness. After the ball, a split screen shows Pierre and Andrei talking about Natasha, while Natasha and her mother discuss Andrei.

The narrator, covering for deletions, notes that three weeks have gone by. Natasha is distraught because Bolkonsky has not come to visit. She wanders about the house, looking sad and alone. In bed with her mother, she vents her angst by talking endlessly. But just when her hopes have nearly been dashed, she hears a carriage: "Bolkonsky is coming!" Andrei, predictably, asks Countess Rostova for Natasha's hand. After her mother tells her the news, Natasha runs to Andrei through darkened halls before bursting into the room. They are shown at opposite ends of the salon in an extreme long shot before they close in on each other. Bondarchuk rarely employs a shot–reverse shot, but he does in this moving scene when Andrei proposes. Then Natasha learns the dreadful news: they must wait a year, and their engagement must be kept secret until then, supposedly because of Andrei's deference to her youth. (He wants her to keep her options open.) What the viewer does not know (although the reader does) is that old Prince Nikolai has denied permission for Andrei to marry Natasha unless there is a one-year deferral. "There was no betrothal," intones the narrator.

A couple of transitional shots show time passing: winter dissolves into spring, spring into summer, summer into fall. The next important episode is the spectacular wolf hunt that caused Bondarchuk so much trouble in production because of the passivity of the borzois. This is an exceptionally good scene, with long traveling shots as the huntsmen, Natasha, and the dogs chase and catch the wolf. It is also especially noisy: bugle blaring, dogs barking, people chattering. An intense, ferocious fight between the wolf and the dog pack brings the hunt to a close.

Even better than the hunt is the lovely scene of Natasha's post-hunt dance, which communicates the film's national theme quite effectively. After the hunt, Natasha and her brother Nikolai go to their uncle's rustic log house to eat supper. A balalaika, an iconic Russian musical instrument, is playing outside. Then Uncle starts strumming his guitar and invites Natasha to dance, Russian style. Here, Natasha reveals that, despite her Westernized appearance, she is essentially Russian. As peasant women gather to watch admiringly, Natasha dances gracefully and, more important, *instinctively* in the Russian way. As the Rostovs leave for home, a folk song plays, reinforcing the Russianness of this episode.

The film moves on to a winter day. Natasha is walking slowly through her house, lonely, thinking about Andrei. She, Nikolai, and Sonya talk about eternity in a very uncinematic scene. Thankfully, this reverie is interrupted when her younger brother Petya throws open the door and announces that the mummers have arrived. The young people join them, troikas racing merrily through the snow. This is like a gift of life for the forlorn Natasha, who longs to end the waiting and return to society.

In the meantime, Andrei is trying, unsuccessfully, to persuade his curmudgeonly father to shorten his enforced separation from Natasha. The old prince sarcastically refuses (he thinks Natasha is too young, and besides, the Rostovs are not nearly as distinguished as the Bolkonskys). When the Rostovs hear that father and daughter Bolkonsky are in Moscow, Count Rostov drags Natasha (against her will) to meet them. The visit is a disaster. The shy and reserved Marya and the normally gregarious Natasha stare at each other uneasily. Prince Nikolai makes a sudden appearance in his nightgown and then exaggerates a patently insincere apology for his rudeness. Natasha is shocked at this demonstration of hostility toward her and leaves in a rush. (In the book, she begins to wonder what impact her father-in-law will have on her marriage.)

Next comes a fateful scene for Natasha (and Andrei). She is at the theater with her father, seated in a box next to Hélène Bezukhova's. Hélène's handsome brother and Pierre's former friend Anatole Kuragin arrives late and seats himself next to Pierre's nemesis, Dolokhov. Both Natasha and Anatole end up in the devious Hélène's box as she plots a romance between them, knowing full well that Natasha and Andrei are engaged.

Then Natasha and Count Rostov go to a recital at the Bezukhovs', a good example of the pretentious French entertainments that were popular at the time. Hélène has also invited Anatole. Standing behind Natasha, he whispers in her ear, and later in the evening they dance (it is not, however, as magical as her dance with Andrei). Anatole declares his love, and they kiss as Hélène watches approvingly from the background, shot in deep focus.

Anatole plans to run away with Natasha. He sends her a note that is intercepted by her cousin Sonya. The screen splits between the misguided, sleeping Natasha and Anatole and his unscrupulous friend Dolokhov, plotting the elopement. Dolokhov, however, is opposed to the scheme because Anatole is already married (to a Polish woman), and he knows that Anatole's passion for Natasha—not to mention his money—will quickly disappear. In

Anatole Kuragin woos Natasha. (Courtesy Photofest)

the meantime, Sonya attempts to remonstrate with her cousin, but Natasha becomes hysterical and declares her love for Anatole. She tells Sonya that she has already broken her engagement to Andrei. Cut to Anatole and his friends carousing to the strains of gypsy music. A beautiful, laughing gypsy woman brings Anatole a sable wrap to give to Natasha. Then Anatole's carriage heads off into the wintry night for the Rostovs', where he intends to retrieve his beloved. But when he is met by a servant, Anatole immediately realizes he has been betrayed and manages to escape. Learning that her new love is lost, Natasha becomes hysterical again. Marya Dmitrievna, at whose house the Rostovs are staying, yells at her, calling her a hussy. "Will you leave me alone?!" screams Natasha, ending a very dramatic scene.

Cut to the Bezukhovs'. An irate Pierre wants to obtain Natasha's incriminating love letters to Anatole and lambastes his brother-in-law for his behavior in the most insulting terms. Predictably, Anatole threatens to challenge Pierre for this assault on his honor, and Pierre sarcastically apologizes. Next we see Andrei returning Natasha's portrait and letters to Pierre. Natasha, who has been very ill, now feels guilty about her treatment of Andrei and wants him to forgive her. She breaks down sobbing when Pierre makes it clear by his silence that forgiveness will not happen. Pierre then declares his love for her, to the extent an honorable, married man can, with these beautiful words: "If I were not I, but the handsomest, brightest, and best man in the world, and I were free, I would go down on my knees this minute and ask for your hand and for your love." On his way home, Pierre sees the Great Comet of 1811; people on the streets are crossing themselves as they watch it.[9] Then on 12 June 1812 French troops cross Russia's border. Part two ends with a long shot of the French moving into the frame.

Although other epics have romantic subplots, Natasha and Andreï's tragic romance is one of the best known in world literature, so it is not surprising that Bondarchuk foregrounds it in part two with grand flourishes and loving detail. Part three ("1812"), however, is devoted to the spectacle of war on a large scale. The credits of "1812" unfold against a backdrop of trees shown by a slowly panning camera. Eventually, head and shoulder shots of soldiers marching are superimposed over the trees.

The film then opens with the ending of part two, a long shot of French troops marching. Until the Battle of Borodino actually commences, part three is constructed of many short scenes of battle preparations intercut with scenes from the home front, an effective device to show the sharp contrast between the headlong plunge into war and the philistine cares of daily life in the two capitals—the actual capital St. Petersburg, and the sacred, historical capital Moscow. For example, a shot of the French soldiers is cut with a scene of courtiers in St. Petersburg dancing the mazurka. Alexander I arrives, and news of the invasion comes. The dance abruptly stops, and the dancers rush in closer so they can hear the reports. It takes war to interrupt their frivolity.

After another shot of the French, we are now at the Rostovs' house in Moscow. Natasha's little brother Petya, barely into his teens, is bursting with desire to volunteer. To the sound of church bells ringing, the citizens of Moscow pour out onto the streets. They head to see the emperor, who has arrived for a religious ceremony on the eve of battle. Petya is wildly enthusiastic, although he does not know which of many gentlemen leaving the Uspensky Cathedral is actually Alexander I. The crowd is likewise ecstatic with love for Alexander. Back in St. Petersburg, at Anna Scherer's salon, a guest is archly criticizing General Kutuzov for having "morals like a dog," referring to his famously scandalous behavior with women.

Now to the Bolkonskys'. Marya reads a pessimistic letter from Andrei, who warns that the city of Smolensk (220 miles from Moscow, but close to

Pierre, dressed in his summer suit, watches the Battle of Borodino. (Courtesy Photofest)

their Bald Hills estate) is about to fall. The family, which includes Andrei's young son Nikolai (Nikolenka), named after his grandfather, is advised to evacuate, but Prince Nikolai will not hear of it, stubbornly refusing to believe the news. To underscore his obduracy, there is a cut to the battlefront, where terrified civilians are brutally scattered from their homes amidst horrific explosions. The old prince goes to his study. Soldiers march. Having trouble sleeping, Prince Nikolai lies on his couch, murmuring, "There's no peace anywhere." He is dying. Marya, now by his bedside, weeps in yet another touching but not overly sentimental scene. "Russia has perished. They've murdered Russia," Nikolai whispers. Cut to the forest, then to the deathbed, back to the woods, then to the sky, and on to soldiers marching. Princess Marya faints. He is gone.

Ever faithful, Pierre appears at the Rostovs'. Natasha, still obsessed with the wrong she has done Andrei, wonders whether he will ever forgive her; she begins sobbing, and Pierre moves in to comfort her. The last scene of the home front before the Battle of Borodino commences is Scherer's salon in St. Petersburg. Kutuzov has been appointed commander of the army, replacing the despised "foreigner" General Mikhail Barclay de Tolly, and he is now being praised by the same man who criticized him earlier. Bondarchuk successfully demonstrates the hypocrisy of the capital's elite nobility.

The focus is now on the battlefront. Bondarchuk is not interested in showing gore and horror in the battle scenes at Borodino; rather, he wants to demonstrate their epic quality.[10] As Kutuzov rides slowly among the soldiers, who are cheering him lustily, he spies Andrei, who brusquely refuses to become Kutuzov's adjutant and pleads with the commander to let him remain with his regiment. Dozens of soldiers strip naked to bathe in the river, singing "As the girls went to the river. . . ." Andrei watches, aloof as always.

As the soldiers are busily constructing defensive fortifications, along comes Pierre, nattily dressed in a cream-colored summer suit and top hat—an incongruous intrusion of the home front into the reality of war. Pierre wants to observe the battle, to see what war is like. In this setting, the soldiers do not fear mocking such a ridiculous gentleman.

Amidst the hubbub of preparations, a religious procession carrying the icon of the Black Virgin of Smolensk (also known as the Holy Mother of Iversky) arrives to bless the proceedings. The men rush toward it, crossing themselves and singing a hymn. Kutuzov struggles up the hill to bow before the icon and kiss it. Cut back to the crowd scene, as dark clouds scud across the sky.

There is a close-up of Andrei, who is thinking about the battle and his possible impending death, as well as the potential loss of Moscow and the fatherland. "I won't exist anymore," he thinks wonderingly. Pierre arrives at Andrei's barracks, and Andrei tells his foolish, curious friend that victory depends not on positions or strategy but on the feelings of the men. A suddenly furious Andrei then subjects the startled Pierre to an angry speech about the dastardly enemy: the French must be exterminated, Andrei insists. (Such overt expression of patriotism is a convention of the national epic.) "War is not a polite recreation but the vilest thing in life," he says.

The battle has begun. Napoleon paces back and forth. As regiments march in step, they are cut down. Pierre is in the midst of the action, watching in disbelief and growing horror, covered in dirt and soot. There is a cavalry charge. Napoleon is surprised when the "Russians stand firm." Pierre sees a man's leg blown off, a surprisingly graphic occurrence for a Soviet film in the mid-1960s. The air is so smoke filled that the soldiers are barely visible, and the blasts of bombs effectively re-create the battle scene The constantly moving cameras show the ravaged landscape, the riderless horses. How can anyone tell which side is which?[11] Kutuzov is told that Bagration, whom he regards as his most important general, has been gravely wounded.

Prince Andreï's regiment has been held in reserve. (Courtesy Photofest)

Andreï's regiment has been held in reserve, but he has already lost a third of his men, who are "sitting ducks" amidst a barrage of gunfire and bombs. He walks slowly among them, anxious to do battle. Elsewhere, Pierre goes to fetch some ammunition for the soldiers. The boxes of ammunition are blown up before his very eyes, and he is knocked unconscious. Cut back to Andrei; a bomb drops near him, spinning crazily. His mortal wounding is presaged by a shot of wind whipping through a birch forest. The bomb goes off. (Andrei is not shown.) Back to Pierre, who gets caught up in hand-to-hand combat with an equally frightened French soldier; they end up crawling away from each other, desperate to save their own lives.

Bondarchuk leaves Pierre and Andrei to focus on the chaos of the battle, which Petritsky's aerial cameras capture magnificently. Bombs are exploding everywhere; the air is filled with clouds of smoke that obscure everything. The ground is in flames. Horses gallop furiously. For Bondarchuk, as for Tolstoy, war is a deadly, meaningless game.

Cut to Kutuzov. Incensed when an officer reports that his men are panicked and retreating, he shouts: "How dare you tell me that!" The old general is mollified when another officer tells him that the enemy has been defeated, and he promises to attack again in the morning. Cut to Napoleon, an isolated figure looking at the carnage through his telescope. He knows that this time, victory has eluded him.

Now the wounded, including Andrei, are being carried off the battle-field as a lullaby, "Sleep My Baby, Sleep," plays on the sound track. In his semiconscious state, Andrei experiences a series of flashbacks, a medley of scenes from his battle experiences. After panoramic shots of the country-side, we see Andrei as a baby. The screen flickers as Andrei loses conscious-ness again. Grim reality sets in at the field hospital. Andrei is placed next to his enemy Anatole Kuragin, whose leg is being amputated, and he suddenly remembers Natasha. His desire for revenge against Anatole melts away.

It is dusk. As the tender lullaby continues on the sound track, the sur-vivors trudge wearily through a devastated landscape. Napoleon is now on horseback, pondering the field of corpses. More bombs explode. Pierre stag-gers through the carnage as night falls. Aerial shots of the battlefield are cut with stills from the battle. Although most historians consider the Battle of Borodino to be a draw militarily, the Russians won a moral victory that day by showing that it was possible to put an end to Napoleon's string of victories. As Andrei implied in his earlier conversation with Pierre about the reasons for victory, Napoleon will eventually fall because the Russians have proved their greater spirit, morale, and grit. An aerial shot shows the desecrated Russian landscape rapidly receding. There is no finer film on early-nineteenth-century warfare than part three of *War and Peace*.

The war continues, but not on the battlefield. The credits for part four ("Pierre Bezukhov") roll past Franz Rubaud's famous Borodino panorama (as mentioned in chapter 1, this vast painting was completed in 1911 for the battle's centenary and is now on display in the Museum-Panorama "Battle of Borodino" in Moscow).[12] This part wraps up *War and Peace* as a war epic quite effectively, focusing on the occupation of Moscow and the French ar-my's retreat. It opens with General Kutuzov and his staff deciding whether to surrender Moscow to the enemy. Reluctantly, Kutuzov gives the fateful order to retreat. After making this painful decision, he puts his head down on his desk and then swears to an aide (in another foreshadowing moment) that regardless of the fate of Moscow, he will punish the French: "I shall make them eat horsemeat like the Turks!"

Moscow is in the midst of an evacuation, shown in a number of short scenes that are reminiscent of Tolstoy's short chapters. Panicked crowds fill the streets as carts carrying the wounded pass by. The Rostovs watch the chaos from their balcony. Pierre asks his servant for peasant clothes and a

Natasha and the mortally wounded Andrei. (Courtesy Photofest)

pistol. Andrei's carriage passes by. The Rostovs have packed up, and as they are on their way out of the city, Natasha spies Pierre from her carriage. He refuses to leave Moscow; his intention (unspoken) is to seek vengeance on Napoleon. (Pierre's motivations for this change of heart are not clearly artic-ulated in the film; the viewer assumes that Pierre now understands that, as a patriot, he must avenge Russia.) There is a shot of a desolate Moscow with its empty streets, followed by shots of the Kremlin's splendor and golden, jeweled icons. An incongruously cheerful march plays on the sound track.

Napoleon has Moscow at his feet—or so he thinks. To his extreme an-noyance, the French emperor learns that Moscow has been abandoned, and there is a long shot of the deserted city. The French enter Moscow in seem-ingly endless lines. At the house where Pierre has taken refuge, a French officer, Captain Ramballe, forces his way in. Pierre saves him from being shot by a drunken old man. Napoleon reaches the Kremlin. Ramballe and Pierre share a table; the Frenchman is expansive and jovial, while Pierre wonders how he got into this situation. Tolstoy's intention was to show that

Pierre rescues a lost child. (Courtesy Photofest)

the French, like the Russians, were being manipulated by their command-ers; they had not given up their humanity. However, this scene is not well integrated into the film and seems extraneous.

Moscow is burning. Sonya tells Natasha the news, but Natasha cares more about the dying Andrei, who is also in the village to which they have fled. Although her parents have ordered her not to see him, she goes anyway, after hearing Andrei's moans through the wall. Because it is late at night, she is dressed in a white nightgown. As she enters his room, she looks like an apparition—or a bride. A sobbing Natasha kisses Andrei's hand, and he whispers, "I love you." His impending death has helped him understand how petty his anger at Natasha was.

Meanwhile, Pierre is on the crowded streets of the rapidly burning city. It is a conflagration; ashes fill the air. People are rushing to escape while the buildings burn ferociously. A frantic mother asks Pierre to rescue her child, who has been separated from her. As the French soldiers are busily looting, packing their booty into carts, one of the looters leads Pierre to the little girl, who is crying in a garden. When Pierre returns to the street with the child in his arms, he finds that her mother is gone. The wind is whipping the fire to extraordinary proportions. A French soldier is harassing an exotic, veiled Armenian woman, and Pierre comes to her rescue. A fight ensues, and Pierre is arrested. Against a backdrop of French looting and riotous drunken merriment, we see a close-up of the feet of a hanged man. Russian civilians are being executed by the French.

In St. Petersburg, however, the situation is starkly different. Life goes on as usual at Anna Scherer's salon. The death of Pierre's wife Hélène is mentioned in passing; this fact becomes important later in the film. Meanwhile, the hapless Pierre has been accused of being a spy and is taken away for execution. As French soldiers joke and laugh, the condemned arrive, a pitiful line of cowed men. There is execution after execution, including a terrified adolescent who has been clinging to Pierre.[13] (Some of the French soldiers are clearly disturbed by what they are doing.) Seemingly by chance, Pierre is spared (perhaps the day's quota has been filled) and is thrown into a makeshift prison in a church. There he meets the man who is arguably Tolstoy's favorite character in the novel: the middle-aged peasant-soldier Platon Karataev, who spouts Russian folk wisdom ("Suffer an hour, live for an age"; "Where there's law, injustice will follow") and represents the "real" Russian, earthy and homespun. Karataev shows Pierre how to eat the potatoes the prisoners have been given for food.

Cut to Andrei and Natasha. He declares his love again and kisses her hand, but she knows the end is near. As he lies dying, he has a dream of his death: He sees himself leaving his bed, walking slowly across the room, and opening a door. Death attempts to enter, and try as he might, Andrei cannot hold the door shut. He sees himself walking through the door and disappearing. His sister Marya arrives with his son, Nikolenka, who is frightened by the sight of this haggard man who is a stranger to him. Andrei dies. The screen whitens and is transformed into clouds in the heavens.

Napoleon attempts to reach a peace settlement with Kutuzov, who refuses to negotiate. Napoleon is furious at the Russian's rejection of his efforts to make peace. Kutuzov is sleeping when an officer comes to tell him that the French are finally leaving Moscow. Kutuzov weeps and prays, declaring, "Russia is saved," an example of the melodramatic patriotic dialogue that is intrinsic to the national epic.

Marching in a driving rain, the retreating French give no quarter to the Russian prisoners they have taken with them; they shoot anyone who collapses. Pierre turns away when Platon Karataev falls behind with the little dog he has rescued. Karataev is shot as the dog yelps piteously. Later, an exhausted Pierre starts to laugh hysterically at his plight: "They have taken me prisoner! Me! My immortal soul! It's all that I am!" (This occurs only in the film, not in the novel.)

The Russian partisans begin harassing the French lines. Young Petya Rostov is with them. Out of compassion, he invites a French prisoner, a little boy, to eat with the men in his unit. Petya has trouble going to sleep and then has strange dreams about a forest enshrouded in clouds and fog. As he awakens, his surroundings slowly come into focus. The partisans are preparing to attack. In a scene that plays on the conventions of epic war films, Petya, on horseback, rushes into battle enthusiastically waving his sword. Just as Pierre is freed from French captivity, Petya is killed, almost immediately. Cut to a shot of Countess Rostova (in a superbly acted scene) writhing, sobbing, and screaming hysterically as Natasha tries to calm her. "My son! My son! It's not true! No, it can't be true! No! No!"

The snows have arrived. Napoleon decides to abandon what is left of his frozen army, implying that he is a coward. ("Dies irae" is playing on the sound track.) A long aerial traveling shot shows dozens of bodies littering the snow-covered earth. This is followed by a long tracking shot of the French hacking up their horses for food and fighting among themselves. As Kutuzov predicted, the French will be eating horsemeat. All semblance of discipline and unity has vanished; the greatest army in the world has been reduced to a cold and hungry rabble. (This is in sharp contrast to the disciplined Russian forces.)

Russian troops are passing by the defeated French. In sympathy, the Russians start to sing and are joined by the French. An aerial shot shows the soldiers coming together to form a big circle. A smiling Kutuzov tells his men, "Our victory is complete. Your glory will live for all time!" followed by a cut to the frostbitten faces of the French. Kutuzov continues, "Who asked them to come? They deserved to have their faces in shit."

Moscow is rebuilding after the fire. Pierre goes to offer his condolences to Marya Bolkonskaya. He suddenly becomes aware that Natasha is sitting in the background, and they approach each other. He has a flashback of Natasha at her first ball, and his fervent declaration of love is heard in a voice-over ("If I were not I . . ."). There is a shot of a birch forest, followed by a panoramic aerial shot of the Russian landscape. Cut to Natasha's brother

General Kutuzov passes the wretched French. (Courtesy Photofest)

Nikolai (unlike in the book, he has only a minor role in the film), who is seen shouting, "Hurrah for the whole world!" Clouds close over the Russian land: "Since corrupt people always unite, honest people must do the same. It's that simple."

The narrative sweep of this film is clearly epic. It spans seven momentous years in Russian military history (see chapter 4 for details) and traces the lives of three interconnected families: the Rostovs, the Bolkonskys, and the Bezukhovs. Indeed, Bondarchuk had difficulty compressing these lives into only four parts and sidelined two very important characters from Tolstoy's book: Nikolai Rostov and Marya Bolkonskaya, Tolstoy's ideal man and woman, who end up marrying in the novel. But Bondarchuk tried hard to provide complete stories for his main protagonists: Andrei, Natasha, and Pierre. To achieve this, he constructed many short scenes that impede the overall flow of the film and give it an episodic character; this is particularly pronounced in part four, which feels rushed and probably was. (Remember that Bondarchuk was under pressure to finish the film.) This was not an unusual shortcoming for a film epic, however. Langford notes that the 1950s epic had difficulty "successfully integrating narrative and spectacle"; this was also true of *War and Peace* a decade later.[14]

There can be no doubt that, like a politically astute Soviet director from the 1920s, Bondarchuk preferred large-scale mass scenes over small individual ones, even though the latter were also very good. Despite all his problems with the cast, he managed to elicit remarkable performances from Tikhonov as Andrei, Saveleva as Natasha, Ktorov as old Prince Bolkonsky, and Boris Zakhava as Kutuzov. Bondarchuk himself was also first rate as Pierre (even though he was too old for the part).

The mass scenes display the epic character of the film very clearly, and it is in these scenes that Bondarchuk's genius as a filmmaker truly reveals itself. Indeed, after seeing part three, a reviewer for the *London Daily Mail* noted that the camera and the countryside were the true stars of the picture, and the mass scenes were more significant than the ones with individual actors.[15] As noted in the previous chapter, all critics agreed that the battle scenes were tours de force; Bondarchuk's depiction of the early-nineteenth-century battle—at Schöngraben, Austerlitz, and especially Borodino—has never been equaled or surpassed in the nearly fifty years since the film appeared.[16] His masterly choreography of thousands of Soviet soldiers and cavalrymen makes for exciting viewing. However, Bondarchuk's finely honed sense of spectacle and epic is not limited to the battle scenes. Natasha's ball is a brilliant scene that operates on both the mass level (500 dancers) and the intimate level (Natasha and Andrei falling in love). The evacuation and burning of Moscow are likewise brilliant, both for their scale and for their execution. The pyrotechnics are still impressive, even in today's age of digital effects.

Style

The style of *War and Peace* is also epic in terms of the variety of film techniques employed. Style in the film is deliberately obtrusive: Bondarchuk wanted it to be clear that the film is art, not a crass commercial venture like its Hollywood counterparts. As Elena Prokhorova writes: "Virtually every shot claims aesthetic value. There are dozens of complicated aerial tracking shots, elaborate use of montage in superimpositions and split screen shots, deep focus and point-of-view shots and so forth . . . this visual cornucopia testifies to the technical achievement of *War and Peace*."[17] We cannot separate the success of the film from the artistry of not only Bondarchuk but also Anatoly Petritsky, the director of cinematography, who had a very fine eye for what makes an epic film "epic." Indeed, in his book on epic films, Constantine Santas praises the "spectacular action scenes" and the "excellent cinematography" in *War and Peace*.[18]

Petritsky and Bondarchuk favored the long shot and often the extreme long shot, as seen on the ground or from the air. They are used mainly in the mass scenes, such as shots of battles or of society life in St. Petersburg, to make their mass character abundantly clear; however, we also see the long shot in intimate settings. When Marya and Andrei say good-bye before he heads off to battle at Schöngraben and then at Austerlitz, Andrei is shown in an extreme long shot to emphasize his isolation. Likewise, when Pierre is sitting with Hélène after her birthday dinner, they are depicted in a long shot that focuses on the figurative distance between them, despite the fact that marriage will soon be foisted upon them. Napoleon is first seen in an extreme long shot, which guides the audience to view him as completely insignificant. At Andrei's proposal of marriage, Natasha and Andrei are initially shown in an extreme long shot, which can be interpreted as a sign that their putative union will never be consummated.

Two common shots from Hollywood-style filmmaking are used sparingly: the close-up and the shot–reverse shot. These two shots draw the viewers' focus to the individual actors, whereas Bondarchuk usually wants to direct their attention to the spectacle of the mass scenes.[19] There are, however, exceptions. During Natasha's ball, there are close-ups of her dancing with Andrei while the rest of the dancers are out of focus, which fits the romantic import of the scene. When Natasha meets her future sister-in-law Marya Bolkonskaya for the first time, their mutual trepidation is shown in shot–reverse shot, a rare use of this staple technique in the film. Another example of shot–reverse shot is at the Borodino field hospital, when Andrei and Anatole realize they are lying side by side.

Petritsky and Bondarchuk also favored a constantly moving camera, which complements the narrative sweep and ratchets up the energy and excitement in the action scenes. This is especially true during the battle scenes, where the camera does not linger; instead, it pans and tracks to show the enormity of the human disaster. Petritsky's use of crane shots and aerial shots (from helicopters) is masterly and shows the carnage of battle within panoramic views of the Russian landscape, whose broad valleys and low hills are dear to every Russian.

Scene transitions occur in a number of ways. The cut, most common in ordinary movies, is used sparingly. Bondarchuk prefers dissolves, fades, wipes, and especially black screens. Some of these techniques, especially the wipe, now seem old-fashioned, but in the 1960s they were perceived as innovative uses of almost forgotten practices. Another old-fashioned technique is the split screen, which Bondarchuk sometimes employs instead of crosscutting when two different shots are occurring simultaneously, such as the scene in which Pierre, realizing that he is in love with Natasha, is alone in his study, while Natasha is in her bed dreaming of Andrei. Finally, superimposition is used fairly frequently, such as when the soldiers run toward the Black Virgin of Smolensk icon at Borodino, providing a sense of their vast numbers.

The music and sound direction is similarly epic in scope. Ovchinnikov's score is superdramatic and, at times, overbearingly loud. In addition to the music he composed for the film, he draws from Russian hymns, folk songs, and lullabies to provide a truly national sound track. The sound track is also filled with naturalistic *noise*. Church bells clang, water drips, clocks tick, people chatter, shout, and laugh. The din of battle is enormous and is quite effective in underscoring the calamity shown in the visuals. Finally, very common to epics is the use of the voice-over—sometimes an omniscient narrator intoning lines from Tolstoy, and sometimes the characters, especially Andrei, Natasha, and Pierre, speaking their thoughts.[20]

Virtually any scene can be chosen to illustrate Bondarchuk's overflowing cornucopia of film techniques. When Andrei is shot at Austerlitz, the screen immediately fades to black as he loses consciousness. Then there is a cut to an iris shot of his face. This cuts to a panoramic view of the sky, and blackouts alternate with the sky. Napoleon appears in an extreme long shot, small against the sky, with Andrei's prostrate body in the foreground. The scene ends with an aerial shot of the landscape.

The preliminaries to Natasha's ball are similarly complex in terms of technique. A long shot of everyone getting dressed is followed by a traveling camera going from room to room in the Rostov mansion. This is followed by a medium shot of the family in the carriage. Cut to a long shot of masses of people ascending the staircase. The camera lingers in traveling shots, with very long takes. Natasha appears in medium shot. An extreme long shot takes in the entire ballroom; this is succeeded by a traveling shot of the room and then a close-up of Natasha. As another example of Bondarchuk and Petritsky's technique, there is a long shot of Napoleon arriving on the outskirts of Moscow, followed by a medium shot. Moscow is at his feet. In a close-up, the disbelieving French emperor is informed that Moscow has been abandoned. Next there is a long shot of the streets of the empty city. Cut to Napoleon giving the order to proceed to Moscow. Cut to shots of several Moscow churches (which underscores the sacred character of the city). Cut to the French entering the city.

The calamity of war. (Courtesy Photofest)

But the most virtuosic episode is the Battle of Borodino, comprising a significant number of scenes. The beginning of the battle is in long shot, the camera slowly panning the scene. Cut to Pierre. Cut to Kutuzov. Cut to Napoleon seen in long shot. Groups of soldiers march (long shot), as some are killed and wounded. Cut to Pierre, out of place in the midst of battle. There is a long shot of soldiers, taken with a slowly panning camera. As the battle continues, the camera is constantly moving, trying to keep pace with the soldiers. These shots are punctuated by aerial panoramas of the disaster. There is an extreme close-up of horses' legs, running frantically. Dramatic music plays throughout.

A National Epic

Just as *War and Peace* was entering production, the prominent critic Yury Khaniutin wrote that Bondarchuk hoped to unite an "investigation of the inner life of the hero with the traditions of the epic, monumental cinema of the 1920s and 1930s."[21] As discussed in chapter 1, the Soviet regime's goal in pouring such a colossal amount of resources into a single film was to "reflect the glories of the Soviet state" and show the world, especially the United States, these glories.[22] How could a multipart film based on a dense and convoluted philosophical novel written by an intensely religious nineteenth-century aristocrat achieve this?

During the 1920s, Soviet filmmakers had trepidations about adapting Tolstoy for the screen, and rightly so. They understood the gap between Tolstoy the novelist and Tolstoy the Christian philosopher.[23] In 1928, celebration of the 100th anniversary of Tolstoy's birth marked a new trend in the USSR of privileging the classics over the avant-garde. In the 1930s, monuments to 1812 and the Borodino battlefield were restored, as were the reputations of Bagration and Kutuzov.[24] Still, unease over Tolstoy's religious and moral stances remained.[25]

World War II, the Great Patriotic War, ended that unease. The state hastily ordered the publication of *War and Peace* in vast quantities in 1941, recognizing that Tolstoy's mythologized history of the First Patriotic War could be used to mobilize at least the intelligentsia, if not the masses.[26] By that time, as Stephen Norris notes, Tolstoy's "moral vision in *War and Peace* could now be seen as patriotic."[27] Public readings of the book were held. Historian David Brandenburger argues that even common soldiers drew comparisons between 1812 and World War II: "the historical analogies invoked by many of these soldiers clearly stemmed from sources like Tolstoi's *War and Peace.*"[28]

Bondarchuk's film carries that moral and patriotic vision forward to the 1960s. As Prokhorova asserts: "With its overwhelming focus on war at the expense of peace and community, one way to approach the film is as a literal, visual illustration of a Soviet high school reading of *War and Peace*. The episodes chosen by Bondarchuk for an extensive treatment follow Soviet ideological clichés."[29] It is true that Soviet literary critics of the 1950s and 1960s interpreted the novel "largely in terms of class and country," but did Bondarchuk follow suit?[30]

The manifestations of Russian patriotism and nationalism in Tolstoy's novel particularly intrigued Bondarchuk.[31] He acknowledged that one of his key goals was to transmit the soul of this "deeply national patriotic work."[32] Indeed, Bondarchuk went so far as to say that the "main theme of [Tolstoy's] novel is patriotic," a statement many literary critics would disagree with.[33] However, Tolstoy scholar R. F. Christian sees Tolstoy's *War and Peace* as "an expression of patriotic pride in the glorious achievements of the Russian nation and its moral superiority over the French invaders."[34] Christian describes the book as a historical novel that "became a national epic."[35]

As already noted, a few Soviet critics praised Bondarchuk's *War and Peace* as a "source of national pride," to quote Uran Guralnik.[36] A. Sofronov singled out the film's patriotism and authenticity as particularly valuable.[37] K. Zamoshkin averred that the film's "deeply patriotic thought" was drawn directly from the novel; he also thought that Bondarchuk really understood the Russian national character (*narodnost*).[38] Some of the cast also praised the film's overt patriotism. Liudmila Saveleva, for example, wrote that the "Russian national aspect" was most important for her.[39] Vasily Lanovoi labeled the film "our national pride."[40] Even some American critics saw the film as a "virtual national epic singing the glory of the Russian soldiers and Russian people" and as "quintessentially Russian."[41]

How does the film communicate nationalism? Contemporary Russian critic I. A. Mussky sees the "Russian national character" embodied in Andrei, Natasha, and Pierre.[42] Andrei is perhaps too chilly and reserved to be the ideal Russian, but Russianness certainly seems to be embedded in Natasha, with her predilection for emotion over reason, for action over thought. She also loves the motherland and instinctively understands it, as shown in the hunt scene and her subsequent Russian dance. As for Pierre, he is an inherently moral and serious man trying to do what is right. After all, he evolves from admiring Napoleon to hating him for what he has done to Russia, a point of view that Bondarchuk clearly wanted to transmit.

Surprisingly for a Soviet film, in which the political message is often heavy-handed, there is relatively little dialogue that explicitly propagandizes the national and patriotic ideals of the film. Instead, the visuals communicate the message. This is seen first and foremost in the many panoramic shots of the Russian landscape at peace and at war. Petritsky's camera lingers on scenes of nature: forests, birches (the canonical Russian tree), the grove at Yasnaya Polyana. The land is shown brutalized by the elements, especially wind and snow, in the same way that Napoleon's Grande Armée has brutalized the Russian people and, in the end, nature brutalizes the Grande Armée.

The national and patriotic message is also communicated in the mass scenes that dominate the Battle of Borodino in particular. Although the exploits of Andrei and Pierre are still followed to a certain extent, the real heroes are the rank-and-file Russian soldiers. They are shown in the thousands, to be sure, but also in close-up, unlike the French. The expressive, achingly human faces of the Russian soldiers in battle carry a stronger patriotic message than any words could.

The film is certainly a *Russian* national epic, but is Bondarchuk's *War and*

Peace an especially Soviet epic? There is no question that the film's monumentalism was, historically speaking, the dominant Soviet style, except for the period of Khrushchev's Thaw. Its political origin as an answer to King Vidor's *War and Peace* also marks Bondarchuk's film as a particularly Soviet "weapon" in the cultural Cold War. In addition, the fact that the state opened its coffers to support Bondarchuk and controlled the filmmaking at the ministerial level was characteristic of the Soviet Union during the Cold War 1960s. The massive collective effort of the production also fit Soviet ideology.[43]

It should also be noted, however, that Bondarchuk's *War and Peace* came at a time when monumental spectacles were all the rage in Hollywood and in European cinema. In the early to mid-1950s we saw biblical epics—*Quo Vadis* (1951, Mervyn LeRoy), *The Robe* (1953, Henry Koster), *Demetrius and the Gladiators* (1954, Delmer Daves), and *The Ten Commandments* (1956, Cecil B. DeMille). In the late 1950s to early 1960s there were swords-and-sandals epics such as *Ben Hur* (1959, William Wyler), *Spartacus* (1960, Stanley Kubrick), and, of course, *Cleopatra* (1963, Joseph Mankiewicz). These were followed by other historical epics, some with a national tinge—*El Cid* (1961, Anthony Mann), *How the West Was Won* (1962, John Ford and Henry Hathaway), *Lawrence of Arabia* (1962, David Lean), and *Doctor Zhivago* (1965, David Lean). Finally, there were the World War II patriotic epics—*The Bridge on the River Kwai* (1957, David Lean), *The Longest Day* (1962, Ken Annakin, Andrew Marton, and Bernhard Wicki), and *The Great Escape* (1963, John Sturges).[44] It is still fairly common in Soviet studies to regard the USSR as sui generis, but despite censorship and isolation, Soviet cinema was very much a part of global trends, and sometimes, such as in the 1920s, it was on the leading edge of those trends. Bondarchuk's *War and Peace* fits squarely with other film epics of this period. In short, like all films, it is rooted in the context of its times, both reflecting and reacting to the film culture in which it was born.

Having established that *War and Peace* is a film epic in deed as well as in name, we now turn our attention to the film as an adaptation. As noted in the preceding chapter, Soviet critics were keen that the film should correspond to both the letter and the spirit of Tolstoy's novel.

CHAPTER THREE

WAR AND PEACE AS AN ADAPTATION

The film epic is a bona fide crowd pleaser, but film adaptations generally satisfy no one. Either they are not "true" enough to the original or they are not cinematic enough.[1] The odds of this happening increase when the original work is a classic. And when the original book is *the* national classic, beloved by all, it is virtually inevitable that critics (and audiences) will sharpen their knives.[2] The present-day head of the Mosfilm studio, Karen Shakhnazarov, says it is "impossible to adapt such a colossal novel."[3] As film scholar Joy Gould Boyum notes, "In assessing an adaptation we are never really comparing book with film, but interpretation with interpretation."[4] The director of an adaptation owes the source some degree of respect (otherwise, why adapt?), yet the translation of novel to film requires both creativity and imagination.[5] However, when the book is an exalted classic on the order of *War and Peace*, the filmmaker enjoys less artistic freedom because of the need to incorporate the critical (and political) consensus on its interpretation.[6]

Adaptation Theory

Scholars of film and literature have developed a number of frameworks for judging the merits of an adaptation. Boyum likens adaptation to translation, arguing that the director "must demonstrate allegiance to a previously existing work . . . and he must also . . . create a new work of art . . . in the language of film." In other words, the director needs to give the work a careful reading and seek to preserve its "immanent intention."[7]

Other scholars have created typologies of adaptation. For example, literature specialist Geoffrey Wagner sees three types of adaptation: transposition (a literal translation), commentary (some departures from the text), and analogy (many departures from the text).[8] Film scholar Dudley Andrew believes the only adaptations worth analyzing are those that respect the intent of the original. He too divides adaptations into three "modes": borrowing (both the film and the book gain audiences and prestige from the adaptation), intersection (preservation of what is unique in the text), and fidelity of transformation (literal translation).[9] Russian studies scholars Stephen Hutchings and Anat Vernitskii argue that "Soviet cinema continued to pay lip service to the 'fidelity approach' beyond the Stalin years," and they cite Bondarchuk's *War and Peace* as their main example.[10]

Even though "fidelity of transformation" seems straightforward, film scholar André Bazin would dispute that it is even a legitimate category, writing that "faithfulness to a form, literary or otherwise, is illusory."[11] Even Russian critics have moved away from the fidelity approach. For example, A. Macheret believes that there cannot be an "objective" adaptation because the filmmaker, of necessity, personalizes it, and Maya Turovskaya sees the adaptation as an "individual artistic statement," not a copy.[12]

What follows is an examination of the theory of fidelity of transformation as applied to Bondarchuk's film. Although the film borrows most of its dialogue wholesale and adheres quite closely to the basic elements of the main plot, can it be considered no more than a literal translation of Tolstoy's novel? As film scholar Robert Ray describes the adaptation: "The film adaptation, in Derridean language, is not simply a faded imitation of a superior, authentic original; it is a 'citation' grafted into a new context. Therefore, far from destroying the literary source's meaning, adaptation 'disseminates' it in a process that Benjamin found democratizing."[13] This process of grafting and dissemination is far more difficult than a mere literal translation because, in Andrew's words, "fidelity to the spirit, to the original's tone, values, imagery, and rhythm [is complicated] since finding stylistic equivalents for these intangible aspects is the opposite of a mechanical process."[14] The relationship between Tolstoy's *War and Peace* and Bondarchuk's arguably conforms to Gérard Genette's definition of intertextuality as the "effective co-presence of two texts."[15] For those who have both read the book and seen the film, the novel is reminiscent of the film, and vice versa.

What were Bondarchuk's views on this subject? On the surface, he believed that his *War and Peace* represented fidelity of transformation, writing that the filmmaker should have "profound respect for the author's intended message, careful and sensitive treatment of the original, the wish to get across as fully as possible both its spirit and letter."[16] In constructing his film, he "sought a coordinated unity of all parts" and wanted to make "the mysteries of *War and Peace* . . . visually tangible."[17] He was adamant that he could not claim authorship, believing that this belonged to Tolstoy alone (remember that Tolstoy's name appears before the film's title in each of the four parts). Yet Bondarchuk also considered his *War and Peace* to be both a contemporary work, acknowledging the film's context in the 1960s, and an independent work of art, writing that "art is not illustration."[18] He admitted that he did not rely on Tolstoy's text alone, although he found its prose very "cinemagenic."[19] In addition to studying histories, he immersed himself in the paintings and graphics, music, poetry, and prose of the era to help him transform Tolstoy's words into screen images.[20]

Bondarchuk as an Adapter

Adapting any novel for the screen presents challenges to the filmmaker. These are intensified when dealing with a work that has the scope and depth of *War and Peace*. Bondarchuk wanted to avoid at all costs King Vidor's major mistake of making a film that was a mere illustration of the novel's major plot points. Therefore, instead of a conventional single film, like Vidor's, Bondarchuk decided on an expanded multipart work based on the four-volume structure of the novel. As we know from chapter 1, the multipart format was controversial and may have alienated audiences. Filmmakers generally avoid making multipart films because they realize that "one of the medium's most crucial qualities [is] its immediacy of impact."[21] Another obstacle for the director is the need to find visual equivalents for the written word. Then there is the matter of compressing and cutting the material, whether the film is two hours or eight. An adaptation presents even more challenges: how to capture the tone and style of the original, and how to translate "thought, dream, and interior action" to the screen.[22] Bondarchuk faced all these problems and struggled mightily to devise solutions. His successes and compromises are evident in the film.

Perhaps the most challenging issue was what to cut and why. Not surprisingly, Bondarchuk chose to focus on Andrei, Natasha, and Pierre—clearly the main protagonists in the novel. But the book also has a host of minor characters that Tolstoy develops incisively; each has a purpose in the novel. Some make perfunctory appearances in the film, such as Nikolai Rostov's friend Vasily Denisov, the peasant-soldier Platon Karataev, and Captain Tushin; most of the others are cut completely (the Rostovs' elder daughter Vera, for example). As noted earlier, there were complaints from the critics about the way Karataev and Tushin in particular were minimized because they both represented "real" Russians—Karataev because he was a down-to-earth peasant sharing folksy wisdom with Pierre, and Tushin because he tended to act instinctively on the battlefield rather than obey orders, which was Tolstoy's ideal for a Russian officer.

More critical to the meaning of *War and Peace*, however, is the severe pruning of the roles of Nikolai Rostov and Marya Bolkonskaya. Tolstoy's Nikolai is a man's man—all action, earthy and arrogant. Like Tolstoy himself, Nikolai has no patience for pretense and niceties. In the book, Nikolai feuds with Andrei and resents Natasha's engagement, yet he finds himself attracted to (and finally marries) Andrei's sister Marya, despite his many promises to marry his cousin Sonya, Natasha's dearest friend. Marya models Tolstoy's womanly ideal. She is religious, virtuous, and chaste. She tends to her father despite his cruelty—she even loves him. She is attentive to the needs of beggars and serfs, which is why it is so surprising in the novel when they nearly rise against her when she attempts to flee Bald Hills in the face of the French invasion. All this is absent from Bondarchuk's film, but to be fair, doing justice to Nikolai and Marya probably would have required another two hours of screen time.

Other cuts are made to scenes and entire chapters that do not contribute to the progression of the plot but do contribute to the development of characters and ideas. A good example is the film's compression of the four chapters in volume 1, part 1, of the novel devoted to the death of Pierre's father. The scheming of Prince Vasily Kuragin to gain control of Count Bezukhov's will, which foreshadows his efforts to get Pierre to marry his daughter Hélène, is severely compressed, thereby weakening a key aspect of Prince Vasily's character and motivations.[23] Only someone who has read the novel will be able to infer what is really going on in these scenes.

Pierre's accidental engagement to the beautiful but vacuous Hélène is also compressed, but this time successfully, through the use of the split screen. Tolstoy, who liked to develop leisurely scenes, takes a whole chapter to tell this part of the story, while Bondarchuk condenses it to a pithy six minutes in which what he *shows* is as effective as what Tolstoy *tells*. Pierre, who has been hanging around the Kuragins' home, is hesitant to ask Prince Vasily for his daughter's hand. He desires her but fears she is stupid, and he tries to convince himself that he is in love with her. Tolstoy writes that, at Hélène's name-day party: "Pierre remained alone with Hélène for a long time in the small drawing room, where they were sitting. . . . Some of the nearest relations were still there. They were sitting in the big drawing room. Prince Vasily walked lazily over to Pierre. Pierre stood up and said it was already late. Prince Vasily gave him a sternly questioning look, as if what he had said was so strange that he could not even hear it well."[24] The prince then returns to the large drawing room, where the few remaining guests are still talking. He asks his wife to *"allez voir ce qu'ils font* [go and see what they are doing]. 'All the same,' she said to her husband. . . . Prince Vasily frowned, got up . . . and with a resolute stride walked past the ladies into the small drawing room. He strode quickly, joyfully up to Pierre. . . . 'Thank God!' he said. 'My wife has told me everything.' He embraced Pierre with one arm, his daughter with the other."[25] Pierre's fate is thus sealed. Bondarchuk manages, through the power of his own acting and editing, to communicate the feeling of Tolstoy's chapter, if not all the details.

In many other cases, Bondarchuk chooses to cut rather than compress. For example, most of volume 2, part 2, which develops Pierre's growing involvement with Freemasonry, is cut. This was likely a political decision on Bondarchuk's part; he was well aware of the official Soviet disapproval of secret societies like the Freemasons.[26] This connection with the Freemasons is, however, an important aspect of Pierre's personal evolution from rationalist to Russian, which is of signal importance to Tolstoy. As another example, Kutuzov's death in April 1813 is not mentioned in the film, even though the old general plays such an important part in it. Tolstoy makes it sound as if Kutuzov died because he did not fit into the new age: "Kutuzov did not understand the significance of Europe, balance, Napoleon. He could not understand it. Once the foe was annihilated, once Russia was delivered and placed at the highest degree of her glory, there was nothing more to do. For the representative of the national war, there was nothing left but death. And so he died."[27]

Another issue in the adaptation was the fact that Tolstoy's *War and Peace* is much more than an epic national saga; it is also a *roman à these*. Tolstoy wanted to explore philosophically what it means to be a Russian specifically and a human being generally. Most of these discussions are cut from the film because they are simply not cinematic. One example is the excision of a discourse on idleness in volume 2, part 4: "Biblical tradition says that absence of work—idleness—was the condition of the first man's blessedness before his fall. The love of idleness remained the same in fallen man, but the curse still weighs on man, and not only because we must win our bread in the sweat of our face, but because our moral qualities are such that we should be able to be idle and at peace. A secret voice tells us that we should feel guilty for being idle."[28] This is an almost commonplace observation, but many pithy and revealing lines about the Russian national character also fell by the wayside—for example: "A Russian is self-assured precisely because he does not know anything, because he does not believe it possible to know anything fully."[29] This observation was undoubtedly excised because it hardly fit the Soviet self-image in the mid-1960s or the image the state was trying to project.

Another category of ideas discussed at length in the novel but not in the film is Tolstoy's views on history and historians (explored in the next chapter in more detail). Suffice it to say that these monologues were cut because they are not easily transferred to images and run the risk of boring the viewer (as they might the ordinary reader who is interested in the story but not the philosophy). For example, volume 3, part 1, chapter 1 is entirely devoted to reflections like this: "For us descendants—who are not historians, who are not carried away by the process of research and therefore can contemplate events with unobscured common sense—a countless number of causes present themselves. The deeper we go in search of causes, the more of them we find, and each cause taken singly or whole series of causes present themselves to us as equally correct in themselves and equally false in their insignificance in comparison with the enormity of the event."[30]

Bondarchuk also excised dialogues that are mainly military in focus, covering strategies and encounters between French and Russian officers. He dramatically downplays the role of Napoleon, whom Tolstoy uses as a straw man to set up his ideas about the unimportance of strategy and the pitiful efforts of historians to find the causes of historical events.[31] These passages are especially prevalent in volume 3, which (like part three of the film) covers the French invasion.[32] Two examples from this volume should suffice. The first: "The French had already passed Smolensk and were moving closer and closer to Moscow. Napoleon's historian [Adolphe] Thiers, like other historians, says, trying to justify his hero, that Napoleon was lured to the walls of Moscow involuntarily. He is right, as all historians are right who seek explanations of historical events in the will of one man; he is right, just as the Russian historians are right who maintain that Napoleon was lured to Moscow by the skill of the Russian commanders."[33]

Also omitted is an encounter between Lavrushka, a Cossack orderly who has been captured by the French, and Napoleon: "He blurted out everything that was the talk among the orderlies. Much of it was true. But when Napoleon asked what the Russians thought about defeating or not defeating Napoleon, Lavrushka narrowed his eyes and fell to thinking. He saw a subtle cunning here, as people like Lavrushka always see cunning in everything, so he frowned and paused. 'It's like this: if there's a battle,' he said thoughtfully, 'and at the sooner, then that's just that. Well, but if it happens three days after that same date, then it means that same battle's going to put a drag on things.'"[34] This is translated into French for Napoleon, as though the statement makes sense—an example of Tolstoy's keen sense of irony, which does not make its way into the film.

Finally, Bondarchuk chose to cut the entire ninety-page epilogue. For some readers, the epilogue nearly spoils Tolstoy's book. Here, the reader sees Natasha and Pierre and Nikolai and Marya in 1819—two happily married couples with their children. Unfortunately, Tolstoy transforms the once charming and sprightly Natasha into an obsessive, overbearing domestic; Pierre has become a henpecked husband. Nikolai and Marya, in contrast, are a model of domestic bliss with their calm, balanced relationship. The second part of the epilogue is devoted to Tolstoy's discourse on history. The famous novel ends with these disquieting words, which seem to have nothing to do with the Rostovs, the Bolkonskys, or Pierre Bezukhov: "In the first case [astronomy], the need was to renounce the consciousness of a nonexistent immobility in space and recognize a movement we do not feel; in the present case, it is just as necessary to renounce a nonexistent freedom and recognize a dependence we do not feel."[35]

Not surprisingly, much was omitted in the process of making a seven-hour film based on a 1,215-page novel. Bondarchuk excised subplots and their characters and ruthlessly cut anything that was not cinematic. Although many of these excisions significantly undermined Tolstoy's intentions, in only one instance—Pierre's Freemasonry—can the cuts be identified as political, motivated by the self-censorship that was so common in Soviet cinema. An important question arises: given the extent of the cutting, can one claim that Bondarchuk's work retains the essence or emotional truth (*istina*) of the original?

An affirmative response must be based on what Bondarchuk chose to preserve in the film. As already noted, he compressed or omitted chapters but always kept the main details intact. There is little reinvention in the film, and that which does exist is fairly modest. One example is from the beginning of the film, when Andrei and Pierre stroll past the Winter Palace and the Winter Gardens in St. Petersburg, discussing marriage and women. In the book, this conversation takes place inside, in Andrei's study. Bondarchuk likely wanted to move the action outdoors to display St. Petersburg's ethereal beauty. This change, however, hardly alters the conversation's import.

Certainly, the best example of Bondarchuk's style of reinvention is from the end of the film. In the novel, although Natasha and Pierre meet again at the Bolkonskys and realize they are in love, it is not as simple as Bondarchuk's version. In the novel (volume 4, part 4), both Natasha and Pierre are haunted by guilt and their memories of Andrei, and they feel it is too soon after Andrei's death to claim such happiness.[36] In the film, Pierre appears at the Bolkonskys', and all previous misunderstandings with Natasha vanish wordlessly. Although this is different from the book, it merely simplifies the ultimate point—that Natasha and Pierre will be together.

The most obvious method used by Bondarchuk to retain the heart of the novel is through the dialogue, most of which is appropriated directly from Tolstoy. Some of this verbatim dialogue is revealing, such as when Andrei says to Pierre in the Winter Gardens scene: "You talk of Bonaparte; but Bonaparte when he was working, went step by step towards his goal, he was free, he had nothing except his goal—and he reached it. But bind yourself to a woman—and, like a prisoner in irons, you lose all freedom. . . . Drawing rooms, gossip, balls, vanity, triviality . . . this stupid society, without which my wife cannot live. . . . Egoism, vanity, dull-wittedness, triviality in everything—that's women when they show themselves as they are."[37] However, much of the borrowed dialogue is rather prosaic. As Dolokhov teeters with his bottle in the window at Kuragin's drinking party, he says, straight from the novel: "Away with all of it, otherwise they'll think I'm holding on." And later he says, "If anyone does the same, I'll pay him a hundred imperials. Understood?"[38] Perhaps Bondarchuk and Solovev thought that, out of respect for Tolstoy, they could not come up with better lines.

Bondarchuk also uses voice-overs for purposes of transitions and to supply a brief synopsis of omitted material. The omniscient narrator (as already noted, a common feature in historical epics) generally provides background, context, or explanation of the action, such as: "On the twelfth of June, the forces of western Europe crossed the borders of Russia, and war began, that is, an event took place contrary to human reason and to the whole of human nature."[39] Sometimes the narrator reads the characters' thoughts, such as when Andrei asks Natasha to marry him: "Prince Andrei . . . did not find the former love for her in his soul . . . the former poetic and mysterious delight of desire was not there, but there was pity for her woman's and child's weakness, there was fear before her devotion and trust. . . . The actual feeling, though not as bright and poetic as the former one, was more serious and strong."[40] Elsewhere, the actors voice their own characters' thoughts, such as the dying Lise Bolkonskaya: "I love you all, I did no harm to anyone, why am I suffering? Help me."[41] In all cases, the text is straight from the novel.

One of the most vivid examples of voice-over narration occurs as the camera pans over the sunset view of the Borodino battlefield. Napoleon, ever inscrutable, gazes upon the day's carnage. Bondarchuk preserves Tolstoy's verdict on the battle:

> And not only for that hour and day were reason and conscience darkened in this man, who, more than all the other participants in this affair, bore upon himself the whole weight of what was happening; but never to the end of his life was able to understand goodness, or beauty, or truth, or the meaning of his own actions, which were too much the opposite of goodness and truth, and too far removed from everything human for him to be able to grasp their meaning. He could not renounce his actions, extolled by half the world, and therefore he had to renounce truth and goodness and everything human.[42]

True to Bondarchuk's intentions, the structure and details of most scenes in the film follow the novel closely. One good example is the episode in which Pierre challenges Dolokhov to a duel, fights the duel, and then argues with his wife. First, Pierre and Dolokhov find themselves together at a banquet to honor General Bagration. That morning, Pierre received an anonymous letter about his wife and Dolokhov: "with the mean jocularity of all anonymous letters," this letter claimed that Pierre "saw poorly through his spectacles and that his wife's liaison with Dolokhov was a secret to no one but him."[43] At the dinner, Pierre can think of nothing but the letter, and although he is seething inwardly at the insult, he is afraid of Dolokhov's reputation as a duelist. Dolokhov then proposes a toast: "Well, now to the health of beautiful women. . . . To the health of beautiful women, Petrusha [Pierre], and of their lovers."[44] A servant lays a sheet of paper in front of Pierre, which Dolokhov quickly snatches. (Tolstoy does not tell us what this paper contains.) "Pierre looked at Dolokhov, the pupils of his eyes sank: the something terrible and ugly that had sickened him during dinner rose up and took possession of him. He leaned his entire corpulent body across the table."[45] When Dolokhov refuses to return the paper, Pierre grabs it and challenges him to a duel.

They meet the next day at the Sokolniki woods with their seconds. Pierre has not slept. Attempts at reconciliation fail. Pierre does not know the rules of dueling and does not even know how to shoot a pistol. Tolstoy writes of the scene: "The thaw and the fog persisted; at a distance of forty paces they could not see each other clearly."[46] (In the film there is less fog, allowing the viewer to distinguish the actors.) Dolokhov approaches slowly, and Pierre fires very quickly but awkwardly. "The smoke, especially thick because of

Hélène as a popular high-society matron. (Courtesy Photofest)

the fog, at first prevented him from seeing anything."[47] Then Dolokhov staggers through the mist toward Pierre; he has been hit and falls to the snowy ground. He aims at Pierre, who stands "with a meek smile of pity and regret, his legs and arms spread helplessly, his broad chest exposed."[48] Dolokhov fires and misses, and the confused Pierre staggers through the woods (in the film), muttering, as Tolstoy writes: "Stupid . . . stupid! Death . . . lies . . . [ellipses in the original]."[49]

Upon returning home, Pierre relives the horror and humiliation in his head, but the white-gowned Hélène, in a fury, interrupts his reverie. She denies being Dolokhov's lover, calls Pierre a fool for believing it, and insists that this duel has made her the "laughing-stock of all Moscow."[50] As she continues to attack him, her voice rising shrilly, Pierre feels like he is suffocating (shown by Bondarchuk's expression). Pierre tells Hélène that they should separate, and she sarcastically agrees—if he gives her his money. Finally, he is driven into a rage and threatens to kill her, wrenching the marble top off a table and rushing toward her. Hélène screams and tries to get away. Tolstoy says, "Pierre felt the enchantment of rage" and shouted "'Out!' in such a frightful voice that everybody in the house was terrified on hearing this shout."[51]

Another example of a scene faithfully but beautifully transformed into cinematic language is Natasha's ball, which is even more memorable in the film than in the novel. After Natasha, her mother, and Sonya climb the long staircase, Bondarchuk and Petritsky bring Tolstoy's description to life:

> [Natasha] entered the hall, took off her fur coat, and walked beside Sonya in front of her mother between the flowers on the lighted stairway. . . . Before them, behind them, also talking quietly and also in ball gowns, other guests were entering. The mirrors on the stairway reflected ladies in white, blue, pink dresses, with diamonds and pearls on their bare arms and hands. . . . Everything mixed into one brilliant procession. At the entrance to the first room, the monotonous noise of voices, footsteps, greetings deafened Natasha, the light and brilliance dazzled her still more.[52]

We see Pierre making his way through the crowds, "rolling his fat body," as Tolstoy says. "But before he reached [the Rostovs], Bezukhov stopped beside a very handsome, dark-haired man of medium height, in a white uniform."[53] It is Andrei Bolkonsky.

The first dance is a polonaise, led by Alexander I. Natasha suddenly recognizes that the unthinkable has happened; no one has asked her to dance. Bondarchuk and Solovev borrowed lines from Tolstoy's rendition of Natasha's thoughts: "Can it be that no one will come up to me, can it be that I won't dance among the first, can it be that all these men won't notice me, who now don't even seem to see me, and if they look at me, it's with such an expression as if they were saying, 'Ah! It's not her, there's no point in looking!' No, it can't be," she thought. "They must know how I want to dance, and how well I dance, and what fun it will be for them to dance with me."[54] Pierre, acutely aware of Natasha's fears, asks Andrei to dance with her. Andrei readily agrees to dance a waltz with the "desperate, rapt" girl whose eyes shine with tears unshed. About the dance itself, Tolstoy says only that both Andrei and Natasha are excellent dancers and that, "as soon as he put his arm around her slender, mobile, quivering waist, and she began to move so close to him and smile so close to him, the wine of her loveliness went to his head."[55] (In this case, the prose pales before the visual poetry of the film, with its constantly moving cameras and close-ups.) Natasha dances with other partners as Andrei watches her. At the end of one dance, he thinks, exactly as in the novel: "If she goes to her cousin first and then to another lady, she'll be my wife."[56] He is smitten.

By the end of the ball, Natasha is "in that highest degree of happiness when a person becomes perfectly kind and good, and does not believe in the possibility of evil, unhappiness, and grief."[57] She tries to share her happiness with the glum Pierre, who is irritated by his wife's popularity with other men. Pierre can only smile "distractedly" and murmur, "I'm very glad."[58]

Another good example of the way Bondarchuk appropriated verbatim episodes from the novel is the hunting scene and the subsequent dinner, which occupies seventeen pages of text (and seven minutes of film).[59] Most of the text is description, which showcases Tolstoy's prose very well: "It was already turning winter, morning frosts gripped the earth moistened by autumn rains, the winter wheat was already tufting up and stood out bright and green against the strips of brownish, cattle-trampled winter stubble and pale yellow summer stubble with red strips of buckwheat. The hilltops and woods, which at the end of August were still green islands among the black winter croplands and stubble, had become golden and bright red islands amidst the bright green winter crops."[60] Bondarchuk and Petritsky faithfully capture the beauty of this description by shooting on location. They also replicate the scene of the capture and trussing of the wolf: "They put a stick in the wolf's mouth, tied it with a leash like a bridle, bound his legs, and Danilo rolled the wolf from side to side a couple of times."[61] After the hunters have taken the wolf to the place where the other hunters are assembling, Bondarchuk and Petritsky focus on a close-up of the wolf, "who, lolling his big-browed head with the stick gripped in his mouth, looked with wide, glassy eyes at this whole crowd of dogs and people surrounding him. When touched, he jerked his bound legs and looked at them all wildly and at the same time simply."[62]

The scene at the uncle's lodge also closely replicates Tolstoy's description. A rustic feast is laid before Natasha, Nikolai, and Petya Rostov: "On the tray were an herb cordial, liqueurs, mushrooms, flat cakes made from dark flour and buttermilk, honey in the comb, still and foaming mead, apples, fresh and roasted nuts, and nuts in honey. Then Anisya Fyodorovna brought preserves made with honey and with sugar, and a ham, and a just roasted chicken."[63] Natasha is in "merry spirits" as the coachman plays the song "Barinya" on the balalaika offscreen.[64] The uncle has Anisya fetch his guitar and begins to play "the well-known song, 'Down the ro-o-oadway.'"[65]

The uncle begins a second song but then breaks off and invites Natasha to dance, a pivotal scene in both the movie and the novel that signifies Natasha's Russianness. The film's narrator intones a slimmed-down version of Tolstoy's lines: "Where, how, and when had this little countess, brought up by an émigré Frenchwoman, sucked this spirit in from the Russian air she breathed, where had she gotten these ways . . . ? Yet that spirit and these ways were those very inimitable, unstudied Russian ones which the uncle expected of her."[66] Anisya immediately gives Natasha her kerchief for the dance and weeps as she watches "this slender, graceful countess . . . who was able to understand everything that was in Anisya and in Anisya's father, and in her aunt, and in her mother, and in every Russian."[67] It is a moment of perfect bliss for Natasha, and one of the most beautiful scenes in Bondarchuk's film.

Prince Andreï's death scene is yet one more example of Bondarchuk's appropriation of Tolstoy, especially the important dream sequence when Andrei knows for sure that he will not survive his wounds. Tolstoy wrote: "In a dream he saw himself lying in the same room in which he lay in reality, but he was not wounded, but healthy."[68] After the people Andrei has been talking to leave, he realizes he must lock the closed door in the room. "And a tormenting fear seizes him. And this fear is the fear of death: *it* is standing behind the door."[69] Death is trying to get in, and Andrei is using all the strength left in him to force the door closed. "His last supernatural efforts are in vain, and the two halves open noiselessly. *It* comes in, and it is *death*."[70] This is a scene made for cinematic presentation, and Bondarchuk uses the conventional means of signifying a dream, shooting in soft focus and slow motion. The mise-en-scène is very white, representing Andreï's newfound spirituality after purging himself of envy and vanity, resentment and anger—all because of his love for Natasha. One detail that Bondarchuk leaves out, however, is that Andrei takes communion and confesses before he dies. This omission is curious, because the last rites are shown when Pierre's father dies, and Kutuzov is also shown praying, kissing an icon, and genuflecting, so it was probably not a political decision.

Then there are the episodes that Bondarchuk truly makes his own: the Battle of Borodino and the Moscow fire. Tolstoy tells the story of Borodino from two primary vantage points: Napoleon's and Pierre's. (Andrei figures only at the very end of the episode.) Bondarchuk does not spend much time with Napoleon during preparations for battle or the battle itself. Tolstoy uses Napoleon to support his disparaging views of so-called great men and their useless strategies: "It would seems that, during the battle, Napoleon would be giving all the necessary instructions; but that was not and could not be done, because during the whole time of the battle, Napoleon was so far away from it that . . . the course of the battle could not be known to him and not one of his instructions during the battle could be carried out."[71] Rather than having the narrator offer this explanation, Bondarchuk shows it: Napoleon appears in a long shot, far away from the battle raging below. He is clearly the commander, but he does not appear to be "in command." One shot visualizes an entire chapter that ends with this paragraph: "In the battle of Borodino, Napoleon fulfilled his function as the representative of power. . . . He did nothing to harm the course of the battle; he bowed to the more well-reasoned opinions; he caused no confusion, did not contradict himself, did not get frightened, and did not run away from the battlefield, but with his great tact and experience of war calmly and worthily fulfilled his role of seeming to command."[72]

In contrast, Bondarchuk follows Pierre's exploits as an observer on the battlefield fairly closely. Pierre climbs to the barrow where Kutuzov and staff officers have gathered, and he admires the view: "Now the whole terrain was covered with troops and the smoke of gunfire, and the slanting rays of the bright sun . . . cast over it, in the clear morning air, a piercing light of a pink and golden hue, and long, dark shadows."[73] Although Bondarchuk was accused of using the battle as an excuse for spectacle, Tolstoy also aestheticizes the battle, at least as seen through Pierre's eyes: "*Poof!* Suddenly a round, compact puff of smoke was seen, a play of purple, gray, and milky white, and *boom!*—a second later came the sound of this smoke."[74] Pierre watches most of the battle from the famous Raevsky redoubt, where his civilian clothing and light-colored top hat first amaze and then amuse the Russian soldiers. Bondarchuk and Solovev borrowed liberally from this section of the novel (volume 3, part 2, chapters 31–32), including much of the dialogue. After Pierre engages in his mad hand-to-hand combat with a French soldier, he finds that not a single Russian soldier has survived, and he runs away. Apart from that, the horror of the battle, so brilliantly visualized by Bondarchuk, is largely absent from the novel.

After Pierre's scenes, Bondarchuk was on his own in terms of depicting the carnage on the battlefield, and he did so brilliantly with a relentlessly tracking camera and memorable aerial shots. Tolstoy preferred the individual point of view and returned to Napoleon, but the French emperor needs binoculars (a telescope in the film) to see anything. Likewise, Kutuzov is seated well behind the lines, where he approves or disapproves of what his staff tells him but does not issue orders. In Tolstoy's words, "He understood that one man cannot lead hundreds of thousands of men struggling with death, and he knew that the fate of a battle is decided not by the commander in chief's instructions, not by the position of the troops, not by the number of cannon or of people killed, but by that elusive force known as the spirit of the troops."[75]

Finally, Tolstoy (and Bondarchuk) turns to Andrei's regiment, which has been held in reserve but is nevertheless dying in droves from the cannon fire. For once, Andrei is thinking of nothing when a "shell dully plopped down within two paces of [him]. . . . The shell was smoking, spinning like a top. . . . 'Can this be death?' thought Prince Andrei, gazing . . . at the grass, at the wormwood, and at the little stream of smoke curling up from the spinning black ball."[76] When Andrei is hit, the battle is over as far as Tolstoy is concerned. In the film, Bondarchuk expands Tolstoy's material to a compelling thirty-five minutes of nightmarish battle. The Battle of Borodino is one instance in which Bondarchuk's film outshines Tolstoy's novel.

Another case in which Bondarchuk is actually better than Tolstoy is the Moscow fire, which Tolstoy covers in a mere nine pages. Pierre is trying to find Napoleon in order to kill him, unaware that Napoleon is already in the Kremlin Palace "issuing detailed, thorough instructions."[77] Tolstoy first writes rather mildly of the fire: "The smoke became thicker and thicker. . . . Fiery tongues occasionally soared up from behind the roofs of the houses. There were more people in the streets, and those people were more alarmed."[78] Later, as Pierre tries to find the little girl who has been lost in the chaos, Tolstoy notes, "The whole street was covered with a cloud of black smoke. Here and there tongues of flame burst from this cloud."[79] Pierre sees that French soldiers are looting, but he is focused on his quest to find the girl. At this point, Tolstoy provides his best description of the fire: "The sound of cracking and the crash of falling walls and ceilings, the whistling and hissing of the flames, and the lively cries of the people, the sight of billowing clouds of smoke, now frowningly thick and black, now soaring up brightly, with flashes of sparks, and here and there of solid, sheaf-like red or scaly golden flames, creeping over the walls."[80] This scene cries out for cinematic treatment, and Bondarchuk and Petritsky provide it in spectacular fashion. Their fire is an inferno; the streets are filled with panicked people, swarming aimlessly. The French soldiers, who have abandoned all pretense of respectability, are looting with impunity. The air is filled with ashes and smoke. One of these looters remembers his humanity and helps Pierre find the child. Then Pierre tries but fails to locate the girl's mother, comes to the defense of the Armenian woman, and is arrested as an arsonist.[81]

The people of Moscow try to escape the fires. (Courtesy Photofest)

Another episode with Bondarchuk's personal stamp takes place near the end of the novel, when a frozen and hungry Captain Ramballe and his orderly Morel show up at a Russian encampment. Ramballe, no longer the self-confident man Pierre met in Moscow, is grateful that the Russians do not kill them and even help them. Morel, drunk on the vodka the Russians have given him, begins to sing. Of course, the Russian soldiers cannot understand him, but one gamely tries to copy the French lyrics, to the hilarity of all. "'They're also people,' one of [the Russian soldiers said]. . . . 'Even wormwood grows on its own root.'"[82] Then Bondarchuk adds some flourishes that come straight from the 1960s, a true "kumbaya" moment. All the soldiers, French and Russian, begin to sing together, eventually forming a large circle that is shot from above. The savagery of the war is behind them. Brotherhood reigns. Tolstoy likely would have approved of this sentiment.

French and Russian soldiers sing together. (Courtesy Photofest)

Bondarchuk's *War and Peace* is certainly a "fidelity of transformation" adaptation, but with as much emphasis on *transformation* as on *fidelity*. He tells the story in mainly cinematic terms (the heavy use of voice-over narration is the major exception). The adaptation is both faithful and complex; Bondarchuk wants to do more than merely tell a story in this film. Despite the claims of some Soviet critics, the picture is true to both Tolstoy's rich details and his humanistic spirit. Whether the film is true to history is the subject of the next chapter.

CHAPTER FOUR

WAR AND PEACE AS HISTORY

Sergei Bondarchuk's film succeeds as a literary adaptation, but does it satisfy the historian? As shown in chapter 1, Bondarchuk was interested in getting the historical minutiae right; to ensure that the costumes, set decorations, and weaponry were accurate, actual period pieces were often used. Some Soviet critics attacked him for paying more attention to achieving historical verisimilitude than to bringing the narrative to life (a charge I think is unfair). Of course, historical authenticity in a film is more than just props. This chapter examines the "real" history of the battles of Schöngraben, Austerlitz, and Borodino to determine how faithful Tolstoy and Bondarchuk were to that history. It also presents Tolstoy's philosophy of war and history as explicated in the novel to determine the extent to which these ideas are communicated in the film.

History as Told by Historians

Russia's wars against Napoleon have been heavily mythologized, especially the events of 1812. Tolstoy's *War and Peace* is widely accepted as the single most important mythmaker of Russia's Napoleonic Wars, and present-day historians have disputed his views. As indicated in the last chapter, Tolstoy believed, in the words of historian Dominic Lieven, that "Russian leadership had little control over events and that Russian 'strategy' was a combination of improvisation and accident."[1] Russia therefore won the war because of the indomitable spirit of its people, a military leader (General Mikhail Kutuzov) who embodied that spirit, and the vast expanse of the Russian land (*rodina*). As a result, as Lieven notes, "Russian national myths derived from the Napoleonic War greatly underestimate the Russian [military] achievement in 1812–14."[2] These myths—that Napoleon was defeated by the spirit of the Russian people, the vast landscape, and the harsh climate—were largely generated by *War and Peace*, which, according to military historian Alexander Mikaberidze, "overshadows historical reality and assumed the authority of a historical document."[3] It is telling that Tolstoy's contemporary, General

Mikhail Dragomirov, found the great writer's views on 1812 (as expressed in *War and Peace*) to be "almost juvenile."[4]

The first battle Tolstoy writes about is Schöngraben, which took place on 16 November 1805, setting the stage for Tolstoy's (and Bondarchuk's) version of the Napoleonic Wars. The battle was a good example of the Russian army's strengths and weaknesses. On the positive side, the military possessed "near legendary courage, resilience and loyalty of the rank and file," along with a "habitual calm discipline."[5] On the negative side, an important weakness was the rivalry among the army's generals, which led to fissures in the high command.[6] Another key weakness was an emperor who believed he knew better than his generals. Alexander I did not heed General Kutuzov's advice to retreat and was thus largely responsible for the Russian catastrophe at Austerlitz two weeks after Schöngraben, on 2 December 1805.[7]

Austerlitz figures prominently in both book and film. There, Alexander was heavily influenced by his young and inexperienced adjutants, who had an "appetite for glory." Alexander was caught up in the general excitement that reigned at his headquarters, and he marginalized not only the old generals but also anyone who agreed with them. For instance, Prince Adam Czartoryski found that his long friendship with the emperor was cooling. Czartoryski also disapproved of Alexander's taking command of the coalition forces.[8]

The Battle of Austerlitz began at 7:30 a.m. and was over by early afternoon. The morning was very foggy, which limited visibility. The coalition troops tried to "take the whole [French] army from the side," exposing their flank. When the fog lifted and Kutuzov could actually see what was happening, he wanted the Russian forces to retreat, but Alexander immediately countermanded that order. Catastrophe resulted, and the Russian army was "submerged in a French assault." When the order to retreat was finally given at 11:00 a.m., the Russian army was surrounded and could not execute the command for another two hours. This was not merely a defeat; it was a rout. The emperor, watching his desperate troops trying to retreat amidst total chaos, leaned against a tree and wept.[9]

From the summer of 1810, Alexander had regarded another war with Napoleon as inevitable due to the latter's expansionism and the fraught relationship between the two men. Alexander ordered the military to prepare for this likelihood. By 1812, Russian artillery was in "tip top shape."[10] Besides artillery, another asset was the Russian army's commander, General Mikhail Barclay de Tolly, whom Lieven describes as an "efficient, incorruptible, hardworking and meticulous administrator" and a "front-line soldier

Prince Andrei at Austerlitz. (Courtesy Photofest)

with an outstanding wartime record . . . [and] a solid grasp on tactics."[11] Furthermore, 1.1 million peasants had been drafted as soldiers, creating an army that was nearly twice as big as Napoleon's, even though it was inexperienced.[12]

Nevertheless, in the event Napoleon actually invaded Russia, retreat was discussed as a strategy as early as April 1812, first advanced by General Pyotr Chuikevich. Both Alexander and Barclay de Tolly believed in strategic withdrawal, but they were reluctant to admit this openly; the public was understandably against retreat, and the emperor did not want to lower morale.[13] Tolstoy's view that the retreat after the Battle of Borodino was the result of chance rather than planning is not supported by the historical evidence, as the documents and correspondence of Alexander and Barclay clearly show.[14]

Nonetheless, official Russian military doctrine in 1812 was based on an offensive strategy, derived not only from public opinion but also from the views of generals such as the ambitious and dynamic Pyotr Bagration.[15] Bagration was especially popular with his men and, later, with Tolstoy and Bondarchuk as well. Despite the fact that Bagration was Georgian, he was, according to historian Sean Pollock, the "leader of a 'Russian party' who resented the presence of generals with foreign sounding names."[16]

The War of 1812 began on 24 June when French troops crossed the

The ambitious and dynamic General Bagration. (Courtesy Photofest)

Neman River and marched unimpeded into Russia. When the Russian army finally reached Smolensk, Alexander began to pressure Barclay de Tolly to advance, but after heavy fighting (and heavy losses) in Smolensk on 16–18 August, the beleaguered Barclay ordered a retreat, against the advice of all the other generals. The retreat was well organized and disciplined, garnering the admiration of the French.[17] But as the retreat continued from Smolensk to Borodino, Barclay's popularity, already tenuous, plummeted.[18] Although native born, he was perceived in court circles as a "foreigner" because of his Scottish ancestry; he had been raised in Livonia (present-day Estonia), which was part of the Russian empire, but a "German" part. One of his chief enemies, Bagration, labeled him "that wretch, scoundrel, and vermin Barclay."[19]

Alexander hoped to foment a national war against Napoleon. He issued an imperial manifesto on 19 July that appealed to the patriotism of all segments of Russian society and compared this dangerous moment in Russian history to the seventeenth-century "Time of Troubles," when the nation had faced invasion by the Swedes and especially the Poles.[20] "Russian people!" the manifesto read, "Brave descendants of the Slavs! . . . With the cross in your hearts and weapons in your hands, no human face will be able to vanquish you."[21] The nobility voluntarily contributed cash and goods to the war effort and formed private militias consisting of their own serfs.[22] On 23 July Alexander met the people of Moscow on the steps of the Kremlin Palace on his way to the Uspensky Cathedral, a powerful scene that appears in both the novel and the film.[23]

Amidst this enthusiasm for war, Barclay de Tolly's days were numbered. He was replaced by Kutuzov on 20 August, but Kutuzov did not take actual command until 29 August.[24] This had been a difficult decision for the emperor because he strongly disliked Kutuzov, a fact that appears in neither novel nor film. Kutuzov was a paradoxical figure. As historian Marie-Pierre Rey notes: "Aged 67, blind in one eye, obese and almost impotent, Kutuzov was known for his laziness, his obsequiousness, his taste for luxury, and his sexual appetite."[25] Kutuzov was, however, supported by the nobility in both St. Petersburg and Moscow.[26] There were reasons for this. Very much like his character in both Tolstoy's and Bondarchuk's *War and Peace*, Kutuzov was indeed stout; he "walked heavily, was often out of breath, and had difficulty riding a horse, preferring his carriage . . . [but] below that drowsy and absent-minded appearance was keen judgment, cunning, and patience."[27] He was also a "skilful, courageous, and experienced soldier."[28] In any event, it was thought (wrongly, as it turned out) that his arrival as commander would put an end to the retreat.[29]

Kutuzov selected the village of Borodino as the place to do battle with Napoleon, a choice that was criticized by his generals because it left "both flanks . . . exposed."[30] The fifth and sixth of September were cool, rainy, and misty, as the Russian soldiers busied themselves constructing battle works, especially redoubts.[31] On 6 September, as both Tolstoy and Bondarchuk inform us, a religious procession carried the miracle-working holy icon of the Black Virgin of Smolensk into the camp, which, in the words of participant Aleksandr Muravev, "had a remarkably uplifting effect on the soldiers."[32] Another participant in the battle, Fyodor Glinka, wrote that as the procession passed by, 100,000 soldiers "fell to [their] knees and bowed [their] head[s] to the ground, ready to satiate it with their own blood."[33] Kutuzov reviewed the lines and delivered inspirational speeches to the rank and file: "Lads! You have to defend the motherland, serve faithfully and truthfully, shedding the very last drop of your blood."[34] Afterward, a strange and dramatic event occurred (not depicted in the novel or the film) that some perceived as a lucky portent: "A large eagle soared above [Kutuzov]. Wherever he went, the eagle followed him."[35]

These eyewitness accounts of Borodino are so vivid that they beg for cinematic treatment. Fyodor Glinka's descriptions are particularly cinematic; on 5 September, for example, he watched French troops from a church bell tower, writing: "The fields . . . waved as a golden sea of harvest . . . in the midst of the golden sea was a steel river of bayonets and muskets that glittered under the evening sun"[36] Ilya Radozhitsky wrote that, on the next day, "the fires turned the dark clouds in the sky into a crimson twilight."[37]

Although sources differ with regard to the start of the Battle of Borodino, the most reliable state that it began at 6:00 a.m. on 7 September 1812. The first round was fired by the French and was directed at Kutuzov's headquarters. The attack on the village of Borodino diverted Kutuzov's attention from his weak left flank; the fighting there was particularly chaotic.[38] Kutuzov remained at his command post while Barclay de Tolly and Bagration oversaw the fighting. When Bagration was mortally wounded (he died on 24 September), Barclay took over.[39] (Both Tolstoy and, apparently, Bondarchuk, shared Bagration's disdain of Barclay and left him by the wayside.)

Napoleon had 130,000 soldiers on the field; the Russians had 125,000.[40] Borodino was a "densely packed" battlefield, which gave the French "little room to manoeuvre or to exploit tactical successes."[41] In effect, Napoleon was forced to fight the Russians' preferred style of warfare: close combat.

According to eyewitness accounts, the battlefield was an inferno. Fyodor Glinka described the death of General Aleksandr Tuchkov this way: "Numerous cannonballs and shells, resembling a boiling cloud, fell on the very place where the general lay, and ploughed the earth, burying the general's corpse."[42] Mikhail Petrov wrote that "this devastating day . . . had dampened the fields and ravines of the Borodino environment with blood and covered them with a thick layer of ravaged bodies and bones."[43] Another Russian officer noted that the Russians and French "did not stop fighting when their muskets broke, but carried on, using butts and swords in terrible hand-to-hand combat."[44]

Lest one think the Russian officers were prone to exaggeration about the battle, a Saxon officer fighting for the French offered this compelling description: "The combat was frightful! Men and horses hit by lethal lead fell down the slope and thrashed around among the dead and dying foe, each trying to kill the enemy with their weapons, their bare hands or even their teeth. To add to this horror, the succeeding ranks of assaulting cavalry trampled over the writhing mass as they drove on to their next targets."[45] Summing it up, Waldemar Löwenstern, who was fighting with the Russian army, observed that "at times the battlefield looked like one of those battle drawings that the great painters of the past have left us."[46] The "bloody day" ended when a "thick fog" descended on the battlefield, which stank of rotting corpses that "smothered the area for weeks."[47]

Kutuzov wrote a letter to Alexander that flattered the Russian army's undeniable "gallantry and resolve," without dwelling on the carnage and chaos. Likewise, his official report asserted that Borodino had been a victory for Russia.[48] In fact, the Russian army lost an estimated 44,000 to 50,000 men, compared with French losses of 28,000 to 30,000.[49] Losses of senior officers were "crippling."[50] There were 6,500 casualties an hour, which is a record for a one-day battle.[51] At best, the Battle of Borodino was a draw, but because Alexander I regarded it as a victory, Kutuzov was promoted to field marshal and was awarded 100,000 rubles.[52]

The day after the battle, Kutuzov claimed he wanted to engage the French forces again—a move he knew would be popular among his generals and the public. But as the losses at Borodino became evident, he changed his mind. This was not an easy decision because he firmly believed that if Moscow fell, Russia would be lost.[53] (Tolstoy and Bondarchuk show his angst very well.) Kutuzov's predecessor, Barclay de Tolly, supported Kutuzov's decision to retreat and abandon Moscow to the French, although most of the other generals did not.[54]

The withdrawal from Moscow was rapid, and the evacuees were quickly "overtaken by panic."[55] Russian troops, followed by thousands of wounded soldiers, preceded the city's inhabitants in flight (6,000 wounded Russian soldiers were left behind in Moscow, and most perished in the fires).[56] Napoleon's troops entered a largely deserted Moscow on 14 September: "long lonely streets with house shutters closed, the roll of drums resounding on deaf echoes."[57] Napoleon himself arrived the following day and headquartered himself in the Kremlin, using Alexander I's office there.[58]

Fires broke out around the city almost immediately and burned for six days.[59] Many historians accept the claim that the mayor of Moscow, Count Fyodor Rostopchin, ordered the setting of the fires, although he denied it; most Russians at the time believed the French destroyed the city.[60] As a result of the fires, not to mention the apathy and confusion of the French commanders, the French soldiers transformed from a disciplined army into a dangerous mob. One French officer recalled that "the army had dissolved completely; everywhere one could see drunken soldiers and officers loaded with booty and provisions from houses which had fallen prey to the flames. The streets were strewn with books, porcelain, furniture, and clothing of every kind."[61] The French army also "acted violently" toward the civilian population; not surprisingly, morale among the Russians left behind was low.[62]

France sent reinforcements to Napoleon to make up for the losses at Borodino, bringing the French force to over 100,000 men. Although Kutuzov's army now had only 63,000 soldiers, Napoleon knew any chance to defeat the Russian army had ended in the carnage at Borodino; winter was fast approaching, and the French were not prepared for it.[63] His attempts to get Alexander I to sign a treaty were unsuccessful; Alexander's view had always been that as long as a single enemy soldier remained on Russian soil, there would be no treaty.[64] Napoleon finally realized the futility of his efforts and ordered his army to leave Moscow on 19 October. The French, unlike the Russians, did not know how to manage or execute an orderly retreat. Witness Matvei Platov wrote: "[The French army] is abandoning its baggage, its sick, and its wounded. It leaves behind horrible sights in its wake."[65] As the French left, Russian troops harassed them, especially the so-called partisans, which were actually "units of regular cavalry and Cossacks operating behind enemy lines under the command of regular officers."[66] Peasants joined the attack against the French, making this stage of the crisis a true people's war.[67]

Lieven calls the perception that the Russian winter defeated the French one of the major myths of 1812. The month of October was in fact warmer than usual, as was November. Deep winter did not set in until December.[68] The main peril the French faced in October and November was hunger. On 9 November 1812 Pyotr Konovnitsyn wrote: "The enemy is dying of hunger, they eat not only horses, but even humans who, on several occasions, were found roasted."[69] On 10 November Pavel Pushin wrote about the condition of French prisoners of war, who were half naked and starving: "I saw one of them who died from blood loss, and his comrade was lying next to him in this pool of blood, calmly awaiting the death that would save him from suffering."[70] Ilya Radozhitsky recalled "one particularly awful scene of a French soldier frozen in death at the very moment he was trying to rip the liver out of a fallen horse."[71] By the end of November, Nikolai Kovalsky reported that the French were wearing "women's clothing, priestly garbs, or servants' livery. Some wore female bonnets instead of helmets." He also saw French soldiers with horse intestines wrapped around their heads to provide warmth.[72]

Although some of the generals were scheming to unseat Kutuzov—they thought his performance at Borodino had been subpar and resented that he had stayed at headquarters during the battle, eating delicacies and drinking champagne—the commander was still popular with the rank-and-file soldiers.[73] He traveled down the Russian lines as the army chased the French out of Russia and was met everywhere with "universal joy" and loud cheering. On 15 November Ivan Zhirkevich reported: "When the cry 'Hurrah for the Saviour of Russia' began, Kutuzov yelled, 'This honour belongs not to me but to the Russian soldier! . . . Hurrah, hurrah, hurrah to the good old Russian soldiers!'"[74] Tolstoy and Bondarchuk would heartily agree.

Tolstoy on War and History

As mentioned at the beginning of this chapter, both Lieven and Mikaberidze seek to replace the historical myths of the War of 1812 with a more evidence-based version that is the "true" history of the war.[75] Lieven in particular argues that the Russian army's achievements have been badly underestimated, due in large part to the grip of Tolstoy's novel on the popular imagination. He writes (perhaps wistfully), "*War and Peace* has had more influence on popular perceptions of Napoleon's defeat by Russia than all the history books ever written." By denying that human actors had any rational influence on events in 1812 "and implying that military professionalism was a German disease, Tolstoy feeds rather easily into Western perceptions of 1812, which blame the snow or chance for French defeat."[76] For Lieven, the real reasons for victory are clear-cut (too clear-cut for Tolstoy): Russia's leaders "out-thought" Napoleon, and "deep retreat" was a sound strategy for which Lieven credits Barclay de Tolly, not Kutuzov.[77] In addition, the Russian army fought well in 1812, with "particular stubbornness and ferocity."[78]

How did Tolstoy's ideas on war, particularly the War of 1812, develop? Tolstoy believed in the "fog of war," leading him "to deny the possibility of purposeful leadership." He, like many others in his era, "stressed the eternal truth that morale, motivation, and will were the keys to victory in war."[79] The great writer further believed that "battles are won by superior numbers and by speed and unity of action . . . from simple and flexible tactics . . . [and] from a sense of unity among the national leaders, the officers and the men."[80]

For his interpretation of 1812, Tolstoy conducted extensive research. According to literary scholar Dan Ungurianu, he read "about fifty titles of memoirs, document collections and histories."[81] Tolstoy leaned heavily on the work of Aleksander Mikhailovsky-Danilevsky, the first Russian official historian of the wars of 1812–1814, who argued that "Russian courage and Kutuzov's wisdom saved the country."[82] These views were widely shared in Tolstoy's time.[83] (This is not to say that *War and Peace* did not have its detractors, particularly among veterans of 1812, who were angry that Tolstoy did not sufficiently heroicize the battles.)[84]

In *War and Peace*, Tolstoy concretizes his ideas about war and history, especially by creating an indelible portrait of Kutuzov. His Kutuzov "perfectly represents the will of the people he leads"; therefore, he cannot be "hubristic and power hungry" like the other generals.[85] Kutuzov, in other words, recognized that his power lay in the people. This may appear to be a variation of the traditional "great man" approach to history, which Tolstoy despised, but it is not.[86] Kutuzov is glorified not as an individual but as a representative of the collective will of the Russians. This is distinct from free will, which, according to Tolstoy, is an illusion.[87]

Even war is not the result of individual actions. Tolstoy wrote: "Why does a war or a revolution take place? We do not know; we only know that for the accomplishment of the one action or the other, people form themselves into certain units and all participate; and we say this is so because it is unthinkable otherwise, because it is a law." In other words, *"the event had to take place, simply because it had to take place* [emphasis in the original]."[88]

Tolstoy's philosophy of war is part of his larger philosophy of history, articulated at great length in *War and Peace*. His philosophy of history has been best explicated by philosopher and historian Isaiah Berlin in his brilliant little book *The Hedgehog and the Fox: An Essay on Tolstoy's View of History* (1953). The title comes from the ancient Greek poet Archilochus: "The fox knows many things, but the hedgehog knows one big thing." Berlin sees Tolstoy as a fox who wanted to be a hedgehog, and he argues that this paradox explains Tolstoy's ideas on history.[89]

Tolstoy was obsessed with history because he believed it held the key to life's most vexing questions.[90] Yet he despised professional historians because of their pretense of scientific objectivity.[91] He believed historians led people astray "by their false emphasis and wrong questions."[92] He saw a big difference between the "truth of history and the truth of the historian."[93] In his opinion, historians see only "the conspicuous monstrosities of human life and think that they are life itself."[94] In 1852 Tolstoy wrote: "History is nothing but a collection of fables and useless trifles, cluttered up with a mass of unnecessary figures and proper names."[95] More than fifty years later, in 1908, he had not changed his mind, writing sarcastically: "History would be an excellent thing if only it were true."[96] In *War and Peace*, Ungurianu argues, "Tolstoy strove to demythologize history," even though he "paradoxically created his own myth of 1812."[97]

What else did Tolstoy object to? For one, he felt that historians had not discovered the true principles of historical causation, choosing instead to emphasize superficial economic or political issues.[98] Literary scholar Gary

Saul Morson writes that, for Tolstoy, "myriads of causes" were obscured by conventional historical narrative.[99] Tolstoy also believed that "an event is not caused by a command which precedes it." In other words, power resides in personal relations, not in any one person.[100] He wanted his history "to deflate the importance of the self and to magnify the importance of other phenomena, irrational, intangible, and incomprehensible."[101]

According to Berlin, Tolstoy "contrasted the concrete and multi-colored reality of individual lives with the pale abstractions of scientists or historians, particularly the latter."[102] History should not only be people centered; it should also focus on ordinary people engaged in the mundane tasks of normal life, because these are the individuals who will save their country in times of crisis.[103] This sounds like "history from below," but in writing volume 3 of *War and Peace*—his literary history of 1812—Tolstoy, a fox masquerading as a hedgehog, only partially lives up to his own ideals. We certainly see the "multi-colored reality of individual lives" in Tolstoy's (and Bondarchuk's) *War and Peace*, but these lives are defiantly upper class. (The wise, proverb-spouting POW Platon Karataev is the only peasant who really matters in the novel.)[104] Tolstoy is unapologetic about this, writing: "The lives of officials, merchants, theological students, and peasants do not interest me and are only half comprehensible to me."[105] Tolstoy argues that because "their lives are 'single-faceted' and boring," they carry "less of the imprint of the times" and are, bluntly, "unattractive."[106]

The most fundamental historical question for Tolstoy was, in his words, "What power is it that moves the destiny of peoples?"[107] His answer, despite his criticism of historians, was not multivalent but rather simplistic. He was a determinist who believed that some "natural law," not human volition, set history in stone.[108] He thought that every person has two lives—a superficial individual life and an "elemental swarm life." The former enjoys some freedom; the latter does not.[109] He also believed that the "social, moral, political, [and] spiritual worlds" cannot be known through science.[110]

Tolstoy's theory of history was fundamentally grounded in his anti-intellectualism: "simple people often know the truth better than learned men, because their observation of men and nature is less clouded by empty theories."[111] Yet Tolstoy leaned on the works of many intellectuals to develop his own views: Alexander Herzen, Alexis de Tocqueville, Georg Hegel, Pierre-Joseph Proudhon, Arthur Schopenhauer, Jean-Jacques Rousseau, Stendhal (Marie-Henri Beyle), and especially Joseph de Maistre. In fact, Tolstoy borrowed from some of de Maistre's work almost verbatim in *War and Peace.*[112] Like Tolstoy, de Maistre believed in the "power of natural forces" and distrusted the scientific method, positivism, rationalism, and the like.[113]

As Tolstoy studied the histories written after the war in preparation for writing *War and Peace*, he felt that they failed to capture the "truth" of 1812 and were generally inaccurate.[114] He wanted to be guided by the "truth," not by the documents, but as already mentioned, he conducted painstaking research and borrowed liberally from his readings.[115] The writer went so far as to claim that "whenever historical persons speak or act in my novel, I have invented nothing but have used historical material."[116] Yet his presentation of the historical characters in *War and Peace* "illustrates . . . [his] general thesis of service to the group, in this case the country, not the family."[117] Soviet ideologists found this aspect of Tolstoy's philosophy of history very congenial to the "collectivism" of Marxism.

One concrete result of this distrust of official and academic history was Tolstoy's fabricated depiction of Kutuzov, who is presented as the "father of the Russian people."[118] As Berlin notes, Tolstoy's "Kutuzov is wise and not merely clever . . . and he is not a victim to abstract theory or dogma as the German military experts are; he is unlike them and is wiser than they—but this is not because he knows more facts than they."[119] Kutuzov's strength is that he is attuned to the will of the people; he "*guides* the spirit of the army as far as he is able [emphasis in the original]."[120] In this way, the "simple, intuitively wise," fictional Kutuzov is Tolstoy's vision of a great man. (Napoleon was not, and never could be, a great man.)[121] According to literary scholar Kathryn Feuer, Kutuzov's counterpart from the masses was "the peasant soldier, ignorant, obedient, and instinctive in his patriotism"— in other words a soldier like Platon Karataev.[122]

Bondarchuk as Historian

What about Bondarchuk's version of history? First and foremost, as discussed in chapter 3, he sought to be true to Tolstoy and succeeded. But he also had other masters to consider: Soviet historians, military advisers, and bureaucrats from the studio, the government, and the Communist Party. (He was also mindful of the audience.) It was difficult for a Soviet filmmaker to determine the "right" interpretation of history; hence Bondarchuk omitted most of the history that Tolstoy included. Gone, for example, are Tolstoy's many negative comments about Barclay de Tolly (indeed, Barclay almost disappears from the film) and Mikhail Speransky, a supreme believer in the rule of law and one of the emperor's closest advisers and the de facto prime minister in 1812. Gone is the depiction of the Freemasons' influence on Russian society (not to mention Pierre) at the time. Gone are the endless strategy sessions conducted by the military. (Tolstoy included them to show how pointless they were.) Gone, for the most part, is Alexander I, whose anointing of Kutuzov as commander in 1812 was as fateful a decision as the emperor's bungled command at Austerlitz.

What remains for Bondarchuk are the battles. In his battle scenes—Schöngraben, Austerlitz, Borodino—Bondarchuk eschews strategy in favor of spectacle. And what a spectacle they are!

At Borodino in particular, Bondarchuk almost got it right. He pushed the boundaries in terms of how much "horror" and "negativism" were allowed on Soviet screens at the time. Even so, he could not show horses running roughshod over bodies. He could not show Russian soldiers fighting with their teeth, their weapons useless. He could not show the French roasting a dead comrade or wearing horse intestines around their heads to keep warm. He wanted to be a Goya but could not display such a high degree of realism. Despite the remarkable inroads made by film directors during the Thaw, the false reality of Socialist Realism was still the dominant aesthetic. Bondarchuk pushed these boundaries as far as he could.

Yet the horrors that Bondarchuk does show are remarkable, considering the constraints he was under. The Battle of Borodino is no Battle of Stalingrad, as revisioned by Fridrikh Ermler in a landmark of Stalinist monumentalism, *The Great Turning Point* (*Velikii perevorot*, 1945). Bondarchuk's battle is war at its ugliest, a field of absolute chaos and confusion, of dead and dying. In this, the film strongly resembles the eyewitness accounts already discussed and the accounts of historians such as Lieven and Mikaberidze. Bondarchuk also makes Borodino vivid by personalizing the battle through Pierre's and Andrei's eyes, especially when Andrei is mortally wounded. In addition, the extras—real Soviet army soldiers—are individualized through medium and close-up shots of their war-weary, very Russian faces.

Bondarchuk admirably portrays what it feels like to be in the midst of a terrible battle. What he only rarely shows are the decisions, for good or ill, that lead men to those places where life and death are on the line. Like Tolstoy (but unlike Soviet historians who elevated Kutuzov to the rank of military genius on a par with Napoleon), Bondarchuk lovingly re-creates Kutuzov. His Kutuzov is no schemer or womanizer (like the "real" Kutuzov); he is an old and flawed general. He is not particularly brave or energetic; he never charges out onto the battlefield to take personal command. In fact,

The spectacle of battle. (Courtesy Photofest)

Bondarchuk shows Kutuzov's infamous habit of nodding off during strategy meetings. (This, of course, could be construed as another sign that strategy is worthless in wartime.)

Like the historical figure, Bondarchuk's Kutuzov stays behind the lines during the battle. Bondarchuk also ignores the exploits of Barclay de Tolly, who, unlike many of the other generals, did not try to disguise his rank and wore all his medals and orders proudly on his chest. Instead, Bondarchuk's Kutuzov favors Bagration, who valiantly attempted to control the weak left flank before he was mortally wounded. In sum, Bondarchuk's Kutuzov is very much like Tolstoy's: wise, instinctive, relying on God's plan for Russia. (By emphasizing Kutuzov's religiosity—he bows and prays and crosses himself—Bondarchuk subtly subverts Soviet orthodoxy on religion.)

In contrast to Tolstoy, Bondarchuk seriously reduces Napoleon's part in the story. In Tolstoy's interpretation, although Napoleon considered himself a great man and a military genius, in reality, he was just a little man buffeted by fate. An argument can be made, however, that by not devoting much screen time to the "great man," Bondarchuk underscores the same point. When Napoleon does appear onscreen, he is generally isolated—either on the battlefield or in a capacious room inside the Kremlin. This contrasts sharply with Bondarchuk's depiction of Kutuzov, who is typically surrounded by many people, whether his staff or the soldiers on the field.

Another key historical figure who is mainly absent from the picture is Alexander I. One would hardly know that Russia was an autocracy for all the importance the emperor has in the film. When Alexander does appear onscreen, it is for a fleeting moment and in a long shot, such as at Natasha's ball. When he intervenes in the action—taking command at Austerlitz and ordering Kutuzov to start fighting—the results are distinctly negative. This is perhaps a nod to the Soviet view of the Romanov dynasty (except for Peter the Great).

But there is more "history" in the book and the film than the depiction of the Napoleonic Wars. Tolstoy originally intended to write a novel that focused on the genesis of the 1825 Decembrist Revolt, when liberal-minded military officers and intellectuals staged an abortive coup to topple Nicholas I, Alexander's brother and successor. Some of this remained in the final version of *War and Peace*, especially in the person of Pierre, who, like the Decembrist rebels, flirted with Freemasonry. (Unlike the Decembrists, he came to his senses.) Bondarchuk dropped this important historical issue completely, except for a brief mention by Natasha to her mother in part two. This was definitely done for political reasons. Masonic societies flourished in Russia during Alexander I's reign. As Marxists, leaders of the Soviet state strongly disapproved of spiritual organizations like the Freemasons; therefore, Soviet historians tended to downplay or ignore their influence on Russian society at the beginning of the nineteenth century. Bondarchuk did not need to be reminded that it was not politically expedient to include Pierre's Masonic ties in the film. Although contemporary Soviet critics commented on other important omissions, no one noticed this one—or at least no one said so publicly.

Another key historical omission that reflects obeisance to Soviet ideology is Tolstoy's depiction of the poor peasantry. Far from being a progressive force, most of Tolstoy's serfs simmer with unjustified resentment toward their masters. The best example in the novel is when the peasants at Bald Hills threaten Princess Marya Bolkonskaya and she is saved by Nikolai Rostov, who just happens by. They are a dark, brooding, and potentially violent mass. Yet Bondarchuk's refusal to treat this subject at all might mean that he also rejected the Soviet notion that *War and Peace* was primarily about class relations.

The Russia of 1805–1812 that emerges onscreen would have been quite idyllic, had it not been for the war with the French and the arrogance of St.

Petersburg society. Like Tolstoy's Rostovs, Bondarchuk's are a large, bustling, happy family that is fully engaged in Moscow society, but the money difficulties that torment them (and Nikolaï's gambling problem) are absent from the film. Bondarchuk stresses only their positive attributes. As another example, although the Bolkonskys can hardly be called a happy family, even here, Bondarchuk glosses over their distress through the omission of Tolstoyan details. The relentless authorial and parental attacks on Marya's physical appearance (she is supposedly ugly) are absent; Bondarchuk's Marya is an attractive, if not beautiful, woman. Anatole Kuragin's unfortunate attempt to woo Marya, which ends in the brutal dashing of her hopes, is also absent, as is Prince Nikolaï's cruel flirtation with Marya's companion, Mlle. Bourienne.

In both book and film, the Rostovs and Bolkonskys contrast sharply with the court nobility, who are petty, narcissistic, and thoroughly false and pretentious. This "civilized" rabble is personified by the Kuragins: suave Prince Vasily and his children Anatole and Hélène, who bring unhappiness wherever they go. If Bondarchuk shows class stratification, it is within the elite rather than between the elite and the common people.

In sum, Bondarchuk's depiction of early-nineteenth-century Russian society generally follows Tolstoy's, but it is less complex due to its many omissions. Bondarchuk excels, however, in his ability to visualize this period, especially its material culture (through superior set design and decoration), as well as its manners and mores. With the exception of Hélène, whose bouffant bleached hair and heavy black mascara mark her as a beauty from the 1960s, not the 1810s, the actors look right for their parts, and they are believable as people from that period. Bondarchuk also excels in his ability to accurately capture the big events, such as the battles (especially Borodino) and the Moscow fires.

What about Bondarchuk's views on history, as inferred from the film? As noted in chapter 1, contemporary Soviet critics complained that Bondarchuk did not pay any attention to Tolstoy's ideas about history. This is unfair. It is difficult to imagine how Bondarchuk could have integrated these notions more explicitly, unless he had included even more passages from the novel read in voice-over—hardly a cinematic solution. Director Georgy Daneliya paid Bondarchuk a backhanded compliment by saying that he was not afraid to be boring, but there were limits. Bondarchuk understood that cinema is primarily an art of images, not words, and he communicated Tolstoy's ideas very well by showing, if not by telling.

Bondarchuk does not offer any overt explanation or interpretation of the

A realistic view of war. (Courtesy Photofest)

events of 1812, choosing to place them in the subtext of the film. Masses of French soldiers pour over the Russian border for no discernible reason. There is no announcement that Napoleon or anyone else is responsible. There is no failure of diplomacy. The French are there because they have to be there at that particular historical moment. Likewise, the Russians have to fight to repel the invaders. They have to win, not because their army is stronger or because their generals are more skilled in strategy but because of the soul of the Russian soldier: courageous, self-sacrificing, and filled with love for the motherland. This is also true of the Russian civilians; Bondarchuk shows no dissenters, no collaborators. Kutuzov, that exemplar of the Russian spirit, has to emerge as the commander because he is the right man at the right time; Bondarchuk does not apprise the viewer of Alexander's reluctance to appoint him. War, when it comes, is chaotic, not purposeful. In short, the film's vision of history is purely Tolstoyan in spirit, if not in every detail.

Do Tolstoy's antiwar sentiments emerge in Bondarchuk's film? Some Soviet critics charged Bondarchuk with being more interested in war than in peace. This is a tricky question. As we have seen, one of the state's original objectives in supporting the project was to create a patriotic film epic. In the novel, Tolstoy manages to be patriotic and antiwar simultaneously. Does Bondarchuk? It is true that Bondarchuk lavishes loving attention on his battle scenes and that war dominates the film, making its appearance in the battles of Schöngraben and Austerlitz in part one and being the main subject of parts three and four. There is, however, no glory in Bondarchuk's battles, just as glory is absent in Tolstoy's. Carnage prevails; good men like Prince Andrei die hard deaths for no discernible reason. Bondarchuk also focuses on the aftermath of battle: the conflagration of Moscow; the arbitrary execution of ordinary Russian citizens for arson and espionage; and the brutality of the retreat, where both French soldiers and Russian prisoners of war suffer horrific deaths. In sum, the film, like the novel, shows that although some wars are worth fighting, as this one was, there is no such thing as a "good" war.

Bondarchuk's depiction of Tolstoy's views on war and history shows that he took his responsibilities as an artist very seriously, but his interpretation was affected to some extent by political imperatives. King Vidor was influenced by a different set of imperatives that were no less constraining. In the next chapter, Vidor's War and Peace, widely regarded as less faithful to Tolstoy than Bondarchuk's version, is compared with its Soviet counterpart.

CHAPTER FIVE

BONDARCHUK VERSUS VIDOR

As we know, Bondarchuk's *War and Peace* was con-
ceived as an "answer" to King Vidor's film version of the novel. Composer
Viacheslav Ovchinnikov put it bluntly: "We had to compete with America.
That American film was a big success in our country."[1] It is therefore import-
ant to compare the two films, especially as adaptations. Unlike Bondarchuk,
Vidor had little interest in the novel's historical aspects. Vidor approached
Tolstoy's *War and Peace* respectfully—"I tried to do justice to this tremen-
dous work"—but not as reverently as Bondarchuk did.[2]

Production

As already noted, Vidor's picture was not, strictly speaking, an American
production; it; was an Italian-American coproduction. Although the film
was not made in Hollywood, film scholars Raymond Durgnat and Scott
Simmon call it "the apotheosis of 'Hollywood' style."[3] Vidor claimed that
expensive epic films had to be made in Europe due to escalating costs in
Hollywood.[4] His *War and Peace* was filmed in northern Italy with a largely Italian crew for Carlo Ponti and Dino De Laurentiis Productions; Ponti
bowed out early.[5] Paramount Studios shared some of the costs and picked
up the American distribution rights; it marketed the film as "history's most
awesome spectacle" and as the "motion picture of the century."[6] The film
supposedly took ten years of preparation and nearly two years of production,
but that was just more hyperbole.[7]

Bondarchuk had directed only one picture when he was chosen to make
War and Peace, although he was an experienced actor with eighteen films
to his credit.[8] By contrast, King Vidor had made his first short film in 1913
(seven years before Bondarchuk's birth) in Galveston, Texas, when he was
only nineteen years old. Vidor went on to direct many classics of Hollywood
cinema, both silent and sound. His extensive and impressive filmography
includes *The Big Parade* (1926), *The Crowd* (1928), *Our Daily Bread* (1934),

Stella Dallas (1937), *Northwest Passage* (1940), and *Duel in the Sun* (1947). *War and Peace* (1956) was his fiftieth feature film.

How did Vidor come to make *War and Peace?* Producer De Laurentiis had originally wanted William Wyler to direct, but Wyler's plans for the film were too expensive. Vidor approached De Laurentiis at Paramount and suggested himself as director. Paramount agreed, although the studio thought Vidor was too old (he was sixty) to direct the battle scenes.[9]

Vidor, like Bondarchuk after him, faced numerous challenges in bringing Tolstoy's epic to the big screen. First, there was the "race" to film the novel; it was the era of epics, and filmmakers looking to adapt an epic literary work had relatively few to choose from. Producers Michael Todd and David O. Selznick had each started the preproduction process on their own versions of *War and Peace* at the same time as De Laurentiis. The Italian beat them and was the first to rush his picture into production. This was accomplished in part by using a team of Italian writers to compose the 500-page screenplay. Vidor recalled that each scenarist wrote a section of the script, and these sections were then spliced together. He was extremely unhappy with this screenplay and could not believe that Paramount had approved it. (It turned out that the bureaucrat in charge of foreign production had not actually read it but had been impressed by its bulk.)[10] So Vidor read the novel carefully, prepared his own script outline, and persuaded De Laurentiis to look for another scriptwriter—British playwright R. C. Sheriff, who ultimately refused to leave England for Italy.[11] Paramount intervened and sent in writers Bridget Boland and Robert Westerby, who both received writing credit. Then Irwin Shaw got involved, and the script became even more unworkable, as far as Vidor was concerned. Finally, Mario Soldati, an Italian novelist with a good command of English, was hired, and he and Vidor worked together amicably on the script. Yet when filming began, the screenplay was only 75 percent finished.[12]

Casting was also a problem, especially since De Laurentiis was, in Vidor's words, "very aggressive," as well as temperamental and domineering.[13] Unlike Bondarchuk, Vidor had little control over the casting. De Laurentiis managed to score a coup by enticing Audrey Hepburn to take the role of Natasha, with a promise that Mel Ferrer, her husband at the time, would be offered the part of Prince Andrei.[14] When Hepburn signed with De Laurentiis, Todd and Selznick scrapped the plans for their pictures.[15] As preproduction progressed, Vidor sought to cast Pierre. He talked to both Peter Ustinov and Paul Scofield and had decided on Scofield, but the British actor was already involved in a project and backed out. Again, De Laurentiis interfered and, without Vidor's approval, signed Henry Fonda. Paramount had demanded a big star for Pierre, but Vidor was very unhappy with Fonda and deeply regretted that he had not advocated for Ustinov more strongly. Ustinov, the director believed, "would have been ideal, and would have given the film much more stature."[16] Vidor found Fonda to be was completely uninterested in understanding Pierre's character and his search for truth.[17] When Vidor tried to explain Pierre to Fonda, the famous actor retorted: "I have been listening to you for almost an hour, and I still don't know what the hell you are talking about and doubt I ever will."[18] Finally, De Laurentiis foisted Anita Ekberg on Vidor as Pierre's wife Hélène, after another actress changed her mind about doing the film. Ekberg certainly fit the role physically, but she was just learning English at the time, so her lines had to be dubbed.[19]

Although there is no evidence that the Cold War played any part in the film's conception, it interfered with Vidor's project in an unexpected way. Director and producer found themselves summoned to the US embassy in Rome to answer Ambassador Clare Boothe Luce's questions about how many Communists they had working on the film. She declared it was 20 percent, which was unacceptable because "any project with American dollars behind it would not be associated with the Communists." Vidor thought it was more like 10 percent.[20]

A final problem was that the budget was inadequate for a film of this scope, at least when compared with Bondarchuk's virtually limitless resources. According to Vidor, the budget was only $5 million or $6 million, and he recalled running out of money and being unable to re-create to his satisfaction the scene at the Moscow opera where Natasha meets Anatole Kuragin.[21] Vidor was also limited in the number of takes he was allowed; for the Battle of Borodino, for example, a maximum of three takes was budgeted.[22] In addition, much of the film, including Pierre's duel with Dolokhov in Sokolniki, was shot on a sound stage rather than on location and looked palpably false.[23] These examples illustrate how the production values may have affected the film's critical reception.

Nevertheless, Vidor was able to make the most of his limited budget due to the lower cost of filming in Italy compared with the United States. He supposedly used 15,000 Italian extras, 18,796 horses, 9,359 carriages and wagons, and 33,749 muskets that fired 634,729 rounds of ammunition.[24] With these resources, he was able to create decent special effects for 1956. At Borodino, for example, Vidor employed 5,000 Italian army soldiers and 800 cavalrymen, along with 90 cannons and 2,000 explosions.[25] There were dozens of cameras.[26] Vidor considered his horse falls "the most spectacular that I have ever seen."[27]

Vidor, like Bondarchuk, claimed to be determined to make an "authentic" picture and was proud of his attention to detail. He had Napoleon's coach carefully reconstructed and period costumes made in Italian and Swiss factories.[28] It took ninety tailors seven months to make the costumes.[29]

Above all, Vidor believed in clarity. For example, he kept the "direction in which any individual or group is moving consistent and simple"; thus, the French soldiers in his film always moved from left to right, and the Russians moved in the opposite direction.[30] This enabled audiences to distinguish between them, and as a result, his battlefield was nowhere near as chaotic as Bondarchuk's. Rather, it was "so obviously timed, so carefully controlled," and so unlike the historical Borodino.[31]

Although the director was obsessed with period authenticity, unlike Bondarchuk, he was not so concerned about being true to the novel. (After all, this was not a canonical novel for Americans.) In this, he had the support of his producer. De Laurentiis scoffed: "I came to realize that fifty percent of the episodes [in the novel] could easily be eliminated, reshuffled or forgotten."[32]

Some American critics found fault with this attitude. Philip Hamburger wrote in the *New Yorker* that Tolstoy's humanity was lost in the film: "Tolstoy loved people . . . he was forever trying to figure them out . . . and . . . the glorious uncertainty of life. Well, the boys who produced this film have practically knocked themselves senseless in reducing the characters to stereotypes."[33] *New York Times* critic Bosley Crowther found the acting and character development ineffective, the plotting mechanical.[34] The *Saturday Review* called the film "a sort of pictorial sour-mash of the original work" and lambasted the choice of lanky, quintessentially American Henry Fonda to play the roly-poly Pierre as "monstrous physical miscasting."[35] The film was not, however, without its fans. There was praise for the battle scenes and the spectacle, as well as for the acting of Audrey Hepburn (Natasha) and Mel Ferrer (Prince Andrei).[36]

Vidor's Adaptation

Decades after the filming of Bondarchuk's *War and Peace*, Vasily Lanovoi, who played Anatole Kuragin, declared: "The American *War and Peace* has almost nothing to do with Tolstoy."[37] Indeed, the major problem with Vidor's *War and Peace* is that he thought he could improve on Tolstoy's storytelling.

Associate producer Arthur Fellows told *Newsweek*, "We didn't stray at all from the book." Then he admitted, "We did put in one scene that wasn't in the novel. It was a personal scene between Natasha and Pierre. Tolstoy took 250 pages to tell readers that there was a feeling between them. We got it over in one scene in the horse corral at the beginning of the picture."[38] Fellows's remarkable confession explains the underlying problem with the entire movie as an adaptation compared with its Soviet counterpart: Vidor, who was wedded to the strong narrative tradition of Hollywood filmmaking, did not trust Tolstoy. Bondarchuk, who came from an entirely different cinematic tradition, did.

Tolstoy's work is sprawling and untidy, as is Bondarchuk's film. Vidor's film, in contrast, is very "American"—neat and clear. Complexity is downplayed, so there is no ambiguity.[39] The characters are all oversimplified, including Natasha and Andrei, but especially Pierre, who is rendered "perpetually lifeless" by Fonda's wooden impersonation.[40]

Vidor claimed that Pierre's search for truth was his favorite theme in the novel, but Fonda's Pierre, unlike Bondarchuk's, is far from spiritual.[41] As film scholar Trisha Jurkiewicz notes, "Pierre changes only because we are told he changes."[42] Likewise, Hepburn's Natasha does not convincingly evolve from a girl to a woman; she is best in the earliest scenes, and one is always aware that it is *Audrey Hepburn* playing Natasha.[43] (Bondarchuk was wise to choose as unknown actress for this pivotal role.) Ferrer's Prince Andrei is one-dimensional and is given "pseudo-poetic" speeches to recite; the viewer never get a sense of his inner struggle or his metamorphosis over the course of the film.[44]

As detrimental as the static characterization is to the essence of Tolstoy's novel, Vidor also compromises Tolstoy's meaning by the way he cuts, compresses, and invents the narrative. As discussed in chapter 3, cutting material is inevitable when bringing a novel to the screen, and Bondarchuk's omissions have already been detailed. Vidor actually made many changes to the text (not just one, as Fellows claimed), all of them undermining Tolstoy's intentions.

Bondarchuk's film opens with a panorama of the Russian land, whereas Vidor's begins with battlefield paintings of a map of Europe over which a "dark shadow" has fallen (an obvious Cold War flourish). Vidor's many departures from the novel occur immediately. The first scene is not Anna Scherer's salon, which Bondarchuk retains to establish the superficiality and Francophilia of St. Petersburg society. Rather, it is a military parade that Pierre and Count Rostov are watching; Natasha sits in the window, and Petya is out in the street.

The love-struck Pierre with Natasha. (Courtesy Photofest)

Since Vidor chooses not to introduce Andrei to the audience at Scherer's salon (as Tolstoy and Bondarchuk do), he makes his first appearance at
Dolokhov's rooms (actually, they are Anatole Kuragin's rooms in the novel—a meaningless change). He has come to rescue Pierre from the drunken
revelers and to take him to his father's deathbed. As Andrei and Pierre walk,
Pierre introduces the fact of his illegitimacy, saying mournfully, "I disap-
prove of the fact that he didn't marry my mother." Andrei complains about
his marriage. (In the novel and Bondarchuk's film, the conversation occurs
at the Bolkonskys' *before* the party, and Andrei implores Pierre not to go to
Kuragin's.)

Prince Vasily Kuragin (Anatole's father) is present at Count Bezukhov's
bedside (as he is in the novel), but so is his daughter Hélène (not in the
novel). She kisses Pierre when she learns that he is now the sole heir to his
father's estates. Later, we see Pierre, Hélène, and Prince Vasily in a carriage
touring Pierre's property. They run into Andrei, who has delivered his wife
to his family at Bald Hills. All this is designed to provide a rational backdrop for Pierre and Hélène's marriage, rather than the unintentional (and
comical) engagement that occurs in Tolstoy's novel and Bondarchuk's film.
Pierre and Natasha have a conversation about love at the horse paddock,

which does not occur in the book and would be inappropriate, given that Tolstoy's Natasha is supposed to be thirteen years old. When Pierre abruptly tells her of his plans to marry Hélène, her face falls.

Vidor's next episode takes place at Kutuzov's headquarters, where a war council is being held. The Battle of Austerlitz is about to begin (Schöngraben has been cut). Kutuzov predicts that the battle will be lost, without explanation. The battle commences with the armies neatly marching amidst smoke grenades. Andrei carries the banner to urge the men to stop fleeing and attack, but Vidor does not show him being shot down. Napoleon comes by, towering over the wounded Andrei; in Bondarchuk's parallel scene, Napoleon appears small against the sky. As this scene shows, Vidor, unlike Tolstoy and Bondarchuk, definitely believes in "great men."

In the meantime, Pierre is gradually discovering that his wife is not the woman he thought she was. Whereas Hélène had once professed to love the countryside, she now refuses to accompany Pierre to his estates and persuades him to go alone. After Austerlitz, Nicholas (the anglicized form of Nikolai) Rostov and his friend Denisov arrive at the Rostovs'. Nicholas asks Natasha: "Are you still true to Pierre now that he's married?" reinforcing Vidor's invented idea that Natasha and Pierre have always been in love. When Prince Andrei returns to Bald Hills, the viewer is unaware that his family has been told he is dead. The scene of Lise Bolkonskaya's death in childbirth is cut-and-dried, without the emotional underpinnings of Bondarchuk's version. Andrei goes to Lise's bedside, the baby cries, she is dead. Her single bloodcurdling scream seems out of place, given the cold atmosphere of the scene.

Pierre learns of his wife's probable infidelity through an anonymous letter; he then goes to a military dinner in honor of General Bagration (Vidor does not reveal what the banquet celebrates, undoubtedly because his audience has no idea who Bagration was). Dolokhov offers his snide toast about the husbands of beautiful women, and here, Pierre very melodramatically throws his glass of wine in Dolokhov's face (a Vidor touch), prompting the challenge to duel. As noted earlier, the duel is shot indoors in a contrived winter set that is obviously fake, unlike Bondarchuk's, which was shot outdoors.

Vidor has a very superficial idea about the meaning of Russianness. For example, Pierre is next seen at the Rostov house, where he and Count Rostov talk about the duel. All of them are traveling to the country, and Pierre decides to tag along. Cut to troikas traveling quickly across the snow. One driver begins to sing a native tune, one of the few Russian touches in Vidor's film. As Jurkiewicz writes: "In Vidor's film all being Russian means is throwing glasses over a shoulder after downing vodka."[45]

Given the amount of invention in the film, one wonders why Vidor wanted to adapt Tolstoy's novel at all. In the country, Andrei encounters Pierre and the Rostovs, who invite him to join their hunt. The actors are obviously riding mechanical horses in their close-ups, which is both jarring and ridiculous.[46] Bondarchuk keeps this important episode where it belongs: after Andrei's proposal and during Natasha's enforced year-long solitude. There is no dinner at the uncle's lodge and therefore no Russian dance for Natasha. By compressing and rearranging, Vidor has ruined one of the most important scenes in both the book and Bondarchuk's film. This is where Tolstoy and Bondarchuk definitively establish Natasha's Russianness. Vidor, not surprisingly, cares nothing for the national character of Tolstoy's novel, and he cuts all explicit references to it.

After the hunt, Pierre and Andrei are staying overnight at the Rostovs, and Andrei opens his window and listens to Natasha and Sonya conversing. Vidor has the two girls discuss Natasha's love for Andrei, whereas in the book and Bondarchuk's version, Natasha waxes eloquent over the beauty of the night. For Tolstoy and Bondarchuk, this is the point where Andrei's soul begins to stir; Natasha has not yet fallen in love with the prince, nor he with her. (That happens at the ball.)

From here, Vidor continues his strategy of rearranging the source to suit his own purposes and cuts to the ball (identified in the novel as taking place on the eve of the new year 1810), a magical moment for both Tolstoy and Bondarchuk. For some inexplicable reason, Vidor inserts Nicholas into the scene; he walks with Natasha and Sonya as Natasha practices a "disdainful" face that will help her compete with the more sophisticated ladies. This is a nice "Hepburn" moment, but it is not characteristic of Natasha. The next bits are also invented, and again Vidor dims in comparison with Bondarchuk. Natasha worries that no one will ask her to dance, but an old man finally asks her, and the dance is finished. The Hollywood narrative model then has Natasha thinking about her love for Andrei: "Why must I keep thinking of Prince Andrei?" (in the novel, she does not love Andrei yet). Suddenly Andrei approaches her with an uncharacteristic smile (Mel Ferrer looks too friendly in the role of the taciturn prince). They dance in long shot in the middle of the room, losing the exquisite intimacy of Bondarchuk's scene. Afterward, Natasha and Andrei talk until another man approaches the young woman and invites her to dance. Andrei thinks: "If she looks back at me on the next turn, she'll be my wife."

Prince Andrei and Natasha at the ball. (Courtesy Photofest)

After the ball, Natasha and her mother discuss Andrei; Vidor then cuts to Andrei talking to his father about his desire to marry again. Old Prince Bolkonsky sarcastically remarks that the Rostovs are "nothing" and that Count Rostov is a former womanizer and a present gambler. (Bondarchuk deletes this important scene, probably because of his desire to present the Rostovs as a perfect, happy Russian family.) Vidor turns next to the engagement, again making telling excisions. Like Bondarchuk, he cuts Andrei's courting of Natasha. Natasha and Andrei kiss gently before he tells her about the one-year waiting period. "I'll die waiting a year!" wails Natasha. Cut to Tilsit 1807, which in the novel occurs several years *before* the engagement, not after it. (It is not clear why Vidor chose to insert a date marker, especially one that is so obviously out of chronological order.) Directly afterward, Natasha and Count Rostov are at the Bolkonskys'. Here, Vidor (like Bondarchuk) draws directly from the book: the old prince arrives in the parlor in his nightgown, pretending he is unaware that visitors are present, delineating his hostility to Natasha.

Vidor's film falters again. Instead of showing Natasha lonely and waiting and then coming to life in the hunt scene, he cuts straight to the opera, with Natasha seated next to Hélène Bezukhova rather than next to her father in an adjacent box. Because of these changes, Natasha's subsequent infatuation with Anatole Kuragin is completely unexpected and unfounded. Anatole arrives at the opera in the company of Dolokhov. The rake pantomimes to his sister and then joins them in the box, whereupon he brazenly starts to flirt with Natasha. At the recital at Hélène's salon, Anatole sits across from Natasha, commanding her attention. (Bondarchuk positions Anatole very close behind Natasha, as does Tolstoy, which adds an erotic frisson to the scene.) Anatole and Natasha dance alone. She runs away from him; he follows her; they kiss. In Vidor's Hollywoodized version, Hélène is nowhere to be seen, which essentially removes her as a coconspirator with her brother to seduce Natasha.

Vidor's emphasis on narrative unfolds more clearly in the next scene. A horrified Sonya reads Anatole's love letter. "I can't live without him!" screams Natasha. There is a cut to Anatole packing for the elopement; the gypsy woman brings him an ermine (rather than sable) wrap. Instead of having a servant intercept Anatole, Vidor decides that Sonya should ask Pierre for help. (Vidor seems determined to insert Pierre wherever he can, regardless of what happens in the novel.) While Natasha waits behind a locked door, Pierre tries to grab Anatole but is unsuccessful. The cad escapes in the rain (rain was undoubtedly easier for Vidor to replicate than snow).[47] Once the threat of abduction is averted, Pierre tells Natasha that Anatole is already married.

Interestingly, Vidor suddenly turns to Tolstoy in the scene that follows. Natasha has been ill after the abortive elopement, and Pierre comes to visit her. Weeping, she begs Pierre to ask Andrei for forgiveness. Now Vidor relies on Tolstoy for dialogue: "If I were not myself, but the handsomest, cleverest man, I would not hesitate for one moment to go down on my knees to beg for your love." (These are essentially the same lines Bondarchuk uses in this scene.) Upon leaving Natasha, Pierre witnesses the Great Comet. Although Pierre's coachman sees the comet as a sign of war (a Vidor invention), Pierre believes it is a sign of happiness.

The comet is, of course, a sign of war. Here, the Vidor version is more effective. Immediately, the director cuts to Napoleon reading a letter from Alexander I that has been delivered by Andrei. Irritated, Napoleon announces: "Tomorrow at dawn we cross the river." Vidor maintains 12 June (Julian calendar) as the date of the invasion instead of updating it to 24 June (Gregorian calendar), the date always given in Western sources. (One wonders whether the director knew the difference.)

Then Vidor moves the film along at a brisk pace. Kutuzov does not want to fight, but the French are burning and looting Smolensk. The people of Moscow learn that Smolensk has fallen. Pierre goes to church, where a priest delivers a fiery patriotic speech. Afterward, Pierre decides that he is headed for Borodino and tells the Rostovs. Young Petya begs to be allowed to go to war too.

Vidor cuts to Borodino, where Pierre seeks out Andrei. They talk about Natasha briefly; then Andrei predicts that he will perish in this battle, although he believes that victory is possible: "A battle is won by men determined to win it," he tells Pierre. (This conversation is very close to what Tolstoy wrote.) Andrei also articulates his "take no prisoners" philosophy, as he does in Bondarchuk's film. As Pierre prepares to leave, the two friends embrace.

Before the battle begins, Vidor shows Napoleon dictating a speech. An aide brings him a portrait of his baby son, the king of Rome (this scene is in the novel but not in Bondarchuk's film). Cut to Pierre in a top hat and dark suit (less striking than the cream-colored suit he wears in Bondarchuk's film), innocently picking a yellow flower (a Vidor touch). We next see Vidor's orderly, formal arrangement of French and Russian soldiers marching into battle. In supposed horror, Pierre drops the flower. Pierre's subsequent actions closely follow the novel and are therefore similar to Bondarchuk's depiction of this part of the story. All resemblance between the two films ends there, however. Vidor, who personally directed the short (ten minute) battle sequence, is too constrained a filmmaker to let all hell break loose. To be fair, though, De Laurentiis thwarted Vidor's plan to shoot Borodino in a small valley instead of on an expansive Italian military reservation.[48] Regardless, the Battle of Borodino is like the battles in other 1950s film epics—well orchestrated but essentially lifeless. There is no hint of Tolstoy's antiwar sentiments. This is perhaps another sign that Vidor was influenced by Cold War fervor, when antiwar activists were seen as "Communists."

Vidor's evacuation of Moscow is also a controlled event that focuses on the Rostovs fleeing the city rather than on the pandemonium in the streets, which dulls the event's dramatic impact. As the Rostovs pack, Natasha dances with the ball gown she wore on New Year's Eve two years earlier and thinks about Andrei. Sonya spots Andrei on the train of wounded and informs Countess Rostova. Eventually, the Rostovs relinquish their carts over to help transport the wounded; they also give permission for the soldiers to live in their house. Natasha sees Pierre in the street as they are leaving; Sonya abruptly tells Natasha that Andrei is among the wounded. The French enter the Kremlin as Napoleon waits for a deputation from "Moscow the holy" and insists: "There must be a surrender!"

In the meantime, the Rostovs, now safely away from Moscow, can see the glow of the city burning on the horizon. This spurs Petya to join the army, but Natasha is interested only in finding and speaking to Andrei. She hunts for him among the wounded. He is delirious; she is shrouded in darkness, her white cloak barely visible. When Andrei recognizes her, he immediately whispers: "I love you."

The Moscow fires, so vivid in Bondarchuk's film, barely register in Vidor's (lasting only three minutes). There is no conflagration, no chaos, no looting. Even more puzzling is Vidor's treatment of Pierre in Moscow. In a scene from the scriptwriters' imaginations, Pierre comes within shooting distance of Napoleon but finds that he cannot pull the trigger.[49] Pierre does, however, try to help a woman who is being attacked by French soldiers, and he is arrested. (There is no mention of the child Pierre attempts to rescue in the novel and Bondarchuk's film.) Vidor then truncates the execution scene; Pierre watches with more curiosity than fear. Although Tolstoy offers no reason why Pierre is spared, Vidor does: "Orders were to shoot only incendiaries." (Vidor may have been frustrated by Tolstoy's failure to include clear-cut rationales for actions, so he invented his own.) Pierre is next seen in a church that is being used as a makeshift prison, where he meets the peasant-sage Platon Karataev.

Natasha sits by Andrei's bedside knitting; Andrei gives a speech about love and hate. Andrei's sister, here called Mary, arrives with Andrei's son Kolya (a diminutive for Nikolai, but not Tolstoy's Nikolushka) and Natasha's brother Nicholas. Nicholas announces that he and Mary are getting married. (It does not happen so suddenly in the book, and certainly not at Andrei's deathbed.) In Vidor's film, this news comes as a complete surprise to the audience, especially since the director has previously played up the romance between Sonya and Nicholas. Mary brings Kolya in to see his father (Vidor's Kolya is a toddler, whereas he should be about seven years old). We now know for sure that Andrei is dying. He talks about his death dream (remember that Bondarchuk *shows* it).

From this condensed rendition of Andrei's death, we now turn to Vidor's vision of Napoleon, who is waiting for emissaries from Kutuzov. The emperor is angry at the total breakdown of discipline among his soldiers: "They are ragpickers! Junk men!" He threatens to replace his staff. Smoke and flames from the fires are seen through a window. Cut to Kutuzov, who

The French in retreat. (Courtesy Photofest)

mutters: "The French are preparing to leave Moscow." To the strains of the tsarist hymn, Kutuzov reads a dispatch delivered by an aide, confirming his conclusion. He falls to his knees to pray: "Russia is saved," he says, with the tsarist hymn still playing.

Vidor then cuts to the French army as it abandons Moscow with its prisoners in tow, Pierre and Platon Karataev among them. Kutuzov explains the Russian victory to his generals as though they are schoolboys: "Retreat brought about the destruction of the French." This line was doubtless intended to educate members of the audience who had not read Tolstoy.

What follows is the best episode in the film because it is the most realistic. The French army is on the march; the Russian army is tailing them, staggering through the rain and mud. A grim Napoleon rides with his men. A carriage is mired in the mud; horses fall to the ground. Then the snow falls, covering the suffering men. "All stragglers" will be shot. There is an extreme long shot of a line of French soldiers struggling slowly through the snow. The retreating soldiers and their prisoners alike are robbing bodies.

Napoleon leaves his army to go to the front of the line. Platon collapses and leans against a tree, his dog by his side. He crosses himself before he is shot. Pierre looks back, but instead of moving on, as he did in the novel and in Bondarchuk's film, he walks over to Platon's body to get the dog. Again, Vidor seeks to provide a "normal" response to tragedy: surely the kind Pierre would not just leave the dog. Nevertheless, the French "death march" is one of the most effective episodes in Vidor's film. For once, he does not shy away from the ugliness of war.

Vidor's handling of the next episode is unusually sensitive. Petya Rostov arrives at the partisan camp, which is under Dolokhov's command. Petya takes food to a young French prisoner, whereas in Tolstoy's and Bondarchuk's versions, he invites the boy into the officers' hut. At this point, Vidor cuts to the partisans as they attack the French line to rescue the prisoners, including Pierre. As in Bondarchuk's film, Petya is shot as he waves his sword. However, instead of showing his mother screaming her despair, Vidor cuts to Petya being lowered into his grave, which is much less dramatic but perhaps more moving. (Dolokhov, who is now friendly to Pierre, offhandedly tells him that Hélène is dead.) The Russians shoot some of their prisoners, which is in definitely not in Bondarchuk's film. The French start to cross a river, followed by a long shot of masses of soldiers. The Russians attack and bomb the bridge. His face gloomy, Napoleon orders French flags to be burned. Moving from French gloom to Russian jubilation, Vidor presents a smiling Kutuzov shouting, "Hurrah! Hurrah!"

Vidor cuts to the Rostovs' vandalized home. The Rostov family is returning, Mary among them. Countess Rostova weeps in dismay. Natasha, alone, looks pensive and remembers Andrei. When Pierre arrives, he and Natasha embrace and kiss. The last shot is of the two of them wandering in the garden. A narrator says, "The most difficult thing, but an essential one, is to love life."

In terms of literary adaptation, Vidor's *War and Peace* represents frequent borrowing but not fidelity of transformation. It is a very loose adaptation of a few motifs from Tolstoy's novel. Vidor borrows the main characters and some of the major plot points, but he tries to find coherence where there is none to be found. Therefore, he forces a rambling narrative about life and humanity into a form that will be accessible to American viewers: a love story that works commercially if not artistically.[50] Vidor freely moves parts of the story around as if their sequence in Tolstoy's novel does not matter at all. He thought he knew how to tell the story better.

Vidor in fact *did* know how to tell the story better. His *War and Peace* is more fluid and straightforward than Tolstoy's novel and Bondarchuk's film. The narrative is reconstructed so that it fits the Hollywood mold: Natasha and Pierre are meant for each other, but the road to true happiness has twists and turns. Three infatuations (Andrei, Anatole, and Hélène) intervene, as does war with the French. Natasha and Pierre survive all these detours and end up together, their love stronger than ever. This reinterpretation violates the spirit of the novel, but should that matter to the filmmaker? Not if the film is first-rate.

Vidor was a prominent and prolific director who made some undeniably great films. *War and Peace* is not one of them; it is no more than an average representative of Hollywood-style filmmaking. Despite its Italian production team, there is no whiff of the European about it. It is a fairy-tale presentation of a major historical event and of one of the greatest novels in world literature. Stylistically, Vidor's *War and Peace* is craft, not art—a journeyman's effort and a surprising result from such an important director. We have seen that Bondarchuk used all the filmic techniques available to him, and he used them imaginatively. Vidor composed his film in medium and medium-long shots, for the most part, making even less use of the close-up than Bondarchuk did. Vidor's cameras rarely moved, and when they did, only very slowly. He preferred the fade and the black screen to transition scenes, although he also used the ordinary cut.

Visually and aesthetically, Vidor's *War and Peace* was seen by American critics as nothing special, as already noted. Since the mid-1970s, however, a few film scholars have taken a less jaundiced view. Clive Denton believes the film has been "badly underrated" due to a faulty understanding of it as but one in a long line of 1950s "roadshow attractions." Rather, Denton argues that Vidor's movie is an "intelligent, exciting, and moving distillation of its great source material in Tolstoy."[51] In a different vein, Raymond Durgnat and Scott Simmon see the film as presenting the themes in Vidor's oeuvre (individualism, community, societies in crisis) and as a fitting finale to a great career in the movies (it was Vidor's penultimate film). Durgnat and Simmon ignore the fact that Vidor persistently undermined Tolstoy's messages; indeed, they treat the film as though it had no literary source.[52] John Baxter provides a reading of the film that is more in line with my assessment: Vidor's *War and Peace* is "condensed and simplified," the acting is weak (except for Hepburn), the characterizations are facile, and the film lacks drama.[53]

Comparison of the Two Films

Bondarchuk's adaptation is truer to Tolstoy than Vidor's, but is it a better film? The Soviet director was certainly more ambitious than Vidor was, and he had more at stake. He sought to make a masterpiece that was worthy of its literary counterpart—a Russian classic. He also needed to surpass Vidor's film to demonstrate Soviet cinematic superiority. Vidor, constrained by the demands of the Hollywood model of filmmaking, to which De Laurentiis enthusiastically subscribed, was required to turn out a commercial product, a film that would attract viewers and earn a profit at the box office. The film also had to be reasonably short; De Laurentiis made Vidor cut about thirty minutes.[54] Vidor may have protested in interviews that he was unhappy with the film because of his production struggles, but he was an old hand in Hollywood, a commercially savvy director who understood that blockbuster films needed big stars and a big production. Vidor's *War and Peace* had these in abundance, even though he was working with a fairly modest budget for a film epic.

Nevertheless, there can be no question that Bondarchuk's *War and Peace* benefited from the virtually unlimited resources at its disposal, which made Vidor's film look impoverished by comparison. The art direction of the Soviet picture is superb; each set is beautifully constructed and fully dressed, with precise attention paid to period style. Yet there is not one false or overly lavish note; Bondarchuk eschewed visual spectacle for its own sake.

There is also the issue of comparative length. Bondarchuk could obviously fit more of the story into his film, since it was twice as long as Vidor's. Although the Soviet director too had to compress and cut, he did not have to do so to the extent that his film would have been incomprehensible without the reinvention Vidor provided.

The acting in Bondarchuk's film is also of consistently high quality, in contrast to Vidor's, with its international cast and its mishmash of accents and acting styles. Bondarchuk, unlike Vidor, was in control of casting, despite the various troubles he had. Liudmila Saveleva is neither as beautiful as Audrey Hepburn nor as charismatic, but that is all to the good. Natasha is never described as a raving beauty in the novel; she is a pretty, spoiled girl who is used to being the center of attention. Saveleva also had another advantage: she was six years younger at the start of the film than Hepburn was. The fact that Bondarchuk's version was so long in production meant that Saveleva's natural aging made her character's maturation more believable.

Both Sergei Bondarchuk and Henry Fonda were far too old to play Pierre, who was supposed to be younger than Prince Andrei (identified by Tolstoy as thirty-one when he meets Natasha). Bondarchuk was forty-six when the first parts of his film were released; Fonda was even older, at fifty-one. There can be no question that Bondarchuk was superior to Fonda in this challenging role. He was a gifted actor but not a star, and he brought Pierre's vulnerability, naiveté, decency, and compassion to life. Fonda, in contrast, was a twentieth-century American movie star forced to impersonate a nineteenth-century Russian aristocrat.

As noted in chapter 1, although Tikhonov won *Soviet Screen*'s nod as best actor, his acting was criticized by both Bondarchuk and Soviet reviewers as wooden. This is unfair. In the novel, Andrei is portrayed as extremely reserved to the point of rigidity, except when he is with his sister Marya; Tikhonov, who had studied the novel carefully, wisely avoids excessive emoting. Tikhonov's portrayal of Andrei's happiness when he falls in love is likewise restrained—believably so. At the ball, when Mel Ferrer's Andrei approaches Hepburn's Natasha with an almost merry smile, it seems out of character for Andrei. But Tikhonov always seems to be in character, and he understands Tolstoy's Andrei very well.

Bondarchuk's secondary roles are also well played. Vasily Lanovoi makes a memorable Anatole Kuragin, while Vittorio Gassman in Vidor's film is far too flamboyant, even for a nineteenth-century roué. Gassman's loud and lively Anatole would have frightened Natasha, who was, after all, a naïve and sheltered teenager from a good family. Boris Zakhava is an excellent Kutuzov, matching appearance and mannerisms with the historical general; Oscar Homolka, by comparison, plays Kutuzov with exaggerated mannerisms, mugging for the camera. Anatoly Ktorov is a superb Prince Nikolai Bolkonsky, all hard edges on the outside but very human nonetheless; Wilfrid Lawson in Vidor's film is onscreen for too short a time to register. The pattern of Bondarchuk's actors being more believable than Vidor's continues down the ladder. The one exception is John Mills, who turns in a wonderful performance in Vidor's picture in the cameo role of Platon Karataev, the peasant-sage.

Despite Vidor's early success in staging battle scenes in *The Big Parade*, Bondarchuk is a much better director of large-scale action. It is true that Bondarchuk was able to mobilize three times as many extras to participate in the Battle of Borodino (15,000 versus 5,000), which, in the era before computer-assisted effects, meant that Bondarchuk was better able to convince the viewer of the carnage and chaos of warfare. Vidor's battle is a pretty set piece by comparison, and it is certainly much more orderly. His is a dancing master's choreography, whereas Bondarchuk drew on his own experiences as a veteran of World War II. Bondarchuk also understood the novel's potential for spectacle, as his elaborate re-creation of old Moscow for the Moscow fire episode convincingly demonstrates.

Of course, Bondarchuk's *War and Peace* has its flaws. Parts one ("Andrei Bolkonsky) and three ("1812") are better constructed than parts two ("Natasha Rostova") and four ("Pierre Bezukhov"), which suffer from their episodic nature. This is especially true for the last part, which Bondarchuk was under pressure to finish so that it could be released in 1967. Although Tolstoy's novel is constructed in short chapters that tend to jump from one group of characters to the next, this kind of disjuncture works better on the page than it does on the screen. Bondarchuk was clearly trying to mimic Tolstoy's style, but part four and, to a lesser extent, the second half of part two feel disjointed and rushed.

The other element of Bondarchuk's film that some critics consider a flaw is the extensive use of voice-over narration. As already noted, this is a common device in historical epics, utilized to fill in the historical background and to provide transitions between scenes, but it is not, of course, a visual device. Sometimes Bondarchuk shows the passing of time visually (such as the rapidly changing seasons), but more often he resorts to the omniscient narrator. This narrator usually reads lines taken directly from Tolstoy's own narration and is thus one of the chief means of communicating Tolstoy's ideals. Again, Bondarchuk's goal (unlike Vidor's) was to present an adaptation that was true to the spirit and ideas of the novel. Although the Soviet director sometimes found cinematic equivalents to transmit these ideas— such as the virtual omission of Napoleon to show Tolstoy's disdain for great men—there is no question that Bondarchuk relied on the voice-over. This is offset, however, by Bondarchuk's almost encyclopedic array of cinematic devices, as described in chapter 2.

In conclusion, Bondarchuk's *War and Peace* is not only a better adaptation than Vidor's film but also a better piece of filmmaking. Vidor presents a solid but uninspired example of Hollywood realism, with no trace of Italian Neorealist influences, despite its Italian provenance. Bondarchuk, in contrast, presents a film that yearns for greatness and almost finds it. Nearly fifty years later, it is still difficult to imagine that there will ever be a better adaptation of Tolstoy's magisterial work.[55]

The international success of *War and Peace* opened new doors for Sergei Bondarchuk. He was now a major player in European cinema. His stature was confirmed when he was tapped to direct what might be considered a sequel to *War and Peace*: *Waterloo*, a lavish Italian-Soviet coproduction. This is the subject of the last chapter.

CHAPTER SIX

CODA: BONDARCHUK'S *WATERLOO*

Bondarchuk undoubtedly approached the making of *Waterloo* (1970) with high expectations. Here was the opportunity to film an epilogue to *War and Peace* and to establish himself as a leading *European* director by working with an international cast and crew and in English, cinema's global language. This Dino De Laurentiis/Mosfilm coproduction had a big budget—estimated at $25 million to $40 million—which would enable Bondarchuk to make another Napoleonic-era extravaganza. Soviet citizens were proud that Bondarchuk had been chosen as the director of this lavish production.[1] Yet the film did not have great success at the box office and received mostly bad reviews in the United States, Britain, and France, ending Bondarchuk's career as a European filmmaker before it had really begun. Not surprisingly, little has been written about it in the forty-four years since its release.

Production

What happened? Producer De Laurentiis, famed for his lavish spectacles, was proud of the film and especially of the way he engineered Soviet involvement. He had come to the subject by chance: while "flipping through the encyclopedia, . . . my eyes happened to fall on the pages devoted to the Battle of Waterloo. I thought it over: epic scenes, Napoleon, Wellington. . . . Yes, there was a film to be made."[2] Before he invested in a screenplay, however, he thought about the potential costs of such a picture: "we would need thousands of soldiers, thousands of horses. . . . So I told myself, 'I'm going to propose this idea to the Soviets.'"[3] Mosfilm was receptive to the idea and suggested that the picture be filmed in Uzhgorod in western Ukraine, near the place where the Battle of Austerlitz had been shot for *War and Peace*.[4] There was a condition to the Soviets' cooperation, however: De Laurentiis had to choose a Soviet director. "I told them I was happy to use Sergei Bondarchuk, a filmmaker I actually admired," recalled De Laurentiis. "And so the government granted me ten thousand soldiers and shipped them from Moscow to Uzgorod [sic]."⁵

Why did Bondarchuk agree to join a film whose main idea had been plucked from an encyclopedia? He told the Soviet journal *Cinema Art* (*Iskusstvo kino*):

> The shooting of *War and Peace* was enthralling and difficult. It seemed that everything possible was already done. Still, during the shooting of the last shots of the Battle of Borodino, I was thinking regretfully that I would have to leave the theme of the epoch that I have studied so thoroughly and for so long. The suggestion of the Italian colleagues to shoot *Waterloo* allowed me to return to these events and characters that I have studied over many years. Indeed at Borodino began the defeat of Napoleon's army. But in *War and Peace* we showed only the beginning of this defeat, without its logical ending. *Waterloo* allows us to finish this theme of the Battle of Borodino.⁶

Furthermore, Bondarchuk wanted an opportunity to return to Tolstoyan ideals. "I have been 'breathing' Tolstoy and what he has taught me. I could talk about it without stopping," Bondarchuk told *Cinema Art*. He continued, rather grandiosely: "But the main point is that the universality of Tolstoy didn't interfere with his ability to notice the subtle, 'microscopic' movements of the human soul. To follow Tolstoy's method implies combining philosophical intensity with everyday simplicity and cordiality, penetration into the subtle psychology [of the human soul] along with the embracing of the panoramic scope of historic events."⁷

Unfortunately for Bondarchuk, it is doubtful that De Laurentiis shared any of his aspirations for the film. The producer was much more interested in spectacle for its own sake. De Laurentiis biographers Tullio Kezich and Alessandra Levantesi breathlessly proclaim that the set was the "biggest in the history of the world, extending over nearly four square miles and with meticulous attention to detail."⁸ The preparations were overseen by "a squad of Mosfilm officials and four hundred soldiers from the Soviet engineering corps."⁹ In addition to the 10,000 troops, the Soviet government sent 1,500 cavalry, which approached the numbers for *War and Peace*.

The horses created logistical problems. As De Laurentiis remembered it, in his usual hyperbolic style: "Thousands of horses: sheer madness. Thanks to them, however, we were able to realize scenes without any precedent in the history of cinema. And I personally shot the most beautiful cavalry charge."[10] Obviously, De Laurentiis had conveniently overlooked the precedent of Bondarchuk's cavalry charges in *War and Peace*. Sadly, many horses died or were maimed as a result of these "beautiful" scenes.[11]

Authenticity was not De Laurentiis's forte. Bondarchuk had been obsessed with it in *War and Peace*, but he did not have the same resources at his disposal for *Waterloo*. Despite Soviet support for the production, it was not, after all, a Russian subject, let alone an adaptation of a Russian literary classic.[12] Nevertheless, according to Soviet critic S. Chertok, "The movie crew traveled across Europe, studied the archives, historical objects from the museums of France, Belgium, Italy, England and the Soviet Union and explored the details of the surroundings and the clothing."[13]

Waterloo's art director was Mario Garbuglio, who had also worked on Vidor's *War and Peace*. Garbuglio proved to be a master of fakery. For instance, he had 5,000 plastic figures made to play soldiers, both living and dead, explaining that "the whole idea was to scatter corpses across the terrain . . . and to integrate the fake soldiers into the units on the battlefields. Each unit was composed of two real soldiers and eight fake ones. The fakes were in perfect formation, of course, and were held in place by a single wooden plank."[14]

The casting proved to be troublesome. As he had with Vidor's *War and Peace*, De Laurentiis took over. He conceived the film as a vehicle for Richard Burton as Napoleon and Peter O'Toole as Wellington. (What a film that might have been!) However, the Soviets wanted to begin filming immediately to avoid the onset of deep winter, which had caused delays in *War and Peace*. This effectively ruled out both Burton and O'Toole, who were performing in plays in London and could not get out of their engagements. So the producer moved on to his second choices: Rod Steiger (Napoleon) and Christopher Plummer (Wellington). De Laurentiis lamented that although they were "tremendous actors," they lacked the "star power" of Burton and O'Toole.[15]

Steiger (who would be heavily criticized for his portrayal of Napoleon) took his role seriously and prepared by reading biographies.[16] Bondarchuk wanted him to play up the human rather than the military side of Napoleon, and Steiger agreed, at least according to Soviet critic Galina Dolmatovskaya.[17] There seems to be some disagreement, however, about the relationship between the actor and the director. On the one hand, Dolmatovskaya claims that Bondarchuk and Steiger worked well together and that Steiger admired Bondarchuk as both actor and director.[18] On the other hand, Steiger's close friend Tom Hutchinson recalled that *Waterloo* was "not altogether a happy experience" for the actor. For one thing, Steiger was frustrated by Bondarchuk's inability to speak English; the director's English was supposedly limited to "How are you?" and "I come back soon."[19] (The multilingual cast and crew had problems communicating in general.)[20]

Three anecdotes illustrate Steiger's issues with the production. First, during one scene, Bondarchuk suddenly yelled, "Cut!" All five cameras were out of film. According to Hutchinson, the production had been "cutting costs by using short ends, pieces of film left over from longer reels and sold off cheaply." Steiger wept in disappointment.[21] Second, Steiger was annoyed that the role called for him to ride a horse. He had trouble controlling his horse, so for his close-ups, he would sit in a saddle on a sawhorse.[22] Third, Bondarchuk thought Steiger was overacting and therefore "cut many of Steiger's best bits," recalled De Laurentiis.[23] (Bondarchuk also found Christopher Plummer too theatrical for his taste; at the time, the Canadian actor was best known for his seventy-five stage roles.)[24]

Waterloo According to Historians

Despite all these problems, De Laurentiis had at least chosen his subject well. The Battle of Waterloo (18 June 1815) seems tailor made for a movie blockbuster, with its clash of titans (Napoleon Bonaparte and Arthur Wellesley, Duke of Wellington), its epic casualty rate, and its picturesque setting in the verdant farmland near the village of Waterloo, then nine miles from Brussels. The "real" story was rife with drama: Napoleon, just escaped from the island of Elba, where he had been exiled, returned triumphantly to Paris while the Bourbon king, Louis XVIII, ignominiously slinked away. As Napoleon moved his army due north from Paris to Belgium, Wellington, an energetic forty-six-year-old, was called away from the Congress of Vienna to fight him. When Napoleon heard that Wellington was in Brussels, he and his well-equipped army of 124,000 men crossed the Belgian border at 3:30 a.m. on 15 June at Charleroi, which was quickly captured.[25]

As the French army was crossing the border, Wellington was enjoying himself at the famous ball given by Charlotte, Duchess of Richmond, that same night. The ball took place at a makeshift location, a coach maker's depot described by historian Andrew Roberts as "a long, barn-like structure with small old-fashioned pillars."[26] According to Roberts, Wellington attended the ball to "show the citizens of Brussels that there was no need to panic."[27] During the ball, Wellington "affected great gaiety and cheerfulness," but his face also bore an expression of "care and anxiety."[28] He constantly broke away from his conversations with the other guests to give orders to his officers. Yet when the Prince of Orange, commander of the Dutch troops in the coalition, interrupted the duke with the news of Napoleon's advance, Wellington told the surprised prince to go to bed. When the ball was over, Wellington asked Charles Lennox, Duke of Richmond, for a map and reportedly declared about the French advance: "Napoleon has *humbugged* me, by God!"[29]

The next day, 16 June, the situation heated up as the French, commanded by Marshal Michel Ney, and some of Wellington's Anglo-Dutch forces clashed at Quatre Bras; they fought to a stalemate that left 9,000 dead.[30] At the same time, the rest of the French army, led by Napoleon, defeated the Prussian army of Field Marshal Gebhard von Blücher at Ligny. This led Napoleon to underestimate the seventy-two-year-old marshal quite badly.[31] As historian David Chandler writes, although Blücher was "rough [and] ill-educated," he was "endowed with common sense, fiery energy, and indomitable courage."[32]

There was no action on 17 June. Wellington's 112,000 inexperienced troops, about which he openly complained, settled in near the village of Waterloo, chosen for its confined space and proximity to the Mont St. Jean ridge.[33] Wellington situated his troops on the back of the ridge, where they would be out of sight. The Hougoumont chateau and the farm called La Haie Sainte were "strong points to the fore," and Wellington was determined to hold them.[34] What followed, however, exemplified Tolstoy's thesis on war: the unexpected rules a battle.

The troops may have been biding their time on 17 June, but the weather was not. A torrential downpour—described by Roberts as an "apocalyptic" storm—began that day and did not let up until 9:00 a.m. on 18 June, the day of the battle.[35] Historians have described the muddy battlefield as a critical factor. It was "glutinous," and soldiers' uniforms were "caked with several pounds of mud."[36] Shells buried in the deep mud and "exploded up, . . . sending up the mud like a fountain."[37] The mud impeded not only the infantry but also the artillery and the cavalry, which sank deep into the muck.

Another factor the armies had to contend with were the cornfields, made soggy by the rain. The corn was already chest high and impeded the rapid deployment of troops.[38] Roberts notes that the Waterloo battlefield was a "very cramped area for nearly two hundred thousand people to fight on."[39] In this, it resembled the Battle of Borodino, which was also fought in a contained area.[40]

Because of the mud, Napoleon decided not to attack at dawn but rather at 11:30 a.m., which gave the Prussian army five extra hours to make its way to the battlefield.[41] Another problem for the French army was that Napoleon was not his usual self; he was ill and lethargic, lacking in "urgency and energy."[42] He gave Marshal Ney "operational control" over the troops and was stationary for much of the battle, relying on Ney for battle reports—another mistake in judgment.[43] Ney, who apparently suffered from battle fatigue, was a poor choice for commander, but Napoleon's best generals, such as Marshals Louis-Nicolas Davout and Louis-Gabriel Suchet, were occupied elsewhere.[44] Furthermore, according to Roberts, Napoleon's orders that day were "unclear or contradictory" and "strategically inept."[45] Napoleon's reputation for "hubris and arrogance" was much in display; he not only underestimated Blücher but also was dismissive of Wellington.[46]

Although Wellington had an ego of his own and a reputation as a "cool and disdainful British Milord," he fully recognized his foe's military genius.[47] Wellington knew his men did not love him, but he cared not. He cut quite a figure at the battle, dressed in civilian clothes: "blue frock coat, white cravat, leather pantaloons, and Hessian boots."[48] Historian Christopher Hibbert notes Wellington's mannerisms during the battle—he "kept glancing at his watch" and looking through his telescope—but also his great personal courage: "he contrived to look unconcerned, continuously appearing where the fire was hottest."[49] His orders were "all short, quick, and to the point."[50] Everywhere around him, his staff was cut down. A legendary example of Wellington's coolness under fire occurred when his second in command, H. W. Paget, Earl of Uxbridge, had his leg shot off while sitting on horseback beside Wellington. The startled Uxbridge reportedly said with classic British aplomb, "By God, sir, I've lost my leg." Wellington retorted, "By God, sir, so you have."[51]

The battle itself was confused and chaotic.[52] There was too much smoke on the battlefield to see clearly.[53] The din was deafening, and casualties littered the field.[54] Many different actions were taking place simultaneously; for example, the battles for Hougoumont and La Haie Sainte lasted all day.[55]

The British defense of Hougoumont is legendary: the French were slaughtered as they attempted to scale the walls.[56] The fighting at La Haie Sainte was equally intense. At 4:00 p.m., a frustrated Napoleon ordered Ney to capture the farm at any cost.[57] The British valiantly held on, against a heavy assault. There was "much fighting at the entrance to the barn, an entrance blocked with bodies."[58] At around 6:30 p.m., after hours of fighting, Napoleon's forces finally succeeded in taking La Haie Sainte and, according to Roberts, "pulverized the Anglo-Allied centre."[59] Victory, however, came at a heavy price.

The cavalry charges were especially chaotic. The British cavalry, for example, faced a French counterattack "without order and with their horses winded, so that their riders lacked much mobility," writes historian Jeremy Black.[60] The French heavy cavalry tried unsuccessfully to penetrate the British "squares" of infantrymen; casualties were high, but the squares remained intact.[61] Wellington's troops shot at the French cavalry's horses, and "dead and injured horses created a formidable obstacle to French attacks," which led to a "breakdown of unit cohesion."[62] Nevertheless, the squares were hit hard, taking heavy casualties.[63]

Meanwhile, as the battle raged, the Prussians were advancing on Waterloo. Blücher sent his entire army to support Wellington, not the single corps the duke had requested.[64] Prussian cannons were within range at 4:00 p.m., and the first Prussian troops arrived at 4:30.[65] The British began a new advance, and according to Black, the French army "disintegrated under pressure [from Wellington's troops] and a large number of troops rushed to surrender, further increasing the collapse of the French army and the chaos on the battlefield."[66] When Napoleon's guard began to scatter, hindered in their advance by the high corn that hid the Anglo-Allied troops, the French knew the battle had been lost.[67] The Prussians were particularly savage, bayoneting wounded soldiers as they lay on the ground.[68] General Blücher met up with Wellington at 9:00 p.m.; the two men shook hands on horseback, and Blücher reportedly said, "*Mein lieber kamerad! Quelle affaire!*" which Wellington joked were the only two words the old general knew in French.[69]

The killing did not stop with the battle's end. According to Black, "both British and Prussian troops looted the dead and wounded of both sides, sometimes killing the latter of their own side."[70] Belgian civilians also scavenged the battlefield, pillaging corpses and killing the wounded.[71] The scene at Waterloo was grim: "undulating fields . . . were knee-deep in mud and covered with bodies."[72] Casualties were high at Waterloo: 71,000 killed and wounded. Combining the engagements of 15–18 June, there were 119,800 casualties: 67,000 French troops, 30,000 Prussian, and 22,800 Anglo-Allied.[73]

Roberts mentions Bondarchuk's film in his account of Waterloo, calling it "visually superb but historically flawed."[74] He seems to be basing his historical criticism on one scene in particular: when the French cavalry plunges down a ravine. This scene, which is undeniably photogenic, has its place in the mythology of the battle. As Roberts writes: "The more chauvinistic French accounts sometimes claim that there was . . . a 'Ravine of Death' down which Ney's cavalrymen fell head-first to their and their horses' deaths." In fact, the Ohain road, where the ravine was allegedly located, was only "slightly sunken" and an "easy in-and-out jump."[75]

Another historical inaccuracy that Roberts does not mention occurs early in the film, when Napoleon is on the road with his army, looking for more soldiers to join him. Bondarchuk shows Marshal Ney (who has vowed to Louis XVIII that he will bring Napoleon back to Paris in an iron cage) ordering his men to fire on Napoleon. They refuse. In reality, this episode occurred at Grenoble in March 1815, when General Jean-Gabriel Marchand sent a battalion out to meet Napoleon there. As in the film, Napoleon alone walked toward the "menacing muskets." Marchand ordered his troops to fire, but they did not and joined Napoleon instead; Marchand fled. As for Ney, all he needed was a note from Napoleon asking for his services; he abruptly changed sides, forgetting all about his promise to the king.[76]

These are minor "mistakes" in the grand scheme of the battle, and both were doubtless intentional, for the sake of greater drama, rather than out of ignorance. Bondarchuk had already studied the years 1805–1812 very carefully for *War and Peace*; he prepared as studiously for *Waterloo*, going back to his material on Napoleon.[77] Indeed, Bondarchuk worked on H. A. L. Craig's script to make it more authentic historically and more dramatic; the extent to which his changes were accepted is not clear.[78] Bondarchuk strove, as he had in *War and Peace*, for authenticity rather than a pedantic adherence to the historical record.[79]

Bondarchuk's *Waterloo*

Turning to the film itself, *Waterloo* opens with a scene of Marshal Ney and other officers at Fontainebleau, preparing to confront the defeated Napoleon. They inform him of the extent of the foreign opposition and urge him to abdicate. Napoleon stands at some remove from the others, emphasizing his isolation. This scene introduces the clunky dialogue that pervades the film and trivializes the important events taking place. Napoleon asks rhetorically: "What must we do? *Fight!*" When he is told that Wellington is too formidable a foe, the emperor petulantly shouts: "Why is it always Wellington?" and then repeats, rather absurdly, "Wellington, Wellington, Wellington, Wellington!" Ney calmly counters that Napoleon must abdicate, whereupon Napoleon shrieks, "I will not! Not! Not!" Bondarchuk's lack of English is obvious; he could not recognize scenarist Craig's tin ear for natural dialogue in English.

As the defeated emperor turns to walk out the door, we hear a voice-over

Napoleon outside Grenoble. (Courtesy Photofest)

of his thoughts: "Why Elba?" There is a close-up of his face, a device Bondarchuk used sparingly in *War and Peace*. This is the first of many close-ups
of Napoleon, underscoring his isolation. Furthermore, as in *War and Peace*,
Bondarchuk uses close-ups in *Waterloo* to differentiate among Napoleon's
men, such as in the next highly emotional scene in which Napoleon says
farewell to his guards.

Napoleon's exile to Elba is not shown. There is an abrupt cut to his escape. At the Tuileries, Louis XVIII (played by a corpulent Orson Welles,
representing the corruption of the French body politic) is informed that "the

monster has escaped from Elba." Marshal Ney, now serving the Bourbons, boastfully promises to bring Napoleon back to Paris in an iron cage, a remark that, according to the historical record, he actually made.

Cut to an aerial panorama and then zoom in on Napoleon, who is marching on foot with his men. They meet Ney's force. Napoleon's troops present their rifles, but he waves them down. There is a close-up of Napoleon's hands clasped behind his back, nervously twitching. He says to Ney's men: "Do you recognize me? If you want to kill your emperor, here I am." Ney orders them to fire, but no one does. Ney's soldiers shout *"Vive la France!"* and rush toward Napoleon. Ney, on horseback and towering above Napoleon, throws down his sword. Napoleon gives the sword back and asks Ney to follow him to Grenoble. (As noted earlier, this episode actually occurred, but with a different general.)

In the next scene, Napoleon is on a balcony, presumably in Grenoble; Ney joins him, to the delight of the crowd below. "I am France and France is me!" Napoleon exultantly shouts. There is a cut to a subdued Louis XVIII, who is about to steal away into the night, murmuring, "Perhaps the people will let me go."

Mobs throng the streets of Paris when Napoleon arrives in triumph. As discussed with reference to *War and Peace*, Bondarchuk is very good with crowd scenes, and this is no exception; the camera follows the surging people. There is a quick transition to Napoleon forgiving his old associates and taking them back into his confidence: "The most precious quality in life is loyalty," he intones without a trace of irony, even though none of these men has in fact remained loyal to him—or to the Bourbons. Napoleon declares, "I did not usurp the crown. I found it in the gutter. I, I picked it up with my sword." He suddenly shifts gears, lamenting the absence of his son, who is in Austria with his mother. (Screenwriter Craig apparently intended this to be a humanizing moment.) Shifting gears again, Napoleon declares that he will discuss peace only "over Wellington's dead body" and adding, out of the blue: "Everything depends on one big battle, just like Marengo," foreshadowing, perhaps, his defeat at Waterloo.

The following scene, the first one shot, takes place in Brussels.[80] It is the Duchess of Richmond's ball, and Scottish soldiers in their kilts are dancing to the tune of bagpipes. It is a magnificent, large-scale scene with 220 actors, reminiscent of Natasha's ball in *War and Peace*.[81] The Duke of Wellington, very lordly and snobbish, arrives. As mentioned earlier, the historical record indicates that he was unhappy with his troops, and in the film, he complains about them to his hostess: "Nothing but beggars and scum." He

The Duke of Wellington and the Duchess of Richmond at her ball. (Courtesy Photofest)

also laments that he will be forced to fight "Bony" (Napoleon), who is "not a gentleman." There is crosscutting between Napoleon's men, marching in the fog and rain, and the ball, where elegant people are engaged in a stately dance. Scriptwriter Craig introduces a love story involving Lady Sarah, the duchess's daughter, and young Lord Richard Hay, one of Wellington's officers. (The duchess asks Wellington to protect Hay; cold as ever, Wellington makes no effort to do so, and Hay is eventually killed at Waterloo.) A bedraggled officer rushes in to tell Wellington that Napoleon has crossed the Belgian border at Charleroi. Word spreads rapidly, and soldiers leave the dance en masse. Meanwhile, Wellington and the Duke of Richmond are shown poring over a map that Richmond has produced. Wellington portentously circles the village of Waterloo on the map.

The rapid-fire exposition continues. Napoleon and Ney are shown against a devastated landscape; General Blücher, commander of the defeated Prussian forces, orders a retreat. Part of Napoleon's army is off in pursuit. (It appears that the French have won and the Prussians have lost—a situation that will be reversed within a day.) In the meantime, Lieutenant General Sir Thomas Picton openly criticizes Wellington's choice of battlefield because of the forest, which will impede troop movements. This is followed by an odd comedic bit in which an English soldier steals a pig and stuffs it in his knapsack. Wellington catches him, sternly reminds him of the penalty for plundering, and then promotes the befuddled lad to the rank of corporal for his mettle. This ham-fisted scene is designed to soften Wellington or perhaps to highlight his penchant for breaking the rules.

Bondarchuk crosscuts four times between Napoleon and Wellington, who are pondering and strategizing. Wellington explains, for the benefit of audience members who may not know the history of the battle, that victory depends on whether the Prussian army arrives in time. Meanwhile, it is still raining.

Napoleon is ill, but he refuses a doctor. He whispers to his flunkies, "Get out, out, out, out, out," continuing the scenarist's habit of giving Napoleon this verbal tic. As an omen, Napoleon hears thunderclaps and the sound of driving rain. He wonders whether it will ever stop raining.

By dawn, the rain has stopped. Napoleon plans to attack at 9:00 a.m. but is persuaded to wait until the ground dries out a bit, around noon. His officers argue, correctly, that they will be unable to move the cannons unless they delay the start of the battle. Meanwhile, Wellington is lying under a tree with a newspaper over his face. His second in command, Uxbridge, naturally wants to know what the battle plans are. Wellington jauntily replies, "To beat the French." There is a cut to a morose Napoleon, knee deep in mud, thinking about his son.

A camera rapidly pans the terrain, in a shot reminiscent of *War and Peace*'s Battle of Borodino. The film's Battle of Waterloo begins at the historically accurate time of 11:35 a.m., with artillery fire. Now Bondarchuk is in his element: the large-scale battle. This one lasts for forty-two minutes, even longer than Bondarchuk's Battle of Borodino. Cheerful martial music plays as the French lines advance. Bondarchuk focuses on the confusion right away; there is too much smoke on the battlefield to see anything clearly. He employs a lot of crosscutting to show simultaneous events during the battle. For example, the French troops are depicted trying to scale the walls at Hougoumont, followed by a cut to the French marching on the Anglo-Allied lines, then back to Hougoumont.

The cavalry charges are spectacular: horses run at top speed and then get shot down or stuck in the mud. For one charge, Bondarchuk uses slow motion to emphasize the awful beauty of the scene. The afternoon passes

The fog of war. (Courtesy Photofest)

quickly, and the Prussian arrive. Napoleon decides that La Haie Sainte must be taken ("The one who wins the farmhouse wins the battle"). Still bedeviled by stomach pain, Napoleon faints. Ney breathlessly announces: "Wellington's retreating! Wellington's retreating!" He orders a new French cavalry charge. This is where Bondarchuk shows, in a scene of terrible beauty, the so-called Ravine of Death that apparently never existed. Horses and riders plunge headlong and headfirst down a steep ravine; Bonarchuk does not reveal the disastrous consequences.

The British soldiers organize into the square formations; there is a wonderful aerial shot of the battlefield at this point. A solitary British soldier breaks free, clearly shell-shocked: "How can we kill one another?" he cries, "Why? Why?" (This is a Bondarchukian antiwar touch.) At this point, there are lots of aerial shot of the battlefield; smoke and fire fill the air, which is thick with ashes.

The French take La Haie Sainte at 6:00 p.m. Napoleon wants to lead his army forward, but his staff persuades him to turn back to safety, where he is told that the Prussian forces are in the woods. Cut to Blücher, who orders his men: "No pity! No prisoners!" In the midst of all this, Wellington is shown cool and collected, while the men around him are mowed down. There is the famous scene of Uxbridge losing his leg; scriptwriter Craig used the exact language that made its way into the history books: "By God, sir, I've lost my leg!" "By God, sir, so you have!"

Although Napoleon believes the Prussians are too late, he is wrong, and the French Old Guard is broken. Napoleon's officers try to persuade him to escape. Wellington asks the surviving French to surrender; they refuse. Instead of showing the resumption of battle, the camera pans the bodies of the dead Frenchmen, communicating the action in a much more powerful way.

As darkness falls, Wellington rides slowly through the battlefield. He sees the dead and wounded being robbed and dozens of dead and dying horses. There is an aerial shot of the terrible scene, and the sound of bagpipes is heard. The young blond soldier who cried "Why? Why?" is dead, but his words echo. Wellington, looking thoughtful for a change, says, "Next to a battle lost, the saddest thing is a battle won." It start to rain again; thunder crescendos.

We see Napoleon, disconsolate, among the remnants of his men. As Ney watches him closely, the defeated emperor slowly climbs into his carriage. A close-up of his weary face is the final shot in *Waterloo*.

As this synopsis shows, Bondarchuk's film *was* historically accurate as far as the big issues and some of the smaller details are concerned, despite one critic's claim that Bondarchuk and Craig "made a confused mess of events."[82] Bondarchuk lost some opportunities for heightened drama, however. He does not show the cornfields, which played such an important role in the battle. Nor does he emphasize the mud; for example, the soldiers' pretty uniforms are splashed with a little mud, but they are certainly not caked with pounds of it. Of course, this would not have been particularly photogenic. The horror of the bloody battlefield is also minimized, but even in 1970, hard-core realism had not yet become common in films, especially one that was Soviet-financed.

Reception

The film's depiction of the chaos of the great battle was true to the historical record, but Bondarchuk was widely criticized for this. Charles Champlin of the *Los Angeles Times* wrote: "The explicit carnage is more restrained in *Waterloo* than in *War and Peace*, but there are still the endlessly billowing clouds of smoke and the tumbling horses and the confusing hordes of men charging up and down geography which the viewer is never allowed to get straight in his mind."[83] Other American critics concurred. Penelope Gilliat was never "sure which soldier in a battle scene [was] coming from which direction," Stanley Kauffman complained that the "battle tactics are never clear," and Judith Crist noted that "we go back and forth in the smoke of battle and know not whose side we're on."[84]

The film's depiction of Napoleon was also heavily criticized, and most of the blame was laid at the feet of actor Rod Steiger. The word *awful* was frequently employed to describe his performance, as in *Newsweek* critic Paul Zimmerman's assertion that "Steiger is just plain awful as Napoleon."[85] The *Washington Post*'s Michael Kernan labeled Steiger's performance a "disaster," claiming that his "soft and pudgy face under the famous Napoleon hat dangerously resembles Lou Costello."[86] Joseph Gelmis of *Newsday* described Steiger's Napoleon as "grimacing and bellowing like a Bronx butcher."[87] Charles Champlin of the *Los Angeles Times* offered a more nuanced explanation of what went wrong: "Although he looks the part, Rod Steiger's rendition of Napoleon is so histrionic that he never stops being Rod Steiger–acting–Napoleon long enough to *become* Napoleon, and he is never able to suggest the awesome charisma that made Napoleon Napoleon."[88]

This negative commentary notwithstanding, Steiger's Napoleon in fact strongly resembles the Napoleon of the One Hundred Days. The restored emperor was *not* the Napoleon of old. As noted earlier, historians' accounts of the Battle of Waterloo describe him as strangely passive and suffering from a variety of ailments. Yes, there are outbursts of anger, petulance, and hubris in Steiger's portrayal, but these all fit the historical record. Napoleon had become a renegade as far as other European leaders were concerned, and he deeply resented that.

Christopher Plummer's Wellington was also criticized, but not to the same extent. For example, the ascerbic Champlin thought Plummer played the Duke of Wellington "as invented by Noel Coward," while Gelmis saw Wellington as the "most amusing character in the film," based on his lofty self-confidence.[89] Sigmund Glaubmann complained that "Wellington is allowed to be a dandy tossing off *bons mots*."[90] Gordon Gow hated Wellington's "perky smugness."[91] *Variety*'s "Rich," who actually liked the film, thought Plummer played Wellington "coolly and sardonically, rather like a captain amassing his team for victory at a cricket match."[92] Indeed, the "real" Wellington was very much like Plummer's portrayal of him. He was far from a stereotypical military commander and was certainly nothing like Napoleon.

A bit of a dandy and a great lover of amusements, especially balls, Wellington acted as if the battle inconvenienced him. He was cool and reserved, always one step removed from the action, but he possessed keen intelligence and a fine strategic mind, as well as great physical courage.

Did critics like anything about the film? Gow acknowledged that "some trouble has been taken to reconcile the splurge of spectacle with latter-day recognition of the fact that war is unbecoming to humanity." He found the technical aspects of *Waterloo* "commendable," complimenting the many pans, zooms, and aerial shots.[93] Champlin described the cinematography as "often stunning," especially when "a helicopter ris[es] to reveal more and more and more of the battlefield.[94] The *Saturday Review*'s critic also thought the aerial shots were impressive: "There must be thousands of men and hundreds of horses on the screen. Shots burst in mid-air and through clouds of white smoke, one clearly perceives a strategy that went awry."[95]

There was an eerie silence in the contemporary Soviet film press about *Waterloo*; neither of the two major journals, *Cinema Art* and *Soviet Screen*, reviewed it. Later Soviet critics focused on *Waterloo* as an antiwar movie and as the follow-up to *War and Peace*.[96] Nina Tolchenova applauded the way Bondarchuk emphasizes the senselessness of the French sacrifice, seeing in *Waterloo* the same universal themes that are present in *War and Peace*.[97] She saw *Waterloo* as a "weighty, intelligent" film.[98] Galina Dolmatovskaya thought Bondarchuk's masterful battle scenes in *Waterloo* demonstrated his antiwar sentiments.[99]

Despite the opprobrium of some Western critics, the film won three prizes: British Academy of Film and Television Arts (BAFTA) Awards went to Mario Garbuglia for art direction and Maria De Matteis for costume design, and *Waterloo* was a cowinner of the David Di Donatello Award for best Italian picture, tying with the acclaimed movies *The Garden of the Finzi-Continis* (*Il giardino dei Finzi-Contini*, Vittorio De Sica, 1970) and *The Conformist* (*Il conformista*, Bernardo Bertolucci, 1970).[100]

De Laurentiis claimed the film did not suffer a loss, at least from his personal perspective: "There was no way I could lose money on the production because I had passed on the gross costs to the Russians. . . . In the USSR the film was a success: Bondarchuk was a mythical figure in that part of the world."[101] Under the terms of his deal with Mosfilm, De Laurentiis could not claim any of the Soviet revenues, but he insisted that the film did well in the English-speaking world (this is open to debate), although he admitted it fared poorly in French-speaking countries.[102] (Dolmatovskaya confirms that *Waterloo* was heavily criticized in the French press.)[103]

Waterloo is a better film than its reception indicates, but overall, it must be judged a disappointment. It cannot compare to *War and Peace*. More than anything, Bondarchuk feared making a film that did not find an audience: "Unfortunate is the movie director whose movies no one attends."[104] In the end, it seems that the great director found himself working in a system he did not understand and that, ironically, gave him less creative freedom than the Soviet system.

Bondarchuk rebounded from this setback, although he did not return to coproduction until his illustrious career was nearing its end. By then, the director of *War and Peace* found himself in the glasnost era, a time of "openness" that was not very friendly to an establishment figure like Bondarchuk. The story of his later career and the twenty-first-century reevaluation of *War and Peace* are the subjects of the conclusion.

CONCLUSION

After the failure of *Waterloo*, Bondarchuk returned to work as an actor, performing in twenty more films before his death from heart failure in 1994 at age seventy-four. His best-known roles were Dr. Astrov in *Uncle Vanya* (*Diadia Vania*, Andrei Konchalovsky, 1971), Ivan Zviagintsev in *They Fought for the Motherland* (*Oni srazhalis na rodinu*, Bondarchuk, 1975), Emelian in *The Steppe* (*Step*, Bondarchuk, 1979), Father Sergius in *Father Sergius* (*Otets Sergii*, Igor Talankin, 1979), and Boris Godunov in *Boris Godunov* (Bondarchuk, 1986). He directed only five more pictures: *They Fought for the Motherland*, *The Steppe*, *Boris Godunov*, *Red Bells* (*Krasnye kolokoly*, 2 parts, 1982–1983), and *Quiet Flows the Don* (*Tikhii Don*, released posthumously in 2006). The last two were international coproductions that led to trouble for Bondarchuk, as we shall see. The unsung masterpiece (in the West) among this group of later works is *They Fought for the Motherland*, a brilliant World War II film set on the eve of the Battle of Stalingrad and starring the great Vasily Shukshin in his final role.[1]

Bondarchuk's last years were not happy. Because he was very close to government and Communist Party officials, he alienated the younger generation of filmmakers who were poised to become the leaders of cinema when Mikhail Gorbachev came to power in 1985.[2] In May 1986, accumulated envy and resentment came to a head at the Fifth Congress of Filmmakers when the director of *War and Peace* was not even elected as a delegate. Director Nikita Mikhalkov, who has now become his own kind of establishment figure, was the only attendee who came to Bondarchuk's defense. Mikhalkov declared: "The fact that he [Bondarchuk] was not reelected as a deputy of the Congress of Soviet Filmmakers, a man who created *The Fate of a Man*, *War and Peace*, and *They Fought for the Motherland*, is an act of childishness that discredits all sincere and noble attempts to revitalize the bleak and formal atmosphere that reigns in our Union of Cinematographers."[3]

After a number of speeches in which Bondarchuk was not mentioned, director Vladimir Menshov, maker of the hit *Moscow Does Not Believe in Tears* (*Moskva slezam ne verity*, 1979) took issue with Mikhalkov's remarks by attacking Bondarchuk's *Red Bells*, which was based in part on John Reed's *Ten Days That Shook the World*. Menshov called the picture a travesty, especially its portrayal of Lenin, and he was outraged that the film had received a State Prize. Menshov hinted at elements of coercion in the film's reception: "We were insistently convinced that it worked out well, though the viewers sluggishly agreed with this 'well.' Ah, so we will give him the State Prize, so that everyone would know that it was 'very good!'"[4] The resentment and envy were obvious.

This incident must have been quite a blow for the sixty-six-year-old actor and director. Just as bad was the imbroglio concerning his final film, *Quiet Flows the Don*, based on Mikhail Sholokhov's classic novel. Mosfilm's general director Karen Shakhnazarov says, whimsically, that the film was "arrested in the West." The Italian producer went bankrupt, and creditors seized the film.[5] It eventually appeared twelve years after Bondarchuk's death as a 364-minute television serial and a 160-minute feature film.[6] Reviews were mixed.[7]

Of the three masterpieces to his credit—*The Fate of a Man, War and Peace*, and *They Fought for the Motherland*—Bondarchuk's place in the history books is probably most deserved for his sole international hit, *War and Peace*. But given the varied response among Soviet critics and audiences at the time, this is far from obvious. That the film has aged well became apparent in 2000 when Mosfilm undertook to preserve it for its archives in a $100,000 restoration project, supported in part by Goskino.[8]

War and Peace was the first movie Mosfilm chose for its restoration project. Shakhnazarov considers it the quintessential Soviet film—one that could only have been made in the USSR, and one that everybody wanted to see. The restoration was difficult. According to Shakhnazarov, *War and Peace* "practically did not exist." Mosfilm did not have the original negatives; some of the negatives were found in Kiev, and a copy of the film was obtained from Soveksportfilm, the film export agency. Mosfilm made half a dozen copies on 35mm Kodak film; one copy was deposited at Gosfilmofond, the national film archive. The Russian Cinema Council (Ruscico) used the Mosfilm restoration for its 2002 DVD. As Shakhnazarov puts it, *War and Peace* is a "unique film" with an "absolutely special place in the history of Russian and Soviet cinema."[9]

With the restoration—and the passage of nearly five decades—the generation of Soviet filmmakers who were young back in the 1960s appreciates it at last. Well-known cinematographer Vadim Yusov represents a typical case. When *War and Peace* first appeared, he thought it did not do justice to Tolstoy. Indeed, Yusov believed Bondarchuk was such a poor Pierre that he went to Mosfilm's Artistic Council to complain about the portrayal. Now, with the director and the system that gave life to the film long gone, Yusov sees *War and Peace* as a "global and authentically deep work of cinema," and he considers any talk about defects in the picture to be ridiculous. The spate of favorable post-Soviet, Russian reinterpretations of Bondarchuk cited in this book supports Yusov's views.

Shakhnazarov claims an "absolutely special place" for *War and Peace* in Soviet film history. Most obvious is the fact that it was the most expensive film ever made in the USSR and one of its biggest hits, at least the first two parts. This was the first time the state literally opened its coffers for a film project. Bondarchuk had the rare opportunity to realize his filmic vision without monetary constraints, and it paid off. The film was exactly what the state had in mind when it first commissioned *War and Peace*: a national epic that surpassed all other national epics, a sensitive adaptation of Tolstoy's classic novel that preserved both the letter and the spirit of the original, and a well-researched historical film that celebrated one of the legendary military victories in Russian history. It was a tribute to the might and righteousness of the Russian people, which fit well with the Russocentrism of the USSR in the late 1960s under Brezhnev. A Russian victory *was* a Soviet victory. As film scholar David Gillespie points out: "Bondarchuk's *War and Peace* contains some of the most thrilling and large scale battle scenes ever filmed, but it remains a paean to Russian military might and the strength of the Russian 'soul.'"[10]

Yet Bondarchuk's film differs in important ways from the monumentalism of Soviet epics before and after it. The differences between *War and Peace* and a Stalinist epic like *The Fall of Berlin* (*Padenie Berlina*, Mikhail Chiaureli, 1949) are extreme. *The Fall of Berlin* epitomizes the hero worship that *War and Peace* argues so strenuously against.[11] But in its lyricism and humanism, *War and Peace* is also different from the most important epic that followed it, Yury Ozerov's *Liberation* (*Osvobozhdenie*, 1970–1972), an eight-hour, five-part World War II film that was commissioned for the twenty-fifth anniversary of Victory Day and was clearly intended to be the Great Patriotic War's *War and Peace*. But without clearly developed individual characters, *Liberation* failed to capture the hearts of the audience, and after an initially strong showing, attendance plummeted for the last three parts. (Workers were "encouraged" by Communist Party organizations to attend, which was not the case for *War and Peace*.)[12]

Indeed, *War and Peace*'s lyricism and humanism, along with its aestheticism, mark it as a Thaw film, even though it is absent from analyses of the cinematic Thaw. Bondarchuk wanted to do more than thrill audiences with his superb battle scenes. He hoped to touch them emotionally and make them think. The lively debate over *War and Peace* indicates that he certainly achieved the latter. The intimacy of the scenes between Andrei and Natasha, Andrei and Pierre, and Pierre and Natasha sharply contrast with the monumentalism of the battle scenes. And Bondarchuk and Petritsky's sense of style—all the cinematic devices they employed so successfully—are reminiscent of some of the great Thaw films.

Globally, *War and Peace* screened to enthusiastic critics and did well at the box office for a foreign movie, except in the United States, where the film had been badly dubbed. Nevertheless, even in the United States the film was seen as an "event," with a lavish premiere and high ticket prices. The disappointment of lukewarm American reviews was forgotten when the film won the Oscar for Best Foreign Language Film. This was a first for Soviet cinema and a point of enormous pride, not only for Bondarchuk but also for the Soviet state, which had invested so much in the picture. For one brief moment, it appeared that the USSR had won the cinematic Cold War.[13]

For this reason alone, *War and Peace* is an important film. The premise of this study, however, is that this film is one of the great epics produced during the era of cinematic epics in the 1950s and 1960s. Bondarchuk's ability to choreograph large-scale scenes is second to none, and he succeeds in imparting a love for Russia and Russians that is patriotic without being overtly propagandistic—no easy feat. Furthermore, the film combines superb battle scenes with an antiwar message that subverted the military fervor of the Brezhnev regime.

Of course, Bondarchuk benefited enormously from having a great novel to adapt. Tolstoy's *War and Peace* posed many challenges, not the least of which was its length. Even though Bondarchuk, unlike Vidor, had the luxury of creating four films to interpret the novel, his cutting and compressing made for some difficult choices, which he resolved as well as anyone could. The hard necessity of cutting meant that criticism was inevitable among an audience with a deep knowledge of and love for Tolstoy. He thus ran the risk of deleting everyone's favorite passages. Nevertheless, Bondarchuk and his coscenarist Solovev succeeded in crafting a coherent narrative while preserving the major ideas of the novel and striving to communicate them cinematically rather than verbally. It is the best adaptation of this complex work and is likely to remain so.

Historians are notoriously harsh critics of historical films, often demanding of films what they cannot give. Is *War and Peace* historically accurate? To a certain extent, Bondarchuk was constrained by Tolstoy's interpretation of the events of 1812. Yet the director's extensive research into the period is apparent in every scene, and the contours of the much-analyzed Battle of Borodino are preserved and bear close resemblance to eyewitness accounts. In particular, Zakhava's Kutuzov corresponds to the historical figure, as does Bagration. The vaunted battle scenes are also historically authentic. Like Tolstoy's novel, Bondarchuk's *War and Peace* creates an indelible impression of Russia in the years 1805–1812.

War and Peace has been rehabilitated in post-Soviet Russia and restored to the pantheon of great Soviet films. As I hope this study demonstrates, it also deserves to be resurrected in the West as one of the greatest epics ever made.

APPENDIX

WAR AND PEACE CREDITS

Director: Sergei Bondarchuk
Screenplay: Sergei Bondarchuk, Vasilii Solovev
Music: Viacheslav Ovchinnikov
Cinematography: Anatolii Petritskii, Yu-Lan Chen, Aleksandr Shelenkov
Editing: Tatiana Likhacheva
Production Design: Mikhail Bogdanov, Aleksandr Dikhtiar, Said Menialsh-
chikov, Gennadii Miasnikov
Set Decoration: Georgii Koshelev, V. Uvarov
Costume Design: Vladimir Burmeister, Nadezhda Buzina, Mikhail Chiko-
vani, V. Vavra
Makeup: Mikhail Chikirev
Assistant Director: Vladimir Dostal
Cast: Sergei Bondarchuk (Pierre Bezukhov), Liudmila Saveleva (Nata-
sha Rostova), Viacheslav Tikhonov (Andrei Bolkonskii), Boris Zakha-
va (General Kutuzov), Anatolii Ktorov (Nikolai Bolkonskii), Anastasiia
Vertinskaia (Lise Bolkonskaia), Antonina Shuranova (Marya Bolkon-
skaia), Oleg Tabakov (Nikolai Rostov), Viktor Stanitsyn (Count Rostov),
Kira Golovko (Countess Rostova), Irina Skobtseva (Hélène Bezukhova),
Boris Smirnov (Vasilii Kuragin), Vasilii Lanovoi (Anatole Kuragin), Iri-
na Gubanova (Sonia Rostova), Aleksandr Borisov (Uncle Rostov), Oleg
Efremev (Dolokhov), Giuli Chokhonelidze (Prince Bagration), Vladislav
Strzhelchik (Napoleon), Angelina Stepanova (Anna Scherer), Nikolai Tro-
fimov (Tushin), Nikolai Rybnikov (Denisov), Jean-Claude Ballard (Ram-
balle), Elena Tiapkina (Marya Dmitrevna), Sergei Ermilov (Petia Rostov),
Nonna Mordiukova (Anisia), Mikhail Khrabov (Platon Karataev)

Source: http://www.imdb.com/title/tt0063794/fullcredits?ref=tt_cl_sm#cast, accessed
24 June 2013.

NOTES

INTRODUCTION

1. This section is drawn in part from my books *Russian War Films: On the Cinema Front, 1914–2005* (Lawrence: University Press of Kansas, 2007), 107–109, and, with Tony Shaw, *Cinematic Cold War: The American and Soviet Struggle for Hearts and Minds* (Lawrence: University Press of Kansas, 2010), 47–55.

2. Miriam Dobson, *Khrushchev's Cold Summer: Gulag Returnees, Crime, and the Fate of Reform after Stalin* (Ithaca, NY: Cornell University Press, 2009), 15.

3. Polly Jones, "Introduction: The Dilemmas of De-Stalinization," in *The Dilemmas of De-Stalinization: Negotiating Cultural and Social Change in the Khrushchev Era*, ed. Polly Jones (London: Routledge, 2006), 11.

4. Ilia Ehrenburg, *The Thaw*, trans. Manya Harari (Chicago: Regnery, 1955).

5. Jones, "Introduction," 4.

6. The best work on Thaw cinema is Josephine Woll, *Real Images: Soviet Cinema and the Thaw* (London: I. B. Tauris, 2000). For an excellent examination of Soviet cinema as an institution and Soviet movie culture under Khrushchev and Brezhnev, see Kristin Roth-Ey, *Moscow Prime Time: How the Soviet Union Built the Media Empire that Lost the Cultural Cold War* (Ithaca, NY: Cornell University Press, 2011), chaps. 1–2.

7. Alexander Prokhorov, "The Unknown New Wave: Soviet Cinema of the 1960s," in *Springtime for Soviet Cinema: Re/Viewing the 1960s*, ed. Alexander Prokhorov (Pittsburgh: Pittsburgh Russian Film Symposium, 2001), 12–13.

8. Paul Babitsky and John Rimberg, *The Soviet Film Industry* (New York: Praeger, 1955), 51.

9. Woll, *Real Images*, 3–11.

10. Prokhorov, "Unknown New Wave," 8.

11. Woll, *Real Images*, 30–31.

12. Jones, "Introduction," 12.

13. Ibid., 14.

14. Woll, *Real Images*, 203–204.

15. For details, see Nina Tumarkin, *The Living and the Dead: The Rise and Fall of the Cult of World War II in Russia* (New York: Basic Books, 1994).

16. Anna Lawton, *Kinoglasnost: Soviet Cinema in Our Time* (Cambridge: Cambridge University Press, 1992), 9–10.

17. Ibid., 11.

18. Running time is based on the Russian Cinema Council version, which was made from the Mosfilm/Goskino restoration. Bondarchuk himself cut the picture by one hour for American distribution.

CHAPTER 1. FROM INCEPTION TO SCREEN

1. Sergei Kudriavtsev, *3500: Avtorskaia kniga kinoretsenzii*, vol. 1, A–M (Moscow: n.p., 2008), 185. This review also appears in Sergei Kudriavtsev, *Svoe kino* (Moscow: Dom

Khanzhonkova/Kinovideotsentr, 1998), 38. It was originally published in *Ekran i tsena*, 1997.

2. Valérie Pozner, ed., *Tolstoï et le cinema. Cahiers Léon Tolstoï*, vol. 16 (Paris: Institute d'études slaves, 2005), 92.

3. A. Vystorobets, *Sergei Bondarchuk: Sudba i filmy* (Moscow: Iskusstvo, 1991), 101.

4. Pozner, *Tolstoï et le cinema*, 92–93; Vystorobets, *Sergei Bondarchuk*, 102. Vystorobets provides some different details about these first films; I have followed Pozner where the details differ.

5. Kudriavtsev, *3500*, 185.

6. Fedor Razzakov, *Gibel sovetskogo kino: Intrigi i spory: 1918–1972* (Moscow: Eksmo, 2008), n.p. (in caption to photo insert).

7. Iurii Tiurin, "*Voina i mir*," in *Rossiiskii illiuzion*, ed. L. M. Budiak (Moscow: Materik, 2003), 417. This museum houses Franz Rubaud's famous panorama, measuring 15 meters high and 115 meters long, that shows the French attack on the village of Semenovskoe. See Alexander Mikaberidze, *The Battle of Borodino: Napoleon against Kutuzov* (Barnsley, UK: Pen and Sword, 2007), 195. Mikaberidze renders the artist's name "François Rubeau"; I have used the more common spelling.

8. Fedor Razzakov, *Nashe liubimoe kino: O voine* (Moscow: Algoritm/Eksmo, 2005), 6.

9. Vladimir Solovev, "*Voina i mir i my*," in *Sergei Bondarchuk v vospominaniiakh sovremennikov*, ed. Olga Palatnikova (Moscow: Eksmo, 2003), 21; Sergei Bondarchuk, *Zhelanie chuda* (Moscow: Molodaia gvardiia, 1981), 188.

10. Razzakov, *Nashe liubimoe kino*, 7.

11. Quoted in Stephen M. Norris, "Tolstoy's Comrades: Sergei Bondarchuk's *War and Peace* and the Origins of Brezhnev Culture," in *Tolstoy on Screen*, ed. Lorna Fitzsimmons (Evanston, IL: Northwestern University Press, forthcoming), ms. 1. My thanks to Professor Norris for letting me see his article in advance of publication.

12. Kristin Roth-Ey, *Moscow Prime Time: How the Soviet Union Built the Media Empire that Lost the Cultural Cold War* (Ithaca, NY: Cornell University Press, 2011), 52.

13. Ibid., 30.

14. Norris, "Tolstoy's Comrades," ms. 6; Razzakov, *Nashe liubimoe kino*, 6. Norris says the reformers "wanted someone else [besides Pyrev] to reach the 1960s Soviet citizen."

15. Razzakov, *Nashe liubimoe kino*, 7.

16. Solovev, "*Voina i mir i my*," 122.

17. Razzakov, *Nashe liubimoe kino*, 7.

18. Bondarchuk resisted joining the Communist Party until 1970, when he decided that the lack of party membership would hurt his career.

19. Bondarchuk, *Zhelanie chuda*, 188.

20. "Sergei Bondarchuk," bonus disc, *Voina i mir* (Ruscico [Russian Cinema Council], 2002), DVD.

21. Iurii Khaniutin, *Sergei Bondarchuk* (Moscow: Iskusstvo, 1962), 10.

22. Presentation by Irina Skobtseva in "Interviews," *Voina i mir* bonus disc.

23. Khaniutin, *Sergei Bondarchuk*, 10; John Lind, "Sergei Bondarchuk: The Road to Waterloo," *Focus on Film* 4 (October 1970): 27.

24. Khaniutin, *Sergei Bondarchuk*, 10. According to Marina Mednikova, he grew up

on the steppe in Kherson oblast; see her "Sergei Bondarchuk," *Soviet Film* 312 (1983): n.p. Mednikova writes, "Wherever he went his beautiful steppe and the pure sky of the motherland were with him."

25. Khaniutin, *Sergei Bondarchuk*, 11. Lind, "Sergei Bondarchuk," 27, says he performed his first role as a first-grader.

26. "Sergei Bondarchuk," *Voina i mir* bonus disc.

27. Lind, "Sergei Bondarchuk," 27.

28. Ibid.

29. Ibid.

30. Ibid.; Khaniutin, *Sergei Bondarchuk*, 20.

31. Galina Dolmatovskaya and Irina Shilova, *Who's Who in the Soviet Cinema: Seventy Different Portraits* (Moscow: Progress, 1979), 28.

32. Lind, "Sergei Bondarchuk," 27.

33. Khaniutin, *Sergei Bondarchuk*, 25.

34. Lind, "Sergei Bondarchuk," 27; Dolmatovskaya and Shilova, *Who's Who in the Soviet Cinema*, 29.

35. Khaniutin, *Sergei Bondarchuk*, 57.

36. Lind, "Sergei Bondarchuk," 28; Khaniutin, *Sergei Bondarchuk*, 67.

37. Quoted in Lind, "Sergei Bondarchuk," 29.

38. Ibid., 28; Dolmatovskaya and Shilova, *Who's Who in the Soviet Cinema*, 29.

39. Khaniutin, *Sergei Bondarchuk*, 67.

40. Russia-InfoCentre, "Sergei Bondarchuk," http://russia-ic.com/people/general/b/2010, accessed 25 June 2013.

41. Dolmatovskaya and Shilova, *Who's Who in the Soviet Cinema*, 29.

42. Lind, "Sergei Bondarchuk," 29. In the mid-1950s Bondarchuk also played Ivan Franko in the film of the same name, which was directed by Timofei Levchuk. See Dolmatovskaya and Shilova, *Who's Who in the Soviet Cinema*, 30.

43. Russia-InfoCentre, http://russia-ic.com/people/general/b/2010, accessed 25 June 2013.

44. Kudriavtsev, *3500*, 185; Elena Prokhorova, "*War and Peace*," in *Directory of World Cinema: Russia*, ed. Birgit Beumers (Bristol, UK: Intellect, 2011), 181.

45. Kudriavtsev, *3500*, 185. The figure of 120,000 is repeated in many sources; see, for example,"The Great Ones: *War and Peace*," *Classic Film Collection* 57 (Winter 1977): 18. The actual number of extras must be less than 20,000; the only concrete number we have is 15,000 soldier-extras in the Battle of Borodino.

46. Prokhorova, "*War and Peace*," 181. According to Vystorobets, *Sergei Bondarchuk*, 121, the film was also shot in 35mm.

47. Kudriavtsev, *3500*, 185.

48. Solovev, "*Voina i mir* i my," 134–135.

49. Ibid., 134.

50. Prokhorova, "*War and Peace*," 181.

51. Viacheslav Ovchinnikov, "Interviews," *Voina i mir* bonus disc.

52. Razzakov, *Nashe liubimoe kino*, 8. That translates to $260,000 (in 2013 dollars). The conversion factor is $8.69 (2013) to one ruble (1961). Furtseva was minister of culture from 1960 until her death in 1974.

53. Solovev, "*Voina i mir* i my," 125.

54. Razzakov, *Nashe liubimoe kino*, 8.

55. Nina Tolchenova, *Mera krasoty: Kino Sergeia Bondarchuka* (Moscow: Sovetskaia Rossiia, 1974), 201.

56. Solovev, "*Voina i mir* i my," 124, 126; Vystorobets, *Sergei Bondarchuk*, 110.

57. Vystorobets, *Sergei Bondarchuk*, 111.

58. Razzakov, *Nashe liubimoe kino*, 11; Vystorobets, *Sergei Bondarchuk*, 111. The date of approval is alternatively given as 20 March; see Ministerstvo kultury Rossiiskoi Federatsii, Nauchno issledovatelskii institut kinoiskusstva, *Letopis rossiiskogo kino, 1946–1965* (Moscow: Kanon+, 2010), 546.

59. Vystorobets, *Sergei Bondarchuk*, 112.

60. Razzakov, *Nashe liubimoe kino*, 11.

61. Ibid.; *The Making of a Film* (Vasily Solovev, n.d.), *Voina i mir* bonus disc.

62. Other actors competing for Andrei were Yury Solomin, Eduard Martsevich, and Andrei Mikhalkov-Konchalovsky. See Natalia Tendora, *Viacheslav Tikhonov: Kniaz iz Pavlovskogo posada* (Moscow: Algoritm, 2008), 87; Viacheslav Ovchinnikov, "Interviews," *Voina i mir* bonus disc.

63. Razzakov, *Nashe liubimoe kino*, 13.

64. Viacheslav Tikhonov, "Pozhaliute v kadr, kniaz!" in Palatnikova, *Sergei Bondarchuk*, 191.

65. Solovev, "*Voina i mir* i my," 131.

66. Tendora, *Viacheslav Tikhonov*, 87.

67. Vasilii Lanovoi, "Interviews," *Voina i mir* bonus disc.

68. Vasilii Lanovoi, "My znaem tsenu dobru," in Palatnikova, *Sergei Bondarchuk*, 255–256. Bondarchuk eventually apologized to Lanovoi, who took over the part after Medvedev was fired. Nikita Mikhalkov was replaced after only one day's work by Sergei Yermolov in the role of Petya; Nikolai Simonov was replaced as Kutuzov by Boris Zakhava, a director at the Vakhtangov Theater who had not acted in years, at the suggestion of the Ministry of Culture. See Razzakov, *Nashe liubimoe kinoe*, 17; Tendora, *Viacheslav Tikhonov*, 89; "*Voina i mir*: Kogda film proshel po ekranam," *Iskusstvo kino* 1 (1968): 38.

69. Tendora, *Viacheslav Tikhonov*, 88.

70. Tikhonov, "Pozhaliute v kadr, kniaz!" 187–188.

71. Ibid., 190–191.

72. Ibid., 192–193. Bondarchuk supposedly wanted Yury Vlasov for Pierre, but he refused. Vystorobets, *Sergei Bondarchuk*, 119; Tendora, *Viacheslav Tikhonov*, 88. Innokenty Smokhtunovsky wrote: "The actor's egoism of Bondarchuk won . . . and as it seems to me, *War and Peace* lost." See Razzakov, *Gibel sovetskogo kino*, 481. Bondarchuk also cast his wife, Irina Skobtseva, as Pierre's wife Hélène after Via Artman had already been hired for the role. See I. A. Musskii, *Sto velikikh otechestvennykh kinofilmov* (Moscow: Veche, 2006), 291. Both Bondarchuk and Skobtseva were at least fifteen years older than their characters, and it showed.

73. Tikhonov, "Pozhaliute v kadr, kniaz!" 194–195; Rianovosti, obituary for Tikhonov, http://en.rian.ru/russia/20091204/157100764.html, accessed 29 July 2013.

74. Razzakov, *Nashe liubimoe kino*, 18–19.
75. Ibid., 11–12; Tendora, *Viacheslav Tikhonov*, 88.
76. Solovev, "*Voina i mir* i my," 129.
77. Liudmila Saveleva, "Bolno…," in Palatnikova, *Sergei Bondarchuk*, 167.
78. Ibid., 167–168.
79. Razzakov, *Nashe liubimoe kino*, 12.
80. Saveleva, "Bolno," 172.
81. Lind, "Sergei Bondarchuk," 35.
82. Antonina Shuranova, "On zhil Tolstym," in Palatnikova, *Sergei Bondarchuk*, 229–232. A telegram arrived that evening (ibid., 233).
83. Ibid., 239.
84. "*Voina i mir:* Kogda film proshel po ekranam," 35. Vertinskaya may have been miffed because she wanted the role of Natasha.
85. Razzakov, *Nashe liubimoe kino*, 10.
86. Ibid., 19.
87. Ibid., 21–22.
88. Anatolii Petritskii, "My na mnogoe smotreli po-raznomu," in Palatnikova, *Sergei Bondarchuk*, 207–214.
89. Ibid., 219–220.
90. Bondarchuk, *Zhelanie chuda*, 132.
91. Vasilii Petritskii, "Interviews," *Voina i mir* bonus disc.
92. Vystorobets, *Sergei Bondarchuk*, 117.
93. Ovchinnikov, "Interviews," *Voina i mir* bonus disc.
94. Bondarchuk, *Zhelanie chuda*, 130.
95. Ovchinnikov, "Interviews," *Voina i mir* bonus disc. Ovchinnikov went on to become an important Soviet composer.
96. Nikolai Ivanov, "Iz dnevnika direktora kartiny," in Palatnikova, *Sergei Bondarchuk*, 144, 147.
97. Ibid., 151.
98. Ibid., 155, 157. Disapproval would have meant going back to the drawing board.
99. Rossiiskii gosudarstvennyi arkhiv literatury i iskusstva (RGALI), f. 2453, op. 4, ed. khr. 239, Mosfilm, 1-oe Tvorecheskoe obedinenie, Stenogramma zasedaniia Khudozhestvenngo soveta ot 19 sentiabria 1961 g. po obsuzhdeniiu literaturnogo stsenariia S. F. Bondarchuka i V. Soloveva *Voina i mir*, pervaia seriia, ll. 5, 14,18.
100. RGALI, f. 2453, op. 4, ed. khr. 239, l. 156. The decision about whether to divide the film into four parts was postponed until after the plan for three parts had been evaluated (ibid., l. 162).
101. Ivanov, "Iz dnevnika direktora kartiny," 159.
102. Tendora, *Viacheslav Tikhonov*, 58.
103. Ivanov, "Iz dnevnika direktora kartiny," 157–158.
104. Tendora, *Viacheslav Tikhonov*, 58.
105. "The Great Ones: *War and Peace*," 18–19; Theodore Shabad, "'War and Peace' on Native Soil," *New York Times*, 12 January 1964.
106. Shabad, "'War and Peace' on Native Soil."

107. Tendora, *Viacheslav Tikhonov*, 95. The number of soldiers' uniforms claimed by Tendora does not jibe with the fact that 15,000 soldier-extras participated in the Battle of Borodino sequence.

108. Petritskii, "Interviews," *Voina i mir* bonus disc.

109. Razzakov, *Nashe liubimoe kino*, 16–17.

110. Ivanov, "Iz dnevnika direktora kartiny," 149.

111. Ibid., 148–149; Razzakov, *Nashe liubimoe kino*, 16.

112. Razzakov, *Nashe liubimoe kino*, 16.

113. Ibid., 17.

114. Saveleva, "Bolno," 178; *The Making of a Film*, *Voina i mir* bonus disc.

115. Razzakov, *Nashe liubimoe kino*, 19.

116. Petritskii, "Interviews," *Voina i mir* bonus disc.

117. Petritskii, "My na mnogoe smotreli po-raznomu," 213; Petritskii, "Interviews," *Voina i mir* bonus disc.

118. Petritskii, "Interviews," *Voina i mir* bonus disc.

119. Razzakov, *Nashe liubimoe kino*, 16–17.

120. Ibid., 18.

121. Ivanov, "Iz dnevnika direktora kartiny," 151.

122. Razzakov, *Nashe liubimoe kino*, 21.

123. The park also refused to accommodate the number of latrines needed. Petritskii, "Interviews," *Voina i mir* bonus disc.

124. Petritskii, "My na mnogoe smotreli po-raznomu," 214.

125. Razzakov, *Nashe liubimoe kino*, 23–24; Petritskii, "My na mnogoe smotreli po-raznomu," 218.

126. *The Making of a Film*, *Voina i mir* bonus disc.

127. Petritskii, "Interviews," *Voina i mir* bonus disc.

128. Razzakov, *Nashe liubimoe kino*, 23.

129. Petritskii, "Interviews," *Voina i mir* bonus disc.

130. Razzakov, *Nashe liubimoe kino*, 27.

131. Ivanov, "Iz dnevnika direktora kartiny," 157.

132. Petritskii, "Interviews," *Voina i mir* bonus disc.

133. "*Voina i mir*: Kogda film proshel po ekranam," 41. Miasnikov said the set was not a copy of Catherine's Hall of Columns, as some believed.

134. Razzakov, *Nashe liubimoe kino*, 28; Ivanov, "Iz dnevnika direktora kartiny," 159.

135. Petritskii, "My na mnogoe smotreli po-raznomu," 218–219; Petritskii, "Interviews," *Voina i mir* bonus disc. This was Petritsky's second favorite scene, after the Battle of Borodino.

136. Saveleva, "Bolno," 176; Tikhonov, "Pozhaliute v kadr, kniaz!" 196; Petritskii, "Interviews," *Voina i mir* bonus disc.

137. Razzakov, *Nashe liubimoe kino*, 29; Ivanov, "Iz dnevnika direktora kartiny," 160; Petritskii, "My na mnogoe smotreli po-raznomu," 220. Bondarchuk's daughter confirms that his first words were about Gerasimov; see Natalia Bondarchuk, *Edinstvennye dni* (Moscow: Astrel, 2010), 161. Ivanov says that Bondarchuk collapsed from overwork the following fall, but this event was not as serious as the first heart attack.

138. Razzakov, *Nashe liubimoe kino*, 30; Ministerstvo kultury Rossiiskii Federatsii, *Letopis rossiiskogo kino*, 666.

139. V. I. Fomin and A. S. Deriabin, eds., *Letopis rossiiskogo kino, 1946–1965: Nauchnaia monografiia* (Moscow: Kanon+, 2010), 670.

140. Razzakov, *Nashe liubimoe kino*, 32.

141. RGALI, f. 3173, op. 1, ed. khr. 189, Stenogramma vstrechi presedatelia komiteta po kinematografii pri SM SSSR A.V. Romanova s uchastnikami vypusnikov stsenarnogo otdeleniia kursov i stsenarnogo fakulteta VGIKa v Repino, 8–15 maia 1967 g., l. 20.

142. The publicity consisted mainly of photo spreads containing both stills and photos of the shooting.

143. Petritskii, "Interviews," *Voina i mir* bonus disc.

144. Ivanov, "Iz dnevnika direktora kartiny," 161.

145. Petritskii, "Interviews," *Voina i mir* bonus disc.

146. Ivanov, "Iz dnevnika direktora kartiny," 163; Razzakov, *Nashe liubimoe kino*, 33–34.

147. Ivanov, "Iz dnevnika direktora kartiny," 163; Razzakov, *Nashe liubimoe kino*, 34; Norris, "Tolstoy's Comrades," ms. 15. Razzakov gives the date as 17 October. Impressive amounts of pyrotechnic material were required to obtain the necessary effects; see the list in Ivanov, 164.

148. Petritskii, "My na mnogoe smotreli po-raznomu," 222; Petritskii, "Interviews," *Voina i mir* bonus disc.

149. Ivanov, "Iz dnevnika direktora kartiny," 164.

150. RGALI, f. 3173, op. 1, ed. khr. 189, l. 20.

151. Ibid.

152. It was generally conceded that the multiple parts did not work. See Norris, "Tolstoy's Comrades," ms. 25.

153. Razzakov, *Nashe liubimoe kino*, 35–36. Examples of billed costs were the actors' salaries, which were very modest. Bondarchuk received 20,100 rubles for playing Pierre (and 21,679 rubles as the director); Tikhonov, 22,228 rubles; and Saveleva, a pittance—10,685 rubles. In the words of Tendora, *Viacheslav Tikhonov*, 86: "If the film had been made in Hollywood, each actor taking part in it would have become millionaires."

154. Kudriavtsev, *Svoe kino*, 413.

155. Shakhnazarov interview, *Voina i mir* bonus disc.

156. Razzakov, *Nashe liubimoe kino*, 36; Tikhonov, "Pozhaliute v kadr, kniaz!" 196. Also see Roth-Ey, *Moscow Prime Time*, 21.

157. Saveleva, "Bolno," 184.

158. Tendora, *Viacheslav Tikhonov*, 92.

159. Saveleva, "Bolno," 183. See also Tikhonov, "Pozhaliute v kadr, kniaz!" 201. Shuranova was chagrined that some of her "snob-friends" claimed that "the American *War and Peace* is authentic. But ours—an illustration." Shuranova, "On zhil Tolstym," 241.

160. Ivanov, "Iz dnevnika direktora kartiny," 164.

161. Tolchenova, *Mera krasoty*, 219.

162. Lind, "Sergei Bondarchuk," 26.

163. Bondarchuk, *Zhelanie chuda*, 200.

164. Kira Golovko, "On byl absoliutno mkhatovskii," in Palatnikova, *Sergei Bondarchuk*, 267.

165. Nikolai Trofimov, "Veroval!" in Palatnikova, *Sergei Bondarchuk*, 277–279.

166. Saveleva, "Bolno," 174, 178.

167. Shuranova, "On zhil Tolstym," 233–234, 236–237.

168. Bondarchuk, *Zhelanie chuda*, 191. In an article Bondarchuk was writing for the journal *Cinema Art* (*Iskusstvo kino*), he was forced to change his use of "I" to "we." See RGALI, f. 2962, op. 1, ed. khr. 90, Redaktsiia zhurnala *Iskusstvo kino*, Sergei Bondarchuk, "Khudozhnik dolzhen iskat," ll. 16–17. This file has no date.

169. Trofimov, "Veroval!" 281. Trofimov, perhaps parroting Bondarchuk, wrote that although Tikhonov was a good actor, he had troubling maintaining a consistently noble affect (ibid.).

170. Shuranova, "On zhil Tolstym," 244.

171. Tikhonov, "Pozhaliute v kadr, kniaz!" 194–195.

172. Ibid., 198.

173. Ibid., 199–200.

174. Tendora, *Viacheslav Tikhonov*, 86.

175. Lind, "Sergei Bondarchuk," 37; Valeriia Gorelova, "Viacheslav Tikhonov," in *Akterskaia entsiklopediia kino Rossii*, pt. 1 (Moscow: Materik, 2002), 135. Fortunately, Tikhonov did not quit acting. He went on to become a People's Artist (like Bondarchuk) in 1974, and in 1984 he was honored as a Hero of Socialist Labor (Gorelova, "Viacheslav Tikhonov," 136). He also became a cult figure playing the role of Stirlitz in Tatiana Lioznova's enormously popular television serial *Seventeen Moments of Spring* (*Semnadtsat mgnovenii vesny*, 1973).

176. Tendora, *Viacheslav Tikhonov*, 91–92.

177. RGALI, f. 3173, op. 1, ed. khr. 189, l. 20. Roth-Ey says there were more than 100 newspaper reviews; see *Moscow Prime Time*, 52n120.

178. Tendora, *Viacheslav Tikhonov*, 92. She notes that an American critic praised the sacking and burning of Moscow as "incomparable" and praised Natasha's ball as "one of the most romantic moments in the history of the screen" (ibid., 85).

179. Ibid., 92. Tendora gives no reason for this.

180. Rostislav Iurenev, *Iskusstvo, rozhdennoe oktiabrem* (Moscow: Biuro propagandy Sovetskogo kinoiskusstva, 1968), 96. This well-placed Soviet film historian writes that there were complaints about Bondarchuk as Pierre, Tikhonov as Andrei, and Oleg Tabakov as Nikolai. But he compliments Saveleva and Ktorov and the battle scenes, the Moscow fire, and Natasha's ball.

181. Norris, "Tolstoy's Comrades," ms. 19.

182. Tendora, *Viacheslav Tikhonov*, 94.

183. K. Zamoshkin, "Vo imia sveta: Zametki o *Voina i mira*—roman i kinofilm," *Smena* 23 (December 1967).

184. A. Sofronov, "Velichie dukha," *Ogonek* 27 (2 July 1967): 16–17. Stills from *War and Peace* adorned the front and back covers of this issue.

185. Khamil Iarmatov, "Sobytie," *Iskusstvo kino* 9 (1965): 12–13.

186. Tendora, *Viacheslav Tikhonov*, 91.

187. Ibid., 89; Musskii, *Sto velikikh otechestvennykh kinofilmov*, 291.

188. Bondarchuk, *Zhelanie chuda*, 127, 129.

189. S. Ermolinskii, "V preddverii novykh stranits," *Iskusstvo kino* 9 (1965): 7–8.

190. Norris, "Tolstoy's Comrades," ms. 18–19.

191. Ibid., 25.

192. Georgii Daneliia, "Ne boias literaturu...," *Iskusstvo kino* 9 (1965): 10. See also Tendora, *Viacheslav Tikhonov*, 94.

193. Igor Zolotusskii, "Dobavlenie k eposu (Tolstoi v romane i Tolstoi v filme)," *Novyi mir* 6 (June 1968): 271, 273–275.

194. Ibid., 280.

195. Claude Autant-Lara, "Dukh epokhi," *Iskusstvo kino* 9 (1965): 13–14; Tendora, *Viacheslav Tikhonov*, 94.

196. Tendora, *Viacheslav Tikhonov*, 95.

197. James Oldridge, "Mysl v deistvii," *Iskusstvo kino* 9 (1965): 12.

198. Tino Balio, *The Foreign Film Renaissance on American Screens, 1946–1973* (Madison: University of Wisconsin Press, 2010), 13.

199. Ibid.

200. Ibid., 220.

201. Ibid.

202. Ibid., 221.

203. Renata Adler, "*War and Peace*," *New York Times*, 29 April 1968, 50. Adler thought the filmmakers were talented but "without genius." She also complained that the money spent to make the film could have paid for a poverty program.

204. Beau, "*War and Peace*," *Variety*, 1 May 1968, 6.

205. Stanley Kauffman, "Take a Giant Steppe," *New Republic*, 18 May 1968, 24. Kauffman wrote that "the two-hour . . . break . . . was like a breather in an arduous unfinished job."

206. Penelope Gilliatt, "The Russians' Monument," *New Yorker*, 4 May 1968, 163.

207. Joseph Morgenstern, "The Biggest Movie," *Newsweek*, 6 May 1968, 120. Morgenstern concluded that the film was "not bad."

208. See, for example, Hollis Alpert, "Clash by Night," *Saturday Review*, 11 May 1968, 56–57.

209. Balio, *Foreign Film Renaissance*, 221.

210. Mosk, "*War and Peace*—Part III." *Variety*, 10 May 1967, 6.

211. Kauffman, "Take a Giant Steppe," 24.

212. Elena Bauman, "Close-up: Our Contemporary Sergei Bondarchuk," *Soviet Film* 296 (1982): 6.

CHAPTER 2. *WAR AND PEACE* AS A FILM EPIC

1. *The American Heritage Dictionary of the English Language*, 3rd ed. (Boston: Houghton Mifflin, 1992), 204.

2. Raphaëlle Moine, *Cinema Genre*, trans. Alistair Fox and Hilary Radner (Malden, MA: Blackwell Publishing, 2008), 144. Moine argues that *blockbuster* is currently the preferred term for a film epic.

3. Barry Langford, *Film Genre: Hollywood and Beyond* (Edinburgh: Edinburgh University Press, 2005), 251.

4. Constantine Santas, *The Epic in Film: From Myth to Blockbuster* (Lanham, MD: Rowman and Littlefield, 2008), 1.

5. Ibid., 89.

6. Langford, *Film Genre*, 242.

7. Robert Burgoyne, "Introduction," in *The Epic Film in World Culture*, ed. Robert Burgoyne (New York: Routledge, 2011), 3.

8. Nature was an important symbol in Thaw-era films in general. See Alexander Prokhorov, "The Unknown New Wave: Soviet Cinema of the 1960s," in *Springtime for Soviet Cinema: Re/Viewing the 1960s*, ed. Alexander Prokhorov (Pittsburgh: Pittsburgh Russian Film Symposium, 2001), 12. This was different from pre-Thaw Soviet films, in which nature merely provided a "picturesque background." See Evgenii Margolit, "Landscape with Hero," ibid., 31.

9. The comet was last seen in Russia in August 1812. Tolstoy calls it the Comet of 1812.

10. Nina Tolchenova, *Mera krasoty: Kino Sergeia Bondarchuka* (Moscow: Sovetskaia Rossiia, 1974), 217.

11. American critic Hollis Alpert praised this "vast, confusing sweep and swirl of regrettable battle" in "Clash by Night," *Saturday Review*, 11 May 1968, 56–57.

12. Stephen M. Norris, "Tolstoy's Comrades: Sergei Bondarchuk's *War and Peace* and the Origins of Brezhnev Culture," in *Tolstoy on Screen*, ed. Lorna Fitzsimmons (Evanston, IL: Northwestern University Press, forthcoming), ms. 11.

13. In the novel, Tolstoy focuses on the death of a factory worker, not a boy. Bondarchuk's version is much more dramatic.

14. Langford, *Film Genre*, 244.

15. Anatolii Petritskii, "My na mnogoe smotreli po raznomu," in *Sergei Bondarchuk v vospominaniiakh sovremennikov*, ed. Olga Palatnikova (Moscow: Eksmo, 2003), 215.

16. One critic complained that instead of being a turning point, as it was in the novel, the Battle of Borodino was "like all the other battles, only bigger." Igor Zolotusskii, "Dobavlenie k eposu (Tolstoi v romane i Tolstoi v filme)," *Novyi mir* 6 (June 1968): 274.

17. Elena Prokhorova, "*War and Peace*," in *Directory of World Cinema: Russia*, ed. Birgit Beumers (Bristol, UK: Intellect, 2011), 181.

18. Santas, *The Epic in Film*, 209.

19. According to Norris, the film is the "patriotic celebration of the collective over the individual." Norris, "Tolstoy's Comrades," ms. 25.

20. Santas harshly (and in my view, unfairly) criticizes the use of the voice-over in the film:"Voice-overs turn out tiresome simplicities, and the film needs the voice-over to convey thought and action." Santas, *The Epic in Film*, 209. These "tiresome simplicities" are straight from Tolstoy.

21. Iurii Khaniutin, "Sergei Bondarchuk," *Iskusstvo kino* 7 (1962): 99.

22. Norris, "Tolstoy's Comrades," ms. 7.

23. Ibid., 2–3.

24. David Brandenburger, *National Bolshevism: Stalinist Mass Culture and the Formation of Modern Russian National Identity, 1931–56* (Cambridge, MA: Harvard University Press, 2002), 92.

25. Norris, "Tolstoy's Comrades," ms. 3.

26. As an example, 100,000 copies of L. N. Tolstoi, *Voina i mir* (Leningrad: OGIZ/ Gosudarstvennoe izdatelstvo khudozhestvennoi literatury, 1941), were printed—an enormous print run.

27. Norris, "Tolstoy's Comrades," ms. 4.

28. Brandenburger, *National Bolshevism*, 165, 172.

29. Prokhorova, "*War and Peace*," 181.

30. R. F. Christian, *Tolstoy: A Critical Introduction* (Cambridge: Cambridge University Press, 1969), 145.

31. Patriotism and nationalism are frequently conflated in the Soviet debates.

32. Sergei Bondarchuk, "Otkrytie chuvstv," *Ogonek* 4 (24 January 1965): 28.

33. Bondarchuk quoted in I. A. Musskii, *Sto velikikh otechestvennykh kinofilmov* (Moscow: Veche, 2006), 29. For example, Kathryn B. Feuer, quoting Tolstoy, sees the novel as being about "the struggle and choice between good and evil." Kathryn B. Feuer, *Tolstoy and the Genesis of War and Peace*, ed. Robin Feuer Miller and Donna Tussing Orwin (Ithaca, NY: Cornell University Press, 1996), 145.

34. Christian, *Tolstoy*, 145.

35. Ibid., 99.

36. Uran Guralnik quoted in Norris, "Tolstoy's Comrades," ms. 21.

37. A. Sofronov, "Velichie dukha," *Ogonek* 27 (2 July 1967): 17.

38. K. Zamoshkin, "Vo imia sveta: Zametki o *Voine i mire*—roman i kinofilm," *Smena* 23 (December 1967): 27, 30.

39. "*Voina i mir*: Kogda film proshel po ekranam," *Iskusstvo kino* 1 (1968): 34.

40. Vasily Lanovoi, "Interviews," bonus disc, *Voina i mir* (Ruscico [Russian Cinema Council], 2002), DVD.

41. See, for example, Theodore Shabad, "*War and Peace* on Native Soil," *New York Times*, 12 January 1964; Renata Adler, "*War and Peace*," *New York Times*, 29 April 1968, 50; Beau, "*War and Peace*," *Variety*, 1 May 1968, 6.

42. Musskii, *Sto velikikh otechestvennykh kinofilmov*, 29.

43. Zamoshkin, "Vo imia sveta," 30. According to American critic Fred Myers, "The film remains . . . as much endeavor as achievement." Fred Myers, "Monumental," *Christian Century* 85 (1968): 1248.

44. Film scholar Frank Manchel, e-mail to author, 6 August 2013.

CHAPTER 3. *WAR AND PEACE* AS AN ADAPTATION

1. Joy Gould Boyum, *Double Exposure: Fiction into Film* (New York: Universe Books, 1985), 15.

2. Bondarchuk claimed that he loved the "wonderful arguments" that arose whenever Tolstoy's work was filmed. See Sergei Bondarchuk, "Leo Tolstoy and the Cinema," *Soviet Film* 255 (1978): 12.

3. Karen Shakhnazarov, "Interview," bonus disc, *Voina i mir* (Ruscico [Russian Cinema Council], 2002), DVD.

4. Boyum, *Double Exposure*, 61.

5. Ibid., 40, 64.

6. Ibid., 64, 77.

7. Ibid., 70, 72, 73.

8. Ibid., 69.

9. Dudley Andrew, "Adaptation," in *Film Adaptation*, ed. James Naremore (New Brunswick, NJ: Rutgers University Press, 2000), 30–33.

10. Stephen Hutchings and Anat Vernitskii, "Introduction: The *Ekranizatsiia* in Russian Culture," in *Russian and Soviet Film Adaptations of Literature, 1900–2001: Screening the Word*, ed. Stephen Hutchings and Anat Vernitskii (London: Routledge Curzon, 2005), 11.

11. André Bazin, "Adaptation, or the Cinema as Digest," in Naremore, *Film Adaptation*, 20.

12. Hutchings and Vernitskii, "Introduction," 11. Boyum agrees that a filmmaker both interprets the source and creates an independent artwork (*Double Exposure*, 73).

13. Robert B. Ray, "The Field of 'Literature and Film,'" in Naremore, *Film Adaptation*, 45.

14. Andrew, "Adaptation," 32.

15. Robert Stam, "Beyond Fidelity: The Dialogics of Adaptation," in Naremore, *Film Adaptation*, 65.

16. Bondarchuk, "Leo Tolstoy and the Cinema," 12.

17. *The Making of a Film, Voina i mir* bonus disc.

18. Sergei Bondarchuk, "Chelovek i istoriia," *Iskusstvo kino* 2 (1981): 29, 35.

19. Sergei Bondarchuk, "Chitaia bessmertnuiu epopeiu," *Iskusstvo kino* 9 (1978): 16.

20. Bondarchuk, "Chelovek i istoriia," 34.

21. Boyum, *Double Exposure*, 78.

22. Ibid., 79–80.

23. Leo Tolstoy, *War and Peace*, trans. Richard Pevear and Larissa Volokhonsky (New York: Alfred A. Knopf, 2007), vol. 1, pt. 1, chaps. 18–21.

24. Ibid., vol. 1, pt. 3, chap. 2, 212–213.

25. Ibid., 213–214.

26. Ibid., vol. 2, pt. 2, chaps. 2–10, 12–21 are omitted.

27. Ibid., vol. 4, pt. 4, chap. 11, 1102.

28. Ibid., vol. 2, pt. 4, chap. 1, 488.

29. Ibid., vol. 3, pt. 1, chap. 10, 639.

30. Ibid., chap. 1, 604.

31. See, for example, ibid., vol. 3, pt. 2, chap. 7.

32. See, for example, ibid., vol. 3, pt. 1, chaps. 4–6, which are omitted from the film.

33. Ibid., vol. 3, pt. 2, chap. 7, 709.

34. Ibid., 710–711.

35. Ibid., epilogue, pt. 2, chap. 12, 1215.

36. Ibid., vol. 4, pt. 4, chaps. 18–20.

37. Ibid., vol. 1, pt. 1, chap. 6, 29.

38. Ibid., 32–33.

39. Ibid., vol. 3, pt. 1, chap. 1, 603. The Russians used the Julian calendar until after the Bolshevik revolution, when they adopted the Gregorian calendar. Thus, 12 June ("old style") is 24 June.

40. Ibid., vol. 2, pt. 3, chap. 23, 479.

41. Ibid., vol. 2, pt. 1, chap. 9, 327.

42. Ibid., vol. 3, pt. 2, chap. 38, 815.

43. Ibid., vol. 2, pt. 1, chap. 4, 311.

44. Ibid., 313.

45. Ibid.

46. Ibid., 315.

47. Ibid., vol. 2, pt. 1, chap. 5, 315.

48. Ibid., 316.

49. Ibid.

50. Ibid., vol. 2, pt. 1, chap. 6, 320.

51. Ibid.

52. Ibid., vol. 2, pt. 3, chap. 15, 456. There are three changes to this description: in the film, Natasha does not take off a fur coat; there are no mirrors along the staircase; and one lady, Hélène, is dressed in black—a crow among the doves.

53. Ibid., 457.

54. Ibid., vol. 2, pt. 3, chap. 16, 459.

55. Ibid., 460.

56. Ibid., vol. 2, pt. 3, chap. 17, 461.

57. Ibid., 462.

58. Ibid.

59. Ibid., vol. 2, pt. 4, chaps. 3–7, 493–514.

60. Ibid., vol. 2, pt. 4, chap. 3, 493.

61. Ibid., vol. 2, pt. 4, chap. 5, 502.

62. Ibid.

63. Ibid., vol. 2, pt. 4, chap. 7, 509.

64. Ibid., 510.

65. Ibid., 511.

66. Ibid., 512.

67. Ibid.

68. Ibid., vol. 4, pt. 1, chap. 16, 985.

69. Ibid.

70. Ibid.

71. Ibid., vol. 3, pt. 2, chap. 26, 783.

72. Ibid., vol. 3, pt. 2, chap. 27, 785.

73. Ibid., vol. 3, pt. 2, chap. 30, 789.

74. Ibid., 790.

75. Ibid., vol. 3, pt. 2, chap. 35, 805.

76. Ibid., vol. 3, pt. 2, chap. 36, 810.

77. Ibid., vol. 3, pt. 3, chap. 33, 924.

78. Ibid., 924–925.

79. Ibid., 926.

80. Ibid., 927.

81. The charge is later amended to spying.

82. Tolstoy, *War and Peace*, vol. 4, pt. 4, chap. 9, 1096.

1. Dominic Lieven, *Russia against Napoleon: The True Story of the Campaigns of* War and Peace (New York: Penguin, 2010), 10.

2. Ibid., 11.

3. Alexander Mikaberidze, *The Battle of Borodino: Napoleon against Kutuzov* (Barnsley, UK: Pen and Sword, 2007), 176.

4. Dominic Lieven, "Tolstoy on War, Russia, and Empire," in *Tolstoy on War: Narrative Art and Historical Truth in* War and Peace, ed. Rick McPeak and Donna Tussing Orwin (Ithaca, NY: Cornell University Press, 2012), 12.

5. Lieven, *Russia against Napoleon*, 39, 37.

6. Ibid., 43.

7. Ibid., 37.

8. Marie-Pierre Rey, *Alexander I: The Tsar Who Defeated Napoleon*, trans. Susan Emanuel (De Kalb, IL: NIU Press, 2012), 166–167.

9. Ibid., 167–168.

10. Lieven, *Russia against Napoleon*, 85, 104.

11. Ibid., 108–109.

12. Mikaberidze, *Battle of Borodino*, 57.

13. Lieven, *Russia against Napoleon*, 134, 143.

14. Lieven, "Tolstoy on War," 14.

15. Lieven, *Russia against Napoleon*, 134.

16. Sean Pollock, "Petr Ivanovich Bagration (1765–1812)," in *Russia's People of Empire: Life Stories from Eurasia, 1500 to the Present*, ed. Stephen M. Norris and Willard Sunderland (Bloomington: Indiana University Press, 2012), 97.

17. Lieven, *Russia against Napoleon*, 159, 165, 157, 187.

18. Ibid., 185.

19. Alexander Muravev quoting Bagration in Alexander Mikaberidze, ed. and trans., *Russian Eyewitness Accounts of the Campaign of 1812* (London: Frontline Books, 2012), 152.

20. Lieven, *Russia against Napoleon*, 217.

21. Rey, *Alexander I*, 249.

22. Lieven, *Russia against Napoleon*, 180, 218.

23. Ibid., 237.

24. Mikaberidze, *Russian Eyewitness Accounts*, 149.

25. Rey, *Alexander I*, 243. Rey, who is very hostile to Kutuzov, goes on to say: "Far from the heroic and mythic picture of him that Tolstoy gave in *War and Peace*, Kutuzov aroused the disapproval, if not revulsion, of many contemporaries" (ibid.).

26. Lieven, *Russia against Napoleon*, 189.

27. Mikaberidze, *Battle of Borodino*, 21.

28. Lieven, *Russia against Napoleon*, 190.

29. Mikaberidze, *Russian Eyewitness Accounts*, 161.

30. Mikaberidze, *Battle of Borodino*, 25.

31. Ibid., 64, 79–83.

32. Ibid., 84; Muravev quoted in Mikaberidze, *Russian Eyewitness Accounts*, 164.

33. Quoted in Mikaberidze, *Russian Eyewitness Accounts*, 185.

34. Mikaberidze, *Battle of Borodino*, 85. Kutuzov also said that this was a battle to save orthodoxy. Lieven, *Russia against Napoleon*, 199.

35. Aleksandr Golitsyn quoted in Mikaberidze, *Russian Eyewitness Accounts*, 172. Presumably, neither Tolstoy nor Bondarchuk knew about this, a singularly dramatic happenstance.

36. Quoted in Mikaberidze, *Russian Eyewitness Accounts*, 185.

37. Ibid., 164.

38. Mikaberidze, *Battle of Borodino*, 99, 105, 112.

39. Lieven, *Russia against Napoleon*, 209.

40. Ibid., 193–195, 198.

41. Ibid., 194.

42. Quoted in Mikaberidze, *Russian Eyewitness Accounts*, 187.

43. Ibid., 181.

44. Quoted in Mikaberidze, *Battle of Borodino*, 160.

45. Ibid., 174.

46. Quoted in Mikaberidze, *Russian Eyewitness Accounts*, 196.

47. Ibid., 198; Mikaberidze, *Battle of Borodino*, 218.

48. Mikaberidze, *Battle of Borodino*, 202.

49. Ibid., 209.

50. Lieven, *Russia against Napoleon*, 209.

51. Mikaberidze, *Battle of Borodino*, 217. Mikaberidze's figures come from *Otechestvennaia voina 1812 goda: Entsiklopediia* (2004), an example of recent Russian research on the subject.

52. Mikaberidze, *Battle of Borodino*, 219.

53. Lieven, *Russia against Napoleon*, 210.

54. Ibid., 210–211.

55. Rey, *Alexander I*, 244.

56. Lieven, *Russia against Napoleon*, 212.

57. Rey, *Alexander I*, 244.

58. Mikaberidze, *Battle of Borodino*, 222; Lieven, *Russia against Napoleon*, 212.

59. Lieven, *Russia against Napoleon*, 212.

60. Mikaberidze, *Battle of Borodino*, 222; Rey, *Alexander I*, 245; Lieven, *Russia against Napoleon*, 213.

61. Mikaberidze, *Battle of Borodino*, 222.

62. Rey, *Alexander I*, 245; Lieven, *Russia against Napoleon*, 221, 234.

63. Lieven, *Russia against Napoleon*, 250.

64. Ibid., 216.

65. Ibid., 257, 261.

66. Lieven, "Tolstoy on War," 19.

67. Rey, *Alexander I*, 247; Sergei Marin quoted in Mikaberidze, *Russian Eyewitness Accounts*, 205; Lieven, *Russia against Napoleon*, 245.

68. Lieven, *Russia against Napoleon*, 265.

69. Quoted in Mikaberidze, *Russian Eyewitness Accounts*, 209. Philosopher Joseph de Maistre, who was the ambassador to Russia from the Kingdom of Piedmont-Sardinia in 1812, wrote: "Someone asserted that he saw a man being roasted; all the stories agree

that Frenchmen were seen lying on the carcass of a horse trying to devour it with their teeth." Rey, *Alexander I*, 248.

70. Quoted in Mikaberidze, *Russian Eyewitness Accounts*, 211.

71. Quoted in Lieven, *Russia against Napoleon*, 265.

72. Nikolai Kovalskii quoted in Mikaberidze, *Russian Eyewitness Accounts*, 217.

73. Aleksandr Voeikov quoted in ibid., 212. Also in Mikaberidze, *Russian Eyewitness Accounts*, see the statements of Ludwig von Wolzogen (199) and Aleksandr Muravev (201). Both Wolzogen and Muravev were staff officers to Barclay de Tolly, which could partially explain their harsh attitudes toward Kutuzov.

74. Ibid., 214.

75. Dan Ungurianu writes about present-day historians of the era: "What is perhaps most astonishing in the revisionist assessments of *War and Peace* is the ease of claiming true knowledge about the epoch in question." Dan Ungurianu, "The Use of Historical Sources in *War and Peace*," in McPeak and Orwin, *Tolstoy on War*, 39. This is certainly the case with Lieven.

76. Lieven, *Russia against Napoleon*, 525.

77. Ibid., 526.

78. Lieven, "Tolstoy on War," 15.

79. Ibid., 12–13.

80. Kathryn B. Feuer, *Tolstoy and the Genesis of* War and Peace, ed. Robin Feuer Miller and Donna Tussing Orwin (Ithaca, NY: Cornell University Press, 1996), 157.

81. Dan Ungurianu, *Plotting History: The Russian Historical Novel in the Imperial Age* (Madison: University of Wisconsin Press, 2007), 113.

82. Lieven, "Tolstoy on War," 17–18.

83. Ibid., 23.

84. Mikaberidze, *Battle of Borodino*, 177.

85. Donna Tussing Orwin, "The Awful Poetry of War: Tolstoy's Borodino," in McPeak and Orwin, *Tolstoy on War*, 125. In the same volume, also see Elizabeth D. Samet, "The Disobediences of *War and Peace*," 168.

86. David A. Welch, "Tolstoy the International Relations Theorist," in McPeak and Orwin, *Tolstoy on War*, 178.

87. Ibid., 180.

88. Quoted in ibid., 182, 183.

89. Isaiah Berlin, *The Hedgehog and the Fox: An Essay on Tolstoy's View of History* (New York: Simon and Schuster, 1953), 1, 4.

90. Ibid., 11. R. F. Christian concurs, noting that "Tolstoy was a lover of history," especially Russian history. R. F. Christian, *Tolstoy's* War and Peace: *A Study* (Oxford: Clarendon Press, 1962), 95.

91. Berlin, *Hedgehog and the Fox*, 12. Most of the historical works that Tolstoy had at his disposal were "imbued with the same chauvinistic, militaristic sentiments which Tolstoy was later to repudiate vehemently." Christian, *Tolstoy's* War and Peace, 60.

92. R. F. Christian, *Tolstoy: A Critical Introduction* (Cambridge: Cambridge University Press, 1969), 161.

93. Christian, *Tolstoy's* War and Peace, 2.

94. Ibid., 21.

95. Quoted in Berlin, *Hedgehog and the Fox*, 13.

96. Ibid.

97. Ungurianu, *Plotting History*, 117, 124.

98. Berlin, *Hedgehog and the Fox*, 21, 15.

99. Gary Saul Morson, *Hidden in Plain View: Narrative and Creative Potentials in "War and Peace"* (Stanford, CA: Stanford University Press, 1987), 105, 114.

100. Christian, *Tolstoy*, 154.

101. Christian, *Tolstoy's* War and Peace, 110.

102. Berlin, *Hedgehog and the Fox*, 29.

103. Ibid., 17.

104. Feuer writes that Karataev "is a clothed idea more than he is a character." Feuer, *Tolstoy and the Genesis of* War and Peace, 147.

105. Quoted in Christian, *Tolstoy's* War and Peace, 22.

106. Feuer, *Tolstoy and the Genesis of* War and Peace, 146.

107. Berlin, *Hedgehog and the Fox*, 23.

108. Ibid., 27.

109. Christian, *Tolstoy*, 155.

110. Berlin, *Hedgehog and the Fox*, 70.

111. Ibid., 45.

112. Ibid., 50. See also Feuer, *Tolstoy and the Genesis of* War and Peace, 182, 208.

113. Berlin, *Hedgehog and the Fox*, 51, 56.

114. Christian, *Tolstoy*, 97.

115. Ibid., 102, 111–115.

116. Christian, *Tolstoy's* War and Peace, 61.

117. Ibid., 106.

118. Ibid., 168.

119. Berlin, *Hedgehog and the Fox*, 65.

120. Christian, *Tolstoy's* War and Peace, 108.

121. Christian, *Tolstoy*, 160.

122. Feuer, *Tolstoy and the Genesis of* War and Peace, 154.

CHAPTER 5. BONDARCHUK VERSUS VIDOR

1. Interview with Viacheslav Ovchinnikov, bonus disc, *Voina i mir* (Ruscico [Russian Cinema Council], 2002), DVD.

2. King Vidor in the trailer for the film, available as bonus material on *War and Peace* (Paramount Pictures, 2002), DVD (hereafter cited as Trailer 1).

3. Raymond Durgnat and Scott Simmon, *King Vidor, American* (Berkeley: University of California Press, 1988), 8.

4. King Vidor, *King Vidor on Film Making* (New York: David McKay, 1972), 79. There was also the competition from television to consider.

5. King Vidor, *King Vidor: Interviewed by Nancy Dowd and David Shepard* (Metuchen, NJ: Directors Guild of America/Scarecrow Press, 1988), 263.

6. Trailer for the film's re-release, available as bonus material on the *War and Peace* DVD.

7. Ibid. Ronald Holloway claims it took less than a year to make the film. See

Ronald Holloway, "Gordost mirovoi kulturu: Lev Tolstoi v kino SShA," *Iskusstvo kino* 9 (1978): 74. Holloway was probably talking about the actual filming, which took about six months.

8. See http://www.imdb.com/namenm0094803/?ref_=nv_sr_2, accessed 28 November 2013.

9. Tullio Kezich and Alessandra Levantesi, *Dino: The Life and Films of Dino De Laurentiis*, trans. James Marcus (New York: Hyperion, 2004), 101.

10. Vidor, *King Vidor*, 263–264.

11. Ibid. 264.

12. Ibid., 266–268.

13. Ibid., 264–265.

14. Ibid., 266–267; Kezich and Levantesi, *Dino*, 102.

15. Vidor, *King Vidor*, 266.

16. Ibid., 268; Kezich and Levantesi, *Dino*, 104.

17. Vidor, *King Vidor*, 269.

18. Vidor, *Vidor on Film Making*, 56.

19. Vidor, *King Vidor*, 271–272; Kezich and Levantesi, *Dino*, 102.

20. Vidor, *King Vidor*, 272. Vidor does not say what, if anything, happened to the Communists among the crew.

21. Vidor, *Vidor on Film Making*, 99.

22. Ibid., 94.

23. Ibid., 98.

24. "Big Screen *War and Peace*," *Newsweek*, 30 July 1956, 53; Philip Hamburger, "Big, Bigger, Biggest," *New Yorker*, 1 September 1956, 55.

25. Vidor, *Vidor on Film Making*, 83, 85.

26. Trailer 1.

27. Vidor, *Vidor on Film Making*, 97.

28. Trailer 1.

29. "Big Screen *War and Peace*," 53.

30. Vidor, *Vidor on Film Making*, 86–87.

31. Trisha Marie Jurkiewicz, "From Epic Novel to Epic Films: Two Cinematic Adaptations of *War and Peace*" (MA thesis, Central Michigan University, 1990), 48.

32. Kezich and Levantesi, *Dino*, 100.

33. Hamburger, "Big, Bigger, Biggest," 55.

34. Bosley Crowther, "*War and Peace*," *New York Times*, 22 August 1956, 26. He also criticized the multiple accents of the characters who were all supposed to be Russian.

35. "Tolstoy in VistaVision," *Saturday Review*, 8 September 1956, 32.

36. Crowther, "*War and Peace*," 25; "Big Book, Big Screen," *Newsweek*, 3 September 1956, 88.

37. Interview with Vasilii Lanovoi, *Voina i mir* bonus disc.

38. "Big Screen *War and Peace*," 55.

39. Jurkiewicz, "From Epic Novel to Epic Films," 35.

40. Ibid., 38.

41. Ibid., 34, 36–38.

42. Ibid., 46.

43. Ibid., 41–42.

44. Ibid., 43–44.

45. Ibid., 34. There is also a Russian Cossack dance at Kuragin's party.

46. Jeremy Brett, who played Nicholas, was the only actor riding a real horse. See http://www.imdb.com/title/tt0049934/triva?ref=tt_ql_2, accessed 15 September 2013.

47. Tolstoy provides no clues about the weather, but given the furs, snow might have been a better option.

48. Vidor, *King Vidor*, 270.

49. There were eight credited scriptwriters: Bridget Boland, Robert Westerby, King Vidor, Mario Camerini, Ennio De Concini, Ivo Perilli, Gian Gaspare Napolitano, and Mario Soldati. See http://www.imdb.com/title/tt0049934/fullcredits?ref_=ttco_sa_1, accessed 9 September 2013.

50. It was also accessible to Russian viewers; Vidor's film enjoyed significant popularity when it was shown in the USSR in 1959. That popularity was due at least in part to the presence of Audrey Hepburn, who had a Soviet following after *Roman Holiday* screened there. See Tony Shaw and Denise J. Youngblood, *Cinematic Cold War: The American and Soviet Struggle for Hearts and Minds* (Lawrence: University Press of Kansas, 2010), 111–112.

51. Clive Denton and Kingsley Canham, *The Hollywood Professionals*, vol. 5, *King Vidor, John Cromwell, Mervyn Leroy* (London: Tantivy Press, 1976), 31–32.

52. Durgnat and Simmon, *King Vidor*, 302–308.

53. John Baxter, *King Vidor* (New York: Monarch Press, 1976), 80–82.

54. Kezich and Levantesi, *Dino*, 106.

55. Television miniseries have tried. The BBC's nearly fifteen-hour *War and Peace* (1972) was contrived as a direct response to Bondarchuk's film. It obviously manages to get more of the story in, but it suffers from low production values and a disastrously miscast Natasha (Morag Hood). It does, however, feature a young Anthony Hopkins, who does a creditable turn as Pierre. Another example is Robert Dornhelm's nearly seven-hour *War and Peace* for RAI (Radiotelevisione Italiana). This international production badly bowdlerizes and sentimentalizes the story, but the cinematography is very beautiful.

CHAPTER 6. CODA: BONDARCHUK'S *WATERLOO*

1. Nina Tolchenova, *Mera krasoty: Kino Sergeia Bondarchuka* (Moscow: Sovetskaia Rossiia, 1974), 227. Tolchenova provides a sovieticized analysis of the film (ibid., 225–256).

2. Tullio Kezich and Alessandra Levantesi, *Dino: The Life and Films of Dino De Laurentiis*, trans. James Marcus (New York: Hyperion, 2004), 183.

3. Ibid., 184.

4. "Ekrannye vesti," *Iskusstvo kino* 2 (1970): 134.

5. Kezich and Levantesi, *Dino*, 184.

6. "Ekrannye vesti," 134, translated by Nadezda Berkovich.

7. Ibid., 135, translated by Nadezda Berkovich.

8. Kezich and Levantesi, *Dino*, 184.

9. Ibid.

10. Ibid.

11. "Rich," *Variety* review in *"Waterloo," Film Facts* 14 (1971): 72.

12. Bondarchuk's copy of the script contained reproductions of battle paintings by Goya and Jacques-Louis David, among others, showing his artistic influences. See S. Chertok, "Bitva pri Vaterloo," *Sovetskii ekran* 17 (1969): 10.

13. Ibid., 13, translated by Nadezda Berkovich.

14. Kezich and Levantesi, *Dino*, 185.

15. Ibid.

16. Tom Hutchinson, *Rod Steiger: Memoirs of a Friendship* (London: Orion, 1998), 132.

17. Galina Dolmatovskaia, *Rod Staiger* (Moscow: Iskusstvo, 1976), 84.

18. Ibid., 88. Evgenii Samoilov recalled that when Steiger was acting, Bondarchuk rarely gave him directions. Olga Palatnikova, ed., *Sergei Bondarchuk v vospominaniakh sovremennikov* (Moscow: Eksmo, 2003), 307.

19. Hutchinson, *Rod Steiger*, 131. Roger Ebert concurs, saying that "Steiger found the making of this film an unpleasant enterprise." *"Waterloo* (1971)," http://www.rogerebert.com/reviews/waterloo-1971, accessed November 5, 2013.

20. Kezich and Levantesi, *Dino*, 185.

21. Hutchinson, *Rod Steiger*, 132.

22. Ibid.

23. Kezich and Levantesi, *Dino*, 185.

24. Dolmatovskaia, *Rod Staiger*, 93.

25. Andrew Roberts, *Waterloo, June 18, 1815: The Battle for Modern Europe* (New York: HarperCollins, 2006), 19, 2; Jeremy Black, *The Battle of Waterloo* (New York: Random House, 2010), 78.

26. Roberts, *Waterloo*, 28

27. Ibid.

28. Christopher Hibbert, *Wellington: A Personal History* (Reading, MA: Addison-Wesley, 1997), 172.

29. Ibid., 172–173.

30. Roberts, *Waterloo*, 32.

31. Hibbert, *Wellington*, 177.

32. David Chandler, *Waterloo: The Hundred Days* (New York: Macmillan, 1980), 47.

33. Black, *Battle of Waterloo*, 91.

34. Ibid., 92.

35. Roberts, *Waterloo*, 51.

36. Ibid.; Chandler, *Waterloo*, 109.

37. Black, *Battle of Waterloo*, 96.

38. Roberts, *Waterloo*, 51.

39. Andrew Roberts, *Napoleon and Wellington: The Battle of Waterloo and the Great Commanders Who Fought It* (New York: Simon and Schuster, 2001), 169. The actual number of troops in the battle was 77,000 for Napoleon, 73,150 for Wellington, and 49,000 for Blücher. Roberts, *Waterloo*, 39–40.

40. Black, *Battle of Waterloo*, 140.

41. Roberts, *Napoleon and Wellington*, 167.

42. Black, *Battle of Waterloo*, 96.

43. Roberts, *Napoleon and Wellington*, 178–179.

44. Chandler, *Waterloo*, 56; Roberts, *Waterloo*, 38

45. Roberts, *Waterloo*, 53.

46. Ibid., 41, 52.

47. Chandler, *Waterloo*, 47.

48. Hibbert, *Wellington*, 176.

49. Ibid., 179.

50. Philip Haythornthwaite, *Wellington: The Iron Duke* (Washington, DC: Potomac Books, 2007), 78.

51. Ibid., 80.

52. Black, *Battle of Waterloo*, 98, 116.

53. Ibid., 101.

54. Ibid., 116.

55. Black, *Battle of Waterloo*, 100–101.

56. Roberts, *Waterloo*, 58.

57. Ibid., 73. According to Black, *Battle of Waterloo*, 112, it was 3:00 p.m.

58. Black, *Battle of Waterloo*, 125.

59. Roberts, *Waterloo*, 97.

60. Black, *Battle of Waterloo*, 106.

61. Ibid., 115; Roberts, *Waterloo*, 82.

62. Black, *Battle of Waterloo*, 116, 120.

63. Ibid., 122.

64. Ibid., 87.

65. Ibid., 131.

66. Ibid., 146.

67. Roberts, *Waterloo*, 103, 109.

68. Ibid., 110.

69. Ibid., 111; Chandler, *Waterloo*, 166.

70. Black, *Battle of Waterloo*, 149.

71. Roberts, *Waterloo*, 120.

72. Black, *Battle of Waterloo*, 140.

73. Roberts, *Waterloo*, 120.

74. Ibid., 86.

75. Ibid.

76. Robert B. Asprey, *The Reign of Napoleon Bonaparte* (New York: Basic Books, 2001), 376–377.

77. A. Vystorobets, *Sergei Bondarchuk: Sudba i filmy* (Moscow: Iskusstvo, 1991), 168. Vystorobets offers one of the few full discussions of the film (167–184).

78. Tolchenova, *Mera krasoty*, 233.

79. Sergei Bondarchuk, *Zhelanie chuda* (Moscow: Molodaia gvardiia, 1981), 30.

80. Chertok, "Bitva pri Vaterloo," 10. Chertok recalls, "I was told that at the first day of shooting, aside from the Italian cultural representatives, there also arrived several

hundred journalists. Such an interest in the movie had to do with the enormity of the artistic task and with the scope of the work, and with the previous work of Bondarchuk's movie *War and Peace*" (translated by Nadezda Berkovich).

81. "Otovsiudu," *Iskusstvo kino* 6 (1969): 145.

82. Sigmund Glaubmann, "*Waterloo*," *Films in Review* 21, 5 (May 1971): 311.

83. Excerpted in "*Waterloo*," *Film Facts* 14 (1971): 72.

84. Quoted in ibid., 71.

85. Ibid.

86. Ibid.

87. Excerpted in ibid., 72.

88. Ibid., 71.

89. Champlin in ibid., 72; Gelmis in ibid., 72.

90. Glaubmann, "*Waterloo*," 312.

91. Gordon Gow, "*Waterloo*," *Films and Filming* 17, 4 (January 1971): 48.

92. Excerpted in "*Waterloo*," *Film Facts* 14 (1971): 73.

93. Gow, "*Waterloo*," 49.

94. "*Waterloo*," *Film Facts* 14 (1971): 72. Champlin, however, found *Waterloo* much less effective than *War and Peace*.

95. Ibid., 73.

96. For example, see Tolchenova, *Mera krasoty*, 227, 232–233, and Vystorobets, *Sergei Bondarchuk*, 169. Bondarchuk had declared to *Cinema Art*: "*Waterloo* is conceived as an anti-war movie that has to show all the monstrosity and bestiality of the rapacious wars, when because of the will of the conspiracy of silence of malicious people, huge masses of people begin to kill other human beings simply because they are dressed in a different color uniform." "Ekrannye vesti," 135, translated by Nadezda Berkovich.

97. Tolchenova, *Mera krasoty*, 234, 254.

98. Ibid., 228.

99. Dolmatovskaia, *Rod Staiger*, 89, 97.

100. "*Waterloo* (1970), Awards," http://www.imdb.com/title/tt0066549/awards?ref_=tt_ql_4, accessed November 5, 2013.

101. Kezich and Levantesi, *Dino*, 185. Joseph Gelmis says that De Laurentiis got his money back "before the film was finished" by selling the distribution rights to Paramount in the United States and Columbia overseas. See "*Waterloo*," *Film Facts* 14 (1971): 72. The alleged Soviet success of the film cannot be corroborated in available Soviet sources. Because the film was a coproduction, it was not considered a domestic film and hence is not included in Sergei Zemlianukhin and Miroslava Segida, *Domashniaia sinemateka: Otechestvennoe kino, 1918–1996* (Moscow: Dubl-D, 1996), an annotated catalog of Soviet films that provides audience figures.

102. Kezich and Levantesi, *Dino*, 186.

103. Dolmatovskaia, *Rod Staiger*, 96.

104. "Ekrannye vesti," 135.

CONCLUSION

1. For an analysis of this film, see Denise J. Youngblood, *Russian War Films: On the Cinema Front, 1914–2005* (Lawrence: University Press of Kansas, 2007), 168–170.

2. Andrei Konchalovskii, "Ia vsegda smotrel na nego s obozhaniem," in *Sergei Bondarchuk v vospominaniiakh sovremennikov*, ed. Olga Palatnikova (Moscow: Eksmo, 2003), 320. Bondarchuk also failed to intervene when other filmmakers got into censorship trouble, such as Konchalovskii with *A Nest of Gentry* (*Dvorianskie gnezdo*) and Andrei Tarkovskii with *Andrei Rublev* (ibid., 321).

3. "V Sezd Kinematografistov," *Iskusstvo kino* 10 (1986): 63, translated by Nadezda Berkovich.

4. Ibid., 115, translated by Nadezda Berkovich.

5. Interview with Karen Shakhnazarov, bonus disc, *Voina i mir* (Ruscico [Russian Cinema Council], 2002), DVD. Also see Peter Rollberg, "Sergei Bondarchuk," in *Historical Dictionary of Russian and Soviet Cinema* (Lanham, MD: Scarecrow Press, 2009), 116.

6. See http://www.imdb.com/title/tt0384712/?ref_=fn_al_tt_1, accessed 12 December 2013.

7. Rollberg, "Sergei Bondarchuk," 116.

8. Lidiia Maslova, "Mosfilm perepechatal *Voinu i mir*," *Kommersant* 120 (2000), http://kommersant.ru/doc/152331, accessed 4 June 2013.

9. Ibid.

10. David Gillespie, *Russian Cinema* (Harlow, UK: Longman, 2003), 18.

11. For a discussion of *The Fall of Berlin*, see Youngblood, *Russian War Films*, 97–102.

12. Ibid., 158–162.

13. In fact, they lost. See Tony Shaw and Denise J. Youngblood, *Cinematic Cold War: The American and Soviet Struggle for Hearts and Minds* (Lawrence: University Press of Kansas, 2010), conclusion.

BIBILIOGRAPHY

ARCHIVAL SOURCE

Rossiiskii gosudarstvennyi arkhiv literatury i iskusstva (RGALI):

    f. 844, op. 4, ed. khr. 334

    f. 2453, op. 4, ed. khr. 239

    f. 2453, op. 4, ed. khr. 253

    f. 2453, op. 5, ed. khr. 24

    f. 2453, op. 5, ed. khr. 36

    f. 2453, op. 5, ed. khr. 698

    f. 2912, op. 1, ed. khr. 90

    f. 3173, op. 1, ed. khr. 189

    f. 3243, op. 1, ed. khr. 359

PRIMARY AND SECONDARY SOURCES

Adler, Renata. "*War and Peace.*" *New York Times*, 29 April 1968, 50.

Alpert, Hollis. "Clash by Night." *Saturday Review*, 11 May 1968, 56–67.

Andrew, Dudley. "Adaptation." In *Film Adaptation*, ed. James Naremore, 28–37. New Brunswick, NJ: Rutgers University Press, 2000.

Anninskii, L. "Lev Tolstoy i my s vami." *Sovetskii ekran* 22 (1966): 9–12.

Asprey, Robert B. *The Reign of Napoleon Bonaparte.* New York: Basic Books, 2001.

Austen, David. "*War and Peace.*" *Films and Filming* 15, 9 (June 1969): 47, 50.

Autant-Lara, Claude. "Dukh epokhi." *Iskusstvo kino* 9 (1965): 13–14.

Babitsky, Paul, and John Rimberg. *The Soviet Film Industry.* New York: Praeger, 1955.

Balio, Tino. *The Foreign Film Renaissance on American Screens, 1946–1973.* Madison: University of Wisconsin Press, 2010.

Bauman, Elena. "Close-up: Our Contemporary Sergei Bondarchuk." *Soviet Film* 296 (1982): 5–7.

Baxter, John. *King Vidor.* New York: Monarch Press, 1976.

Bazin, André. "Adaptation, or the Cinema as Digest." In *Film Adaptation*, ed. James Naremore, 19–27. New Brunswick, NJ: Rutgers University Press, 2000.

Beau. "*War and Peace.*" *Variety*, 1 May 1968, 6.

Berlin, Isaiah. *The Hedgehog and the Fox: An Essay on Tolstoy's View of History.* New York: Simon and Schuster, 1953.

"Big Book, Big Screen." *Newsweek*, 3 September 1956, 88.

"Big Screen *War and Peace.*" *Newsweek*, 30 July 1956, 53–56.

Bilinkis, Ia. "Proza Lva Tolstogo i sovremennoe kino." *Iskusstvo kino* 3 (1964): 65–79.

Black, Jeremy. *The Battle of Waterloo.* New York: Random House, 2010.

Bondarchuk, Natalia. *Edinstvennye dni.* Moscow: Astrel, 2010.

Bondarchuk, Sergei. "Chelovek i istoriia." *Iskusstvo kino* 2 (1981): 28–40.

———. "Chitaia bessmertnuiu epopeiu." *Iskusstvo kino* 9 (1978): 13–29.

———. "Khudozhnik dolzhen iskat." *Iskusstvo kino* 10 (1961): 9.

———. "Leo Tolstoy and the Cinema." *Soviet Film* 255 (1978): 11–12.

———. "Otkrytie chuvstv." *Ogonek* 4 (24 January 1965): 27–28.

———. *Vaterloo*. Atrium DVDArt, n.d. DVD.

———. *Voina i mir*. Ruscico, 2002. DVD.

———. *Zhelanie chuda*. Moscow: Molodaia gvardiia, 1981.

Borokov, Vl. "Vozvrashchenie Anatoliia Ktorova." *Sovetskii ekran* 14 (1967): 6–7.

Boyum, Joy Gould. *Double Exposure: Fiction into Film*. New York: Universe Books, 1985.

Brandenburger, David. *National Bolshevism: Stalinist Mass Culture and the Foundation of Modern Russian National Identity, 1931–56*. Cambridge, MA: Harvard University Press, 2002.

Burgoyne, Robert. "Introduction." In *The Epic Film in World Culture*, ed. Robert Burgoyne, 1–16. New York: Routledge, 2011.

Chandler, David. *Waterloo: The Hundred Days*. New York: Macmillan, 1980.

Chertok, S. "Bitva pri Vaterloo." *Sovetskii ekran* 17 (1969): 10–13, 14.

Christian, R. F. *Tolstoy: A Critical Introduction*. Cambridge: Cambridge University Press, 1969.

———. *Tolstoy's* War and Peace: *A Study*. Oxford: Clarendon Press, 1962.

Crowther, Bosley. "*War and Peace*." *New York Times*, 22 August 1956, 26.

Daneliia, Georgii. "Ne boias literaturu...." *Iskusstvo kino* 9 (1965): 10–11.

Denton, Clive, and Kingsley Canham. *The Hollywood Professionals*, vol. 5, *King Vidor, John Cromwell, Mervyn Leroy*. London: Tantivy Press, 1976.

Dobson, Miriam. *Khrushchev's Cold Summer: Gulag Returnees, Crime, and the Fate of Reform after Stalin*. Ithaca, NY: Cornell University Press, 2009.

Dolmatovskaia, Galina. *Rod Staiger*. Moscow: Iskusstvo, 1976.

Dolmatovskaia, Galina, and Irina Shilova. *Who's Who in the Soviet Cinema: Seventy Different Portraits*. Moscow: Progress, 1979.

Durgnat, Raymond, and Scott Simmon. *King Vidor, American*. Berkeley: University of California Press, 1988.

Ehrenburg, Ilia. *The Thaw*, trans. Manya Harari. Chicago: Regnery, 1955.

"Ekrannye vesti." *Iskusstvo kino* 2 (1970): 134–135.

Ermolinskii, S. "V preddverii novykh stranits." *Iskusstvo kino* 9 (1965): 7–9.

Evtushenko, Evgenii. "Sergei Bondarchuk." *Soviet Film* 348 (1986): 6–7.

Feuer, Kathryn B. *Tolstoy and the Genesis of* War and Peace, ed. Robin Feuer Miller and Donna Tussing Orwin. Ithaca, NY: Cornell University Press, 1996.

Fomin, V. I., and A. S. Deriabin, eds. *Letopis rossiiskogo kino, 1946–1965: Nauchnaia monografiia*. Moscow: Kanon+, 2010.

Gillespie, David. *Russian Cinema*. Harlow, UK: Longman, 2003.

Gilliatt, Penelope. "The Russians' Monument." *New Yorker*, 4 May 1968, 163.

Glaubmann, Sigmund, "*Waterloo*." *Films in Review* 21, 5 (May 1971): 311–312.

Golovko, Kira. "On byl absoliutno mkhatovskii." In *Sergei Bondarchuk v vospominaniiakh sovremennikov*, ed. Olga Palatnikova, 261–275. Moscow: Eksmo, 2003.

Golovnia, Anatolii. "Operatory, kotorykh Ia liubliu." *Sovetskii ekran* 18 (1968): 12.

Gorelova, Valeriia. "Viacheslav Tikhonov." In *Akterskaia entsiklopediia kino Rossii*, pt. 1, 134–136. Moscow: Materik, 2002.

Gorvin, A. "Na peredovoi kino-proizvodstva." *Sovetskii ekran* 6 (1968): 20.

Gow, Gordon. "*Waterloo.*" *Films and Filming* 17, 4 (January 1971): 48–49.

"The Great Ones: *War and Peace.*" *Classic Film Collection* 57 (Winter 1977): 18–19.

Guralnik, Uran. "Potizhenie eposa *Voina i mir:* Film i ego kritiki." *Iskusstvo kino* 8 (1969): 102–117.

———. "Vast as an Ocean." *Films and Filming* 15, 8 (May 1969): 60–63.

Hamburger, Philip. "Big, Bigger, Biggest." *New Yorker,* 1 September 1956, 55.

Hart, Henry. "*War and Peace.*" *Films in Review* 19, 6 (June–July 1968): 373–375.

Haythornthwaite, Philip. *Wellington: The Iron Duke.* Washington, DC: Potomac Books, 2007.

Hibbert, Christopher. *Wellington: A Personal History.* Reading, MA: Addison-Wesley, 1997.

Holloway, Ronald. "Gordost mirovoi kultury: Lev Tolstoi v kino SShA." *Iskusstvo kino* 9 (1978): 74–75.

Hutchings, Stephen, and Anat Vernitskii. "Introduction: The *Ekranizatsiia* in Russian Culture." In *Russian and Soviet Film Adaptations of Literature, 1900–2001: Screening the Word,* ed. Stephen Hutchings and Anat Vernitskii, 1–24. London: Routledge Curzon, 2005.

Hutchinson, Tom. *Rod Steiger: Memoirs of a Friendship.* London: Orion, 1998.

Iarmatov, Khamil. "Sobytie." *Iskusstvo kino* 9 (1965): 12–13.

Iurenev, Rostislav. *Iskusstvo, rozhdennoe oktiabrem.* Moscow: Biuro propagandy sovetskogo kinoiskusstva, 1968.

Ivanov, Nikolai. "Iz dnevnika direktora kartiny." In *Sergei Bondarchuk v vospominaniiakh sovremennikov,* ed. Olga Palatnikova, 141–165. Moscow: Eksmo, 2003.

"Iz otzyvov masterov mirovogo kino." *Sovetskii ekran* 2 (1968): 8.

Jones, Polly. "Introduction: The Dilemmas of De-Stalinization." In *The Dilemmas of De-Stalinization: Negotiating Cultural and Social Change in the Khrushchev Era,* ed. Polly Jones, 1–18. London: Routledge, 2006.

Jurkiewicz, Trisha Marie. "From Epic Novel to Epic Films: Two Cinematic Adaptations of *War and Peace.*" MA thesis, Central Michigan University, 1990.

Kauffman, Stanley. "Take a Giant Steppe." *New Republic,* 18 May 1968, 24.

Kezich, Tullio, and Alessandra Levantesi. *Dino: The Life and Films of Dino De Laurentiis,* trans. James Marcus. New York: Hyperion, 2004.

Khaniutin, Iurii. "Sergei Bondarchuk." *Iskusstvo kino* 7 (1962): 90–100.

———. *Sergei Bondarchuk.* Moscow: Iskusstvo, 1962.

Kolesnikova, N. "Pervyi bal Natashi." *Sovetskii ekran* 12 (1965): 8–12.

———. ". . . pro den Borodina." *Sovetskii ekran* 1 (1964): 13.

Konchalovskii, Andrei. "Ia vsegda smotrel na nego s obozhaniem." In *Sergei Bondarchuk v vospominaniiakh sovremennikov,* ed. Olga Palatnikova, 317–327. Moscow: Eksmo, 2003.

"Konkurs-1966: Itogi." *Sovetskii ekran* 10 (1967): inside front cover.

"Kto budet igrat Natashu Rostovu?" *Sovetskii ekran* 16 (1961): 14.

Kudriavtsev, Sergei. *Svoe kino.* Moscow: Dom Khanzhonkova/Kinovideotsentr, 1998.

———. *3500: Avtorskaia kniga kinoretsenzii,* vol. 1, A–M. Moscow: n.p., 2008.

Kuznetsov, M. "O voine i o mire (Zametki kritika s Moskovskogo kinofestivalia)." *Sovetskii ekran* 16 (1965): 2–3.

Langford, Barry. *Film Genre: Hollywood and Beyond*. Edinburgh: Edinburgh University Press, 2005.

Lanovoi, Vasilii. "My znaem tsenu dobru." In *Sergei Bondarchuk v vospominaniiakh sovremennikov*, ed. Olga Palatnikova, 247–259. Moscow: Eksmo, 2003.

Lawton, Anna. *Kinoglasnost: Soviet Cinema in Our Time*. Cambridge: Cambridge University Press, 1992.

Lesenko, O. "Viacheslav Tikhonov: Tvorcheskii portret." *Sovetskii ekran* 22 (1966): 14–15.

Lieven, Dominic. *Russia against Napoleon: The True Story of the Campaigns of* War and Peace. New York: Penguin, 2010.

———. "Tolstoy on War, Russia, and Empire." In *Tolstoy on War: Narrative Art and Historical Truth in* War and Peace, ed. Rick McPeak and Donna Tussing Orwin, 12–25. Ithaca, NY: Cornell University Press, 2012.

Lind, John. "Sergei Bondarchuk: The Road to *Waterloo*." *Focus on Film* 4 (October 1970): 24–41.

Margolit, Evgenii. "Landscape with Hero." In *Springtime for Soviet Cinema: Re/Viewing the 1960s*, ed. Alexander Prokhorov, 29–50. Pittsburgh: Pittsburgh Russian Film Symposium, 2001.

Maslova, Lidiia. "Mosfilm perepechatal *Voinu i mir*." *Kommersant* 120 (2000). http://kommersant.ru/doc/152331.

McPeak, Rick, and Donna Tussing Orwin, eds. *Tolstoy on War: Narrative Art and Historical Truth in* War and Peace. Ithaca, NY: Cornell University Press, 2012.

Mednikova, Marina. "Sergei Bondarchuk." *Soviet Film* 312 (1983): n.p.

Mikaberidze, Alexander. *The Battle of Borodino: Napoleon against Kutuzov*. Barnsley, UK: Pen and Sword, 2007.

———, ed. and trans. *Russian Eyewitness Accounts of the Campaign of 1812*. London: Frontline Books, 2012.

Ministerstvo kultury Rossiiskoi Federatsii, Nauchno issledovatelskii institut kinoiskusstva. *Letopis rossiiskogo kino, 1946–1965*. Moscow: Kanon+, 2010.

Moine, Raphaëlle. *Cinema Genre*, trans. Alistair Fox and Hilary Radner. Malden, MA: Blackwell Publishing, 2008.

Morgenstern, Joseph. "The Biggest Movie." *Newsweek*, 6 May 1968, 120.

Morson, Gary Saul. *Hidden in Plain View: Narrative and Creative Potentials in "War and Peace."* Stanford, CA: Stanford University Press, 1987.

Mosk. "*War and Peace*—Part III." *Variety*, 10 May 1967, 6.

———. "*War and Peace*—Part IV." *Variety*, 14 February 1968, 120.

Musskii, I. A. *Sto velikikh otechestvennykh kinofilmov*. Moscow: Veche, 2006.

Myers, Fred. "Monumental." *Christian Century* 85 (1968): 1246–1248.

Naremore, James, ed. *Film Adaptation*. New Brunswick, NJ: Rutgers University Press, 2000.

Nash Korr. "Zakonchena kinoepopeia." *Sovetskii ekran* 2 (1968): 8.

Norris, Stephen M. "Tolstoy's Comrades: Sergei Bondarchuk's *War and Peace* and the Origins of Brezhnev Culture." In *Tolstoy on Screen*, ed. Lorna Fitzsimmons. Evanston, IL: Northwestern University Press, forthcoming.

Norris, Stephen M., and Willard Sunderland, eds. *Russia's People of Empire: Life Stories from Eurasia, 1500 to the Present*. Bloomington: Indiana University Press, 2012.

Oldridge, James. "Mysli i deistvii." *Iskusstvo kino* 9 (1965): 11–12.

Orwin, Donna Tussing. "The Awful Poetry of War: Tolstoy's Borodino." In *Tolstoy on War: Narrative Art and Historical Truth in* War and Peace, ed. Rick McPeak and Donna Tussing Orwin, 123–139. Ithaca, NY: Cornell University Press, 2012.

"Otovsiudu." *Iskusstvo kino* 6 (1969): 145.

Palatnikova, Olga, ed. *Neizvestnyi Bondarchuk: Planeta genii.* Moscow: Eksmo/Algoritm, 2010.

———. *Sergei Bondarchuk v vospominaniakh sovremennikov.* Moscow: Eksmo, 2003.

"Parizh smotrit *Voinu i mir:* Iz otklikov frantsuzskoi pressy." *Sovetskii ekran* 15 (1966): 8–9.

Petritskii, Anatolii. "My na mnogoe smotreli po raznomu." In *Sergei Bondarchuk v vospominaniiakh sovremennikov,* ed. Olga Palatnikova, 207–227. Moscow: Eksmo, 2003.

Pollock, Sean. "Petr Ivanovich Bagration (1765–1812)." In *Russia's Peoples of Empire: Life Stories from Eurasia, 1500 to the Present,* ed. Stephen M. Norris and Willard Sunderland, 93–103. Bloomington: Indiana University Press, 2012.

Pozner, Valérie, ed. *Tolstoï et le cinema. Cahiers Léon Tolstoï,* vol. 16. Paris: Institute d'études slaves, 2005.

Price, James. "*War and Peace.*" *Sight and Sound* 38, 2 (Spring 1969): 97–98.

Prokhorov, Alexander. "The Unknown New Wave: Soviet Cinema of the 1960s." In *Springtime for Soviet Cinema: Re/Viewing the 1960s,* ed. Alexander Prokhorov, 7–28. Pittsburgh: Pittsburgh Russian Film Symposium, 2001.

Prokhorova, Elena. "*War and Peace.*" In *Directory of World Cinema: Russia,* ed. Birgit Beumers, 180–182. Bristol, UK: Intellect, 2011.

Ray, Robert B. "The Field of 'Literature and Film.'" In *Film Adaptation,* ed. James Naremore, 38–53. New Brunswick, NJ: Rutgers University Press, 2000.

Razzakov, Fedor. *Gibel sovetskogo kino: Intrigi i spory: 1918–1972.* Moscow: Eksmo, 2008.

———. *Nashe liubimoe kino: O voine.* Moscow: Algoritm/Eksmo, 2005.

———. *Nashe liubimoe kino: Tainoe stanovitsia iavnym.* Moscow: Algoritm, 2004.

Rey, Marie-Pierre. *Alexander I: The Tsar Who Defeated Napoleon,* trans. Susan Emanuel. De Kalb, IL: NIU Press, 2012.

Roberts, Andrew. *Napoleon and Wellington: The Battle of Waterloo and the Great Commanders Who Fought It.* New York: Simon and Schuster, 2001.

———. *Waterloo, June 18, 1815: The Battle for Modern Europe.* New York: HarperCollins, 2006.

Rollberg, Peter. *Historical Dictionary of Russian and Soviet Cinema.* Lanham, MD: Scarecrow Press, 2009.

Root, Robert L., Jr. "Imagining Visual Literacy: The Poetics and Rhetoric of the Image." *CEA Critic* 58, 3 (Spring–Summer 1996): 60–71.

Roth-Ey, Kristin. *Moscow Prime Time: How the Soviet Union Built the Media Empire that Lost the Cultural Cold War.* Ithaca, NY: Cornell University Press, 2011.

Rudnitskii, K. "Anatolii Ktorov." *Iskusstvo kino* 9 (1972): 99–114.

Samet, Elizabeth D. "The Disobediences of *War and Peace.*" In *Tolstoy on War: Narrative Art and Historical Truth in* War and Peace, ed. Rick McPeak and Donna Tussing Orwin, 160–174. Ithaca, NY: Cornell University Press, 2012.

Santas, Constantine. *The Epic in Film: From Myth to Blockbuster*. Lanham, MD: Rowman and Littlefield, 2008.

Saveleva, Liudmila. "Bolno...." In *Sergei Bondarchuk v vospominaniiakh sovremennikov*, ed. Olga Palatnikova, 167–185. Moscow: Eksmo, 2003.

Semenov, E. "Ia snimaius v kino." *Sovetskii ekran* 1 (1965): 4–6.

Shabad, Theodore. "*War and Peace* on Native Soil." *New York Times*, 12 January 1964.

Shaw, Tony, and Denise J. Youngblood. *Cinematic Cold War: The American and Soviet Struggle for Hearts and Minds*. Lawrence: University Press of Kansas, 2010.

Shuranova, Antonina. "On zhil Tolstym." In *Sergei Bondarchuk v vospominaniiakh sovremennikov*, ed. Olga Palatnikova, 229–245. Moscow: Eksmo, 2003.

Sniatkova, T. "Razdumia belykh nochei." *Sovetskii ekran* 17 (1964): 2–3.

Sofronov, A. "Velichie dukha." *Ogonek* 27 (2 July 1967): 16–17.

Solovev, Vladimir. "*Voina i mir* i my." In *Sergei Bondarchuk v vospominaniiakh sovremennikov*, ed. Olga Palatnikova, 117–139. Moscow: Eksmo, 2003.

Stam, Robert. "Beyond Fidelity: The Dialogics of Adaptation." In *Film Adaptation*, ed. James Naremore, 54–76. New Brunswick, NJ: Rutgers University Press, 2000.

Tendora, Natalia. *Viacheslav Tikhonov: Kniaz iz Pavlovskogo posada*. Moscow: Algoritm, 2008.

Tikhonov, Viacheslav. "Pozhaliute v kadr, kniaz!" In *Sergei Bondarchuk v vospominaniiakh sovremennikov*, ed. Olga Palatnikova, 187–205. Moscow: Eksmo, 2003.

Tiurin, Iurii. "*Voina i mir*." In *Rossiiskii illiuzion*, ed. L. M. Budiak, 417–422. Moscow: Materik, 2003.

Tolchenova, Nina. *Mera krasoty: Kino Sergeia Bondarchuka*. Moscow: Sovetskaia Rossiia, 1974.

Tolstoi, L. N. *Voina i mir*. Leningrad: OGIZ/Gosudarstvennoe izdatelstvo khudozhestvennoi literatury, 1941.

Tolstoy, Leo. *War and Peace*, trans. Richard Pevear and Larissa Volokhonsky. New York: Alfred A. Knopf, 2007.

"Tolstoy in VistaVision." *Saturday Review*, 8 September 1956, 32–33.

Trofimov, Nikolai. "Veroval!" In *Sergei Bondarchuk v vospominaniiakh sovremennikov*, ed. Olga Palatnikova, 277–289. Moscow: Eksmo, 2003.

Tumarkin, Nina. *The Living and the Dead: The Rise and Fall of the Cult of World War II in Russia*. New York: Basic Books, 1994.

Ungurianu, Dan. *Plotting History: The Russian Historical Novel in the Imperial Age*. Madison: University of Wisconsin Press, 2007.

———. "The Use of Historical Sources in *War and Peace*." In *Tolstoy on War: Narrative Art and Historical Truth in* War and Peace, ed. Rick McPeak and Donna Tussing Orwin, 26–41. Ithaca, NY: Cornell University Press, 2012.

"V Sezd Kinematografistov." *Iskusstvo kino* 10 (1986): 63.

Vidor, King. *King Vidor: Interviewed by Nancy Dowd and David Shepard*. Metuchen, NJ: Directors Guild of America/Scarecrow Press, 1988.

———. *King Vidor on Film Making*. New York: David McKay, 1972.

———. *War and Peace*. Paramount Pictures, 2002. DVD.

"*Voina i mir*." *Sovetskii ekran* 2 (1968): 9.

"*Voina i mir*: Kogda film proshel po ekranam." *Iskusstvo kino* 1 (1968): 30–45.

Vystorobets, A. *Sergei Bondarchuk: Sudba i filmy.* Moscow: Iskusstvo, 1991.

"*Waterloo.*" *Film Facts* 14 (1971): 70–73.

Welch, David A. "Tolstoy the International Relations Theorist." In *Tolstoy on War: Narrative Art and Historical Truth in* War and Peace, ed. Rick McPeak and Donna Tussing Orwin, 175–189. Ithaca, NY: Cornell University Press, 2012.

Woll, Josephine. *Real Images: Soviet Cinema and the Thaw.* London: I. B. Tauris, 2000.

Youngblood, Denise J. *Russian War Films: On the Cinema Front, 1914–2005.* Lawrence: University Press of Kansas, 2007.

Zamoshkin, K. "Vo imia sveta: Zametki o *Voine i mire*—roman i kinofilm." *Smena* 23 (December 1967): 27–30.

Zemlianukhin, Sergei, and Miroslava Segida. *Domashniaia sinemateka: Otechestvennoe kino, 1918–1996.* Moscow: Dubl-D, 1996.

Zolotusskii, Igor. "Dobavlenie k eposu (Tolstoi v romane i Tolstoi v filme)." *Novyi mir* 6 (June 1968): 269–283.

INDEX

history, *War and Peace* as
  accuracy, 7, 86–87, 130–131
  differences from novel, 85–86,
    87–88
  military consultants, 19
  objects from museum collections,
    19–20, 23
  portrayal of war, 90–91
  research, 130–131
  Russian society, 88–89
  verisimilitude, 19–20, 74, 86
  See also battle scenes
Homolka, Oscar, 108
Hutchings, Stephen, 58
Hutchinson, Tom, 112–113

intertextuality, 58
Ivanov, Nikolai, 20

Jones, Polly, 2–3, 5
Jurkiewicz, Trisha Marie, 96, 99

Kamensky, Anatoly, 10
Karalli, Vera, 10
Kauffman, Stanley, 28, 124, 143n205
Kennedy, John F., 5–6
Kezich, Tullio, 111
Khaniutin, Yury, 53
Khrushchev, Nikita, 1, 2, 4–6
Konovnitsyn, Pyotr, 81
Kovalsky, Nikolai, 81
Kozintsev, Grigory, 15
Ktorov, Anatoly, 17, 26, 50, 108
Kumanov, Yevgeny, 18
Kurasov, V. V., 19
Kutuzov, Mikhail
  command of Russian army, 78, 80,
    81–82, 90
  death, 61, 69
  historical figure, 54, 70–71, 74, 75, 78,
    79, 80, 81–82, 86–87
  portrayal in Bondarchuk film, 32, 33, 40,
    41–42, 43–44, 47, 48, 49 (photo),
    86–88, 90, 131
  portrayal in novel, 70–71, 83, 85
  portrayal in Vidor film, 101–102, 103–
    104, 105, 108

Langford, Barry, 29, 49–50
Lanovoi, Vasily, 15, 55, 95, 108, 138n68
Lawson, Wilfrid, 108
Levantesi, Alessandra, 111
Liberation (Osvobozhdenie), 129
Lieven, Dominic, 74, 75–76, 81, 82, 86
Likhachev, V. A., 23
Likhacheva, Tatiana, 17
literary adaptation, *War and Peace* as
  battle scenes, 69–71, 144n16
  Bondarchuk on, 58–59
  challenges, 59, 61, 130
  characters omitted or reduced, 49,
    59–60
  dialogue, 64, 67–68
  emotional truth retained, 63–64
  fidelity of transformation, 58, 65–71,
    73
  Moscow fire scene, 71
  narration, 64–65, 69, 109
  reinventions, 63–64, 71–72, 144n13
  scenes compressed or omitted, 30,
    60–63, 89, 130
  style, 109
  success, 7, 109, 130
  Vidor film, 59, 92, 95–99, 105–106
London Daily Mail, 50
Los Angeles Times, 123–124
Louis XVIII, King, 113, 117, 118–119
Löwenstern, Waldemar, 79–80
Luce, Clare Booth, 94

Macheret, A., 58
Maichenko, Liudmila, 11
Malenkov, Georgy, 2
Malinovsky, Rodion, 19
Marchand, Jean-Gabriel, 117
Markovich, Markian, 19
Masons. *See* Freemasonry
Medvedev, Vadim, 15
Menshov, Vladimir, 127–128
Miasnikov, Gennady, 22, 140n133
Mikaberidze, Alexander, 74, 82, 86
Mikhailovsky-Danilevsky, Aleksandr,
  82
Mikhalkov, Nikita, 127, 138n68
Mills, John, 108